America's Disconnected Youth

This important book collects a mountain of research by some of America's most respected experts on young people. These experts teach us that our common sense instincts are right: Young people need to know there are real opportunities at the end of the road. Connectedness means positive efforts to connect young people, concretely, to career and work realities and to involve them in extended contact with adults who care about their success. We owe Doug Besharov and the authors a vote of thanks for what they have shared with us.

Peter Edelman, Professor of Law
Georgetown University Law Center

Too often, we seem to assume that the only prevention efforts worth doing are those that focus on very young children. Yet, as this important new book reminds us, it is during adolescence that many are diverted from the path to becoming productive adults. Filled with cutting-edge information and "out-of-the-box" thinking, this volume is sure to become a classic for both researchers and practitioners interested in enhancing the life chances of our nation's youth.

Wade F. Horn, Ph.D., President, National Fatherhood Initiative
Co-author of *The Better Homes and Gardens New Teen Book*

Douglas Besharov has brought together some of the best minds in the country to analyze the data and discuss one of the country's best-kept secrets: youth disconnectedness. *America's Disconnected Youth* offers firm, gripping evidence of the relationship between long-term disconnectedness among young adults and the short-sighted decisions to cut off or shortchange supports to marginally connected youth in the high school and transitional years. If research can have an impact on policy, this volume should.

Karen Johnson Pittman, Senior Vice President
International Youth Foundation

America's Disconnected Youth: Toward a Preventive Strategy

Douglas J. Besharov, Editor

CWLA Press

American Enterprise Institute for Public Policy Research

Washington, DC

CWLA Press is an imprint of the Child Welfare League of America. The Child Welfare League of America (CWLA), the nation's oldest and largest membership-based child welfare organization, is committed to engaging all Americans in promoting the well-being of children and protecting every child from harm.

CHILD WELFARE LEAGUE OF AMERICA, INC.
440 First Street, NW, Third Floor, Washington, DC 20001-2085
E-mail: books@cwla.org

AMERICAN ENTERPRISE INSTITUTE FOR PUBLIC POLICY RESEARCH
1150 17th Street NW
Washington, DC 20036-4670

CURRENT PRINTING (last digit)
10 9 8 7 6 5 4 3 2 1

Cover design by Luke Johnson

Printed in the United States of America

ISBN # 0–87868-756-4

Library of Congress Cataloging-in-Publication Data
America's disconnected youth : toward a preventive strategy / edited by Douglas J. Besharov.
    p.   cm.
    Includes bibliographical references.
    ISBN 0-87868-756-4 (alk. paper)
    1. Teenagers--Services for--United States. 2. Youth--Services for--United States. 3. School-to-work transition--United States.
    I. Besharov, Douglas J.   II. Child Welfare League of America.
    III. American Enterprise Institute for Public Policy Research.
    HV1431.A64   1999   99-20814
    362.7'083--dc21   CIP

Contents

List of Tables

List of Figures

Foreword

Adolescence is a time of both great opportunity and risk, as young people experience physical change, intellectual growth, self-discovery, and growing independence. This is the time where strategic investment in our youth is extremely valuable and an opportunity exists to encourage the formation of healthy behaviors that could last a lifetime. The value of programs and support for young people is increasingly recognized, and new efforts are under way nationally to more fully utilize and understand their broader implications.

Over the past decade, The Commonwealth Fund's Helping Young People Become Productive Adults program developed and tested innovative mentoring programs and supported efforts to understand the factors that help adolescents make a successful transition to adulthood. The Fund has had a strong interest in helping to consolidate the position of mentoring and school-to-work programs within the health care industry, schools, and communities and has sought to inform policy discussions about successful programs for at-risk adolescents through the following multipronged strategy:
- test and evaluate models
- advance knowledge through surveys, evaluation and best practices studies, and research
- inform public policies on youth programs through targeted dissemination efforts.

This interest in youth development has yielded important lessons about how a caring mentor can provide encouragement and guidance during the difficult transition from adolescence to adulthood, while also imparting skills and values needed for later success in school and employment. This knowledge will continue to assist in the development of practical models for providing young people with adult guidance, transferable work skills, and job opportunities.

As part of the documenting lessons learned and building on previous Fund-supported research, the American Enterprise Institute is publishing *America's Disconnected Youth: Toward a Preventive Strategy*. Some of the papers in this volume were first presented at a May 1996 Fund-supported conference of the same name. The Institute's findings, primarily based on the National Longitudinal Survey of Youth (NLSY), stress the importance of young people's involvement in at least one mainstream sphere of activity, such as school, work, military service, or marriage. The findings additionally emphasize the importance of building on a system that is already established to create an environment that enables growth, development, and opportunity. An example of a prime institution that interfaces with youth is the education system. Those working in this system see our children daily and have repeated opportunities to influence their lives. This system must be harnessed—not simply within the classroom but broadly, including both in- and out-of-school activities.

America's Disconnected Youth: Toward a Preventive Strategy has growing relevance, especially as prevention is increasingly seen as an activity emphasized for very young children. Prevention strategies for youth should continue well past the early years, into the tumultuous time of adolescence, where development and change continue full force. It is important to not give up on our children and continue to support their healthy development in constructive ways that help them stay in school and make a successful transition toward productive adulthood.

Because *America's Disconnected Youth: Toward a Preventive Strategy* focuses on the importance of a strategy of prevention rather than crisis intervention in configuring youth-related services, its ideas are hopeful and encouraging. It will be an important resource to policymakers, youth program leaders, and the public alike.

Karen Davis
President, The Commonwealth Fund

Acknowledgments

This book reports on the first stages of a project to increase our understanding about why some young people have difficulty making transitions to productive adulthood—and how to help them make more successful transitions. When we began, we decided to call these young people "disconnected," and defined them as 16- to 23-year-olds who were not in school, working, or married for at least six months in any calendar year. We rejected other terms, such as "idle youth," because they suggested that these young people were doing nothing at all, which is not the case. We are pleased that others have begun using the term disconnected as well.

Our first step was to estimate the nature and scope of youthful disconnectedness and to identify some of the factors associated with it. We asked Brett Brown of Child Trends, Inc. to conduct this research. His thoughtful and meticulous analysis of the National Longitudinal Survey of Youth provided many new insights about this population and laid the factual foundation for our project. Kristin Moore, Executive Director at Child Trends, Inc., was an important source of guidance and wisdom.

An advisory committee assisted us to plan and interpret the Child Trends research. The members of the committee were Jim Connell, then senior vice president for research, Public/Private Ventures; Felton Earls, professor, Harvard School of Public Health; Ronald Ferguson, associate professor, John F. Kennedy School of Government; Frank Furstenberg, professor of sociology, University of Pennsylvania; Ricardo Galbis, director, Andromeda Hispano Mental Health Center; Michael

Lamb, chief of social and emotional development, National Institute of Child Health and Human Development; Robert Lerman, director of human resources policy, The Urban Institute; Ronald Mincy, program officer, The Ford Foundation; Karen Pittman, then vice president, the Academy for Educational Development; and Freya Sonenstein, director of population studies, The Urban Institute. Collectively and individually, this group helped us conceptualize the problem and guided us in the preparation of our final report.

In May, 1996, we held a day-long policy conference on the subject at the American Enterprise Institute (AEI). The conference, "America's Disconnected Youth: Toward a Preventive Strategy," was attended by more than 100 researchers and policymakers. The keynote speaker was Representative William Goodling of Pennsylvania, chairman of the relevant committee of the House of Representatives, at that time called the Committee on Economic and Educational Opportunities.

Many of the papers from this conference also appear in this volume. The conference also benefitted from three papers, not included here, on the effects of taxes and income transfers on family formation by Stacy Dickert-Conlin, assistant professor of economics, University of Kentucky; Eugene Steuerle, senior fellow, The Urban Institute; and Timothy Sullivan, instructor of economics, Southern Illinois University. In addition, Gary Walker, president of Public/Private Ventures, presented a paper on the merits of mentoring programs. Four discussants provided the programmatic, social, and political contexts for the papers: Amy Bentanzos, president, Wildcat Service Corporation; Peter Edelman, former assistant secretary for planning and evaluation, U.S. Department of Health and Human Services; Kevin Garvey, director of training and career development, United Parcel Service; and Mark Lopez, assistant professor of public affairs, University of Maryland.

At AEI, the project was initially in the capable hands of Lisa Laumann, who is now a doctoral student in psychology at the University of Virginia. In addition to serving as the principal contact with Child Trends researchers and the advisory committee, Lisa helped draft the introduction to this volume. Final editing of the chapters was admirably performed by Dana Lane, Ann Petty, and Cheryl Wiseman of AEI and Cathy Corder of the Child Welfare League of America. Shelley Obringer, of AEI, ably and cheerfully marshalled all file chapters—and authors—as we completed the manuscript and made final revisions. Susan Brite, the League's director of publications, supported the publication of this book from the beginning, and efficiently squired it though all stages of production.

As mentioned above, this book is the first major product of a long-term project on the prevention of youthful disconnectedness. The Commonwealth Fund generously supported the first stage of this project, which included the Child Trends research, the policy conference, and the publication of this book. The Fund's president, Karen Davis, contributed the Foreword to this volume and has been a constant source of encouragement and guidance. Many members of the Fund's staff helped us throughout the project, especially Karen Fulbright, Shawn LaFrance, and Kathryn Taaffe McLearn. Besides helping deal with the administration of the grants, each provided advice on how to interpret and present our findings.

As suggested by the contents of this book, our research on disconnected youth is now focusing on the potential of career-oriented education. With support from the Charles Stewart Mott Foundation, we are now analyzing data from a number of national data sets to determine the current universe of career-oriented education and its effects on educational, labor market, and social outcomes.

At the Mott Foundation, Jack Litzenberg immediately appreciated the importance of career-oriented education and helped us conceptualize the project. Christine Sturgis, also at Mott, reviewed our research plans as well as the manuscript for this book and offered helpful suggestions about additional research that might be included.

I also want to express thanks to the authors of the papers that appear in this book, not only for their insights—but also for their patience in responding to our numerous requests for changes in their papers. They were invariably cooperative and good natured.

And most special thanks go to Karen N. Gardiner, my long-time friend and colleague, who recently departed AEI for The Lewin Group. Karen assumed responsibility for this project when Lisa Laumann left AEI. With her help, we were able to complete the analysis that resulted in the introduction to this volume, as well as various publications. She also worked with the authors to shape and revise their chapters. Throughout, she was a critical eye and careful wordsmith, who cared deeply for the young people who are the subject of this book.

D.J.B.
June, 1999
Washington, D.C.

Introduction: Preventing Youthful Disconnectedness

Douglas J. Besharov & Karen N. Gardiner*

Many American youth are diverted from the path toward becoming productive members of society. Some drop out of high school and are inactive for many years. Others finish school but do not find gainful employment. Some use drugs, go to jail, or both. Some have babies out of wedlock and spend years on welfare. Despite their differences, all these young people have one thing in common: they spend a crucial period of their lives "disconnected" from the broader society.

Disconnectedness is most visible in the contemporary inner city, as William Julius Wilson, Lewis P. and Linda Geyser University Professor at Harvard, suggests in this book's first chapter, "The Plight of the Inner-City Black Male." Wilson describes the deteriorating economic and social status of inner-city black males, tracing this "new urban poverty" to the flight of well-paying blue collar jobs. Today's inner-city neighborhoods are marked by joblessness, which, he argues, leads to low levels of social organization.

Using data from the Chicago Urban Poverty and Family Life Study, Wilson contends that the image of the inner city—overrun by crime, gang violence, drug trafficking, and family breakups—stigmatizes black males and makes employment difficult. Whereas in the past, employers looked at a job candidate's strength and stamina, employers today judge potential employees by references and connections. Low-income black males, unlike their Hispanic counterparts, lack the informal job

---

* Lisa A. Laumann helped prepare this chapter when she was at the American Enterprise Institute for Public Policy Research. A version of this chapter appeared in the *Children and Youth Services Review*.

1

networks that lead to jobs. As a result, many resort to illicit activities, such as hustling. Wilson proposes educational policies that strengthen the transition from school to work, including national performance standards, policies to equalize public school resources and involve the private sector, and family policies that reinforce learning, such as universal preschool programs.

But the problems of disconnectedness run throughout our society. It is a problem for youth of all racial and ethnic groups. As Wilson notes, joblessness and social disorganization are two markers of disconnectedness.

Risky sexual practices also identify youth who are not connected to mainstream society or values. In this book's second chapter, "Teen Sexuality Among Inner-City White Youth," Patricia Stern, a doctoral candidate in sociology at the University of Pennsylvania, describes the role that sexual activity plays in establishing adult identities for youth in a poor, predominantly white neighborhood in Philadelphia. She notes that youth from myriad socioeconomic, racial and ethnic, and religious backgrounds engage in sexual activity. But neighborhood norms affect how teenagers prepare and respond to the consequences of their behavior. Whereas middle-class youth might actively seek to avoid pregnancy by using contraception, the teens Stern interviewed in Milton (a poor, predominantly Catholic, white neighborhood), eschewed prevention strategies. These youth were uncertain about their futures. Blue collar jobs were vanishing from the neighborhood. There were few role models to demonstrate the benefit of higher education. They felt let down by the adults in their lives. To fill this void, according to Stern, teenagers used sexual activity to exert power and establish some control over their lives. For many young people in Milton, according to Stern, pregnancy and babies often were used as a means to finding love and becoming independent from their families.

The research that undergirds this book also reveals that many youth of all races are disconnected for varying periods of time. Besides focusing on particularly high-risk groups, therefore, societal responses should reflect this broader reality.

Studying "Disconnectedness"

Policymakers have long worried about the consequences of youthful disconnection, as evidenced by high-profile efforts to combat drug abuse, teenage pregnancy, and youth crime. Studies focusing on dysfunctional or high-risk behavior among youth have informed, or in some cases been the impetus for, many of these efforts. Much of this research, however, portrays youth behavior at only one point in time. The Center for Disease Control's Youth Risk Behavior Survey, for example, highlighted the prevalence of frequent sexual activity, drug use, and other risky behaviors among high school students. But there was little analysis of how these individual behaviors might relate to an underlying problem (like disconnection from mainstream society) or how they might dim the future life prospects of the youth. Similarly, although many longitudinal studies have detailed the characteristics, behaviors, and later life histories of subsets of youth (such as low-income teenage mothers, young unwed fathers, idle youth, and unemployed youth), none, to our knowledge, has followed an entire cohort of youth.

To address both gaps, researchers at Child Trends, Inc., and AEI analyzed data from the National Longitudinal Survey of Youth (NLSY), one of the most comprehensive data sources for tracking the transition of youth into the labor force. Since 1979, the NLSY has annually tracked a group of about 12,000 males and females, ages 14 to 21, to create a comprehensive, longitudinal record of their activities. Blacks, Hispanics, and poor whites were oversampled to facilitate analysis of these groups. As of 1991, 90% of the sample was still being interviewed.

In collaboration with Brett Brown and his colleagues at Child Trends, we followed 4,000 youth from 1979, when they were 14, 15, and 16 years old, through 1991, when they were in their mid-to-late 20s. Most of our analyses focused on youth aged 16 to 23 because, developmentally, it is a difficult period of transition during which young people struggle to become adults.

To define disconnectedness, we first identified those activities that connect young people to mainstream society: school (secondary and postsecondary), work, and military service. There are, of course, other activities that can connect someone to the broader society, but these behaviors were the most telling and capable of reasonably accurate measurement within the NLSY. After careful consideration, we also decided to include marriage as a form of connection. Excluding marriage would have had the effect of classifying homemakers married to working men or students as disconnected women.[1]

The definition of disconnectedness also needed a temporal dimension. One possibility was to count youth as disconnected if they were not involved in any of the four specified activities during the NLSY survey week. This method yielded the largest number of disconnected youth, but it incorrectly labeled as disconnected young people who worked or were in school for much of the year but who, during that one week, happened to be between jobs or taking time off after school graduation. Another possibility was to count youth only if they were disconnected for an entire 52-week period. This definition erred in the other direction: it yielded the smallest number of disconnected youth because it excluded those who were in school or who worked for as little as one week during the entire year.

Clearly, our definition needed to specify a time period between one and 52 weeks. We chose 26 weeks (or more) out of any calendar year, because we hypothesized that young people disconnected for that long were likely to experience serious problems in later life—especially as we considered multiyear spells of disconnection.

Hence, we defined disconnectedness as not being enrolled in school (either having dropped out or not continuing after graduation), not employed, not in the military, and not married to someone who met at least one of the criteria—for 26 weeks or more out of any calendar year. Based on the findings reported below, it appears that this definition successfully distinguished between young people who were actively involved in the broader society (by either working or being engaged in activities that would build human capital) and youth who, for extended periods of time, were not.

Our study sought to answer several questions: How prevalent is disconnectedness? Who are the disconnected youth, and do they share certain characteristics? Are they the urban men described by William Julius Wilson, or a broader group of youth? How do disconnected youth fare in later life? And, most important, how can we prevent disconnectedness? Although not reported here, in examining each issue, we took into account how a different definition would have altered our findings.

Nature and Extent

In this book's third chapter, "Prevalence, Patterns, and Outcomes," Brett Brown, a research associate at Child Trends, and Carol Emig, assistant director for public information and policy there, summarize the main findings of our study.[2]

Youthful disconnectedness is widespread in American society. Even under our relatively narrow definition, many young people went through a period of disconnectedness as they moved from adolescence to adulthood (from ages 16 to 23). In fact, more than one-third (37%) of both males and females were disconnected for at least 26 weeks during one calendar year (see Table 1).

Such short-term disconnectedness was prevalent among all racial groups, but with important differences. For males, rates were 32% for whites, 55% for blacks, and 50% for Hispanics. Rates for white and Hispanic females were about the same as those for their male counterparts. Black females, however, were 22% more likely than black males to have been disconnected (67% compared with 55%).

Why were the black women, unlike the women in the other two groups, more likely to be disconnected than the black men? Part of the difference was due to marital status. When we included marital status in our definition of connectedness, the proportion of women disconnected at age 23 dropped 61% among whites, 53% among Hispanics, but a smaller 31% among blacks. And most of these women were connected through more than one activity: At age 23, about 7% of the sample was connected through marriage only.

Table 1. Prevalence of Disconnectedness for Males and Females in the United States (percent)

	Never (0 years*)	Short-term (1-2 years)	Long-term (3+ years)
All Males	63	24	13
White	67	23	10
Black	45	28	26
Hispanic	50	30	19
All Females	62	24	14
White	68	23	9
Black	33	30	37
Hispanic	50	29	21

* A year is defined as being disconnected for 26 or more weeks out of any given year.

Source: Child Trends, Inc.

Our definition also counted as disconnected the unmarried women who were caring for their children while on public assistance. Black teens are almost three times more likely than non-Hispanic whites to have a baby out of wedlock, which would make them more likely to go on welfare. (In 1996, the rates for 15- to 19-year-olds were 89.2 per 1,000 and 27 per 1,000, respectively) [DHHS 1998]. Other studies indicate that many unmarried fathers have children by more than one woman [Achatz & MacAllum 1994, Anderson 1993]. Moreover, it may be that many unmarried African American fathers (and black males in general) have an easier time finding a job performing manual labor, for example, than do African American single mothers. As William Julius Wilson discusses in his chapter, the lack of informal networks in African American communities to provide job referrals, transportation, and child care place an additional obstacle to black mothers' working. Whatever the explanation is, the difference is large enough to be of concern to policy.

Few youth were disconnected before their third year of high school. At age 16, only 5% of males and 4% of females were disconnected. But the numbers rise quickly thereafter. By age 17, rates of disconnectedness doubled among whites (from 4 to 8%), almost tripled among blacks (5 to 13%), and increased two-thirds among Hispanics (9 to 15%), a smaller increase because the base was higher. (See Figure 1.) And by age 19, almost 17% of both males and females had been disconnected for at least one 26-week period.

Given the importance of these figures to our later recommendations about preventive interventions, we note that they are consistent with the U.S. Department of Education's estimates of high school dropout rates. According to its analysis of the U.S. Census Bureau's Current Population Survey, only 3.7% of 16-year-olds have dropped out. The dropout rate is highest for 18-year-olds (at 12%) [U.S. Department of Education 1993].

To assess the significance of these high rates of disconnectedness, we also examined whether disconnectedness was associated with the youth's later family income, employment stability, and poverty status.[3] As described next, we found that most youth who were disconnected did not suffer severe long-term economic and social problems.

Short-term disconnected youth do not seem to suffer serious social or economic problems. Almost two-thirds of the ever-disconnected males and females were disconnected in only one or two years. For them, disconnectedness did not seem to be associated with long-lasting problems (see Table 2 on page 11).

As young adults (ages 25 to 28), 15% of short-term disconnected males and 22% of their female counterparts were in poverty. The median family income for this group was about $30,000, the same as the median income of all American households [U.S. Bureau of the Census 1992].[4] The vast majority of short-term disconnected women were not relying on federal programs: only 10% were receiving welfare and only 14% were receiving food stamps. (By way of comparison, 11% of American families with children under age 18 were on Aid to Families

Percent

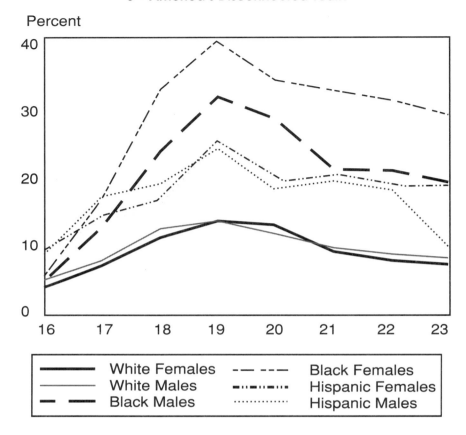

White Females	Black Females
White Males	Hispanic Females
Black Males	Hispanic Males

with Dependent Children [the precursor to Temporary Assistance for Needy Families] in 1990; about 10% of individuals received food stamps.) Many were married: 40% of males and 48% of females. In addition, most men (61%), and almost half the women (48%), were employed full time.

By age 23, most of the short-term disconnected had completed high school or received a General Educational Development (GED) certificate (75% of males and 84% of females). Of these, a sizable proportion had a GED instead of a diploma (more than one-third of males and one-fourth of females). (This is an important finding because researchers who study the education of young people have called into question the value of the GED and whether it is an adequate substitute for a high school diploma.)[5] The proportion of females who gave birth to a child before age 18 (12%) was about the same as for the population of females under age 18 as a whole (11%).

These surprisingly small differences are partly an artifact of our definition of short-term disconnectedness, which encompasses a broad range of youth without serious problems. Our definition, for example, includes a high school graduate who took six months or more to find a first job and a college student who took six months off after graduation to travel.

Nevertheless, those who had been disconnected even for a short time as youth did not fare as well in early adulthood as did youth who had never been disconnected. Very few women who had never been disconnected were in poverty (4%), and fewer were relying on welfare and food stamps when they were ages 25 to 28 (1% and 3%, respectively). The median family income of those who had never been disconnected ($40,000) was above the U.S. average. More men and women worked full time (75% and 61%) and were married (54% and 65%). Ninety-four percent of males who had never been disconnected and 96% of their female counterparts had a high school diploma or a GED. Moreover, fewer of these were GEDs: 8% of males and 9% of females. Only 5% of the females had had a child by age 18.

Although the short-term disconnected seemed to have experienced more problems in early adulthood than youth who had never been disconnected, future research that controls for family characteristics may explain some of this discrepancy. There is likely a selection effect at work: Those young people who were never disconnected probably had various personal and family characteristics that made them more successful in life.

Youth disconnected in three or more years suffer long-term social and economic problems. Youth disconnected in three or more years experienced significant hardship, even into their mid- and late-20s. At ages 25 to 28, median family income was only about $18,000 for men and $15,000 for women. About 44% of the long-term disconnected men and 56%

of the women were in poverty. In addition, many of the long-term disconnected women were still relying on some form of public assistance: 34% received AFDC and 48% received food stamps (see Table 2).

Adult labor force participation continued to be tenuous for those individuals who were disconnected in three or more years in their youth. At ages 25 to 28, only 41% of the men and 21% of the women were employed full-time. Because the vast majority of people have completed their schooling by this age, these very low employment figures are of substantial concern. They indicate that the majority of the long-term disconnected had still not become productive members of mainstream society.

The lower family income of those who had been long-term disconnected youth may also be the result of marital status. They were only about half as likely as connected youth to be married in their late 20s. Less than 30% were married at ages 25 to 28. Moreover, the long-term disconnected who did marry were more likely than those who were never disconnected to be divorced or separated (24% versus 11% for women; 13% versus 10% for men).

Thus, those who were idle for extended periods of time in their youth experienced substantial social and economic hardship as adults. We cannot say definitively why long-term disconnected youth fared much worse as adults than did their short-term disconnected counterparts. We do know that short-term disconnectedness began, on average, at ages 18 to 19, or after high school. Long-term disconnectedness, however, began around age 16. As a result, youth disconnected for the long term were twice as likely to have dropped out of high school. Of those who did graduate, three-quarters had a GED, almost three times the proportion of short-term disconnected youth. Moreover, twice as many long-term disconnected females as short-term ones had had a child before age 18 (24% versus 12%). All these behaviors compromise the development of human capital.

In addition, long-term disconnected males were more likely to have spent time in jail, further reducing their eventual earnings capacity.

Table 2. Measures of Adult Status by Periods of Disconnectedness for Males and Females (percent)

	Never (0 years*)	Short-term (1-2 years)	Long-term (3+ years)
Males			
In poverty	3	15	44
Employed full-time	75	61	41
Married	54	39	23
Females			
In poverty	4	22	56
Receiving welfare	1	10	34
Employed full-time	62	48	21
Married	65	48	28

* A year is defined as being disconnected for 26 or more weeks out of any given year.

Source: Child Trends, Inc.

Over 30% of men who were disconnected in three or more years spent some time in a jail or youth correctional facility, more than six times the rate for the short-term disconnected men (30% versus 5%). As might be expected, women were much less likely than men to have spent time in jail, with only around 3% of even the long-term disconnected women having spent any time in jail as youth.

Again, in interpreting differences between short-term and long-term disconnected youth, we must recognize the probability of a substantial selection effect, as mentioned above. Nevertheless, society should be deeply concerned about the very poor status as adults of the long-term disconnected.

Various social and demographic characteristics identify adolescents at high risk of long-term disconnectedness. We did not conduct multivariate analyses, so we cannot identify those factors that cause youthful disconnection. Nevertheless, our bivariate analyses identified factors so closely associated with later disconnectedness that they may be considered precursors to it (see Table 3). Later, we argue that these precursors should inform a preventive strategy.

Specific aspects of family background are strongly related to long-term disconnectedness.[6] Youth whose parents were high school dropouts, for example, compared with those who had at least one parent who graduated from high school, were almost three times more likely to be disconnected in three or more years (25% versus 9%). Family welfare receipt and poverty status were also strongly associated with long-term disconnectedness. More than 40% of the females who came from families that received welfare were disconnected in three or more years, compared with 11% of females from families that did not. A similar proportion of females who grew up in poor families, 36%, became long-term disconnected, while only about 10% of those who were not poor did so. (Male rates were within 5 percentage points of the females.[7])

Even more than family background, however, intellectual ability or achievement appears to be related to long-term disconnectedness. Over 30% of males and 40% of females who scored in the lowest quartile on the Armed Forces Qualifying Test (AFQT)[8] became long-term disconnected, compared with only 2% of both males and females who scored in the top quartile. Of those youth scoring in the middle two quartiles, about 10% became long-term disconnected.

Dropping out of high school also put youth at risk of long-term disconnection. Four in 10 high school dropouts became disconnected for the long term. By way of comparison, only 5% of males and 8% of females who graduated from high school became long-term disconnected. Moreover, those who were suspended or expelled from school were three and a half times more likely to become long-term disconnected than those who were not.[9]

Considered alone, race was associated with long-term disconnectedness. Black youth were found to be two to four times more likely than white youth to become long-term disconnected. (For men, the figures were 26% compared with 10%; for women, they were 37% versus 9%.)

Table 3. Risk Characteristics (Females)

	% Long-term Disconnected
Parent dropped out of high school	23.6
Parent graduated from high school	8.7
Family poor	35.6
Family not poor	9.7
Family on welfare	40.5
Family not on welfare	10.8
Dropped out of high school	42.8
Graduated from high school	8.1
Gave birth before age 18	36.8
Did not give birth before age 18	11.4

Source: Child Trends, Inc.

Racial differences in rates of long-term disconnectedness, however, diminished substantially when family poverty was taken into account. For both black and white males whose families were poor in 1978, 30% became long-term disconnected. Among the women, however, there was still a large discrepancy between the rates of long-term disconnectedness for poor black and poor white women: 51% versus 23%. As indicated earlier, this result was largely a product of our definition of disconnectedness, which counted unmarried and unemployed mothers caring for their children (presumably while on public assistance) as disconnected.

Racial differences also decreased when intellectual ability or achievement was considered, especially for men. Of black and white males who scored in the top quartile on the AFQT, only 2% became long-term disconnected. For women, there was a greater disparity between the races: about 2% of white females who scored in the top quartile became disconnected for the long term, while 13% of their black counterparts did so. Again, this difference is likely due to the black females' higher rates of nonmarital births and subsequent welfare recipiency.

Drug use was also related to long-term disconnectedness, but only for males. More than one-fifth of males who had used drugs before age 16 became long-term disconnected, compared with 11% of males who did not use drugs. Among females, there was no statistically significant difference in rates of long-term disconnectedness by reported use of drugs.

Early parenthood also seemed to be associated with long-term disconnectedness. Almost 40% of females who gave birth before age 18 became long-term disconnected compared with 11% of females who did not give birth. For men, 35% who fathered a child before age 18 became long-term disconnected, compared with 12% of those who did not. We cannot tell from our analysis whether the teenagers were married at the time they gave birth. The vast majority of births to younger teens, however, are out of wedlock. The National Center for Health Statistics reports that in 1996 (the most recent data available) 86% of births to 16-year-olds were out of wedlock, as were 82% of births to 17-year-olds [DHHS 1998].

Combining two risk categories identified the youth who were at especially high risk of becoming long-term disconnected. For instance, of the youth who came from welfare families and who scored in the lowest quartile on the AFQT, more than 50% of men and 68% of women became disconnected for the long term (compared with about 11% of youth who had neither of these characteristics). Furthermore, of the women who came from welfare families and had a baby before age 18, 66% became long-term disconnected.

All these characteristics, of course, are highly related to each other, making it difficult to differentiate paths of causation. More significantly, many young people growing up in inner-city neighborhoods live under such circumstances without spending appreciable time being disconnected. Chapters 4 and 5 identify some of the prime factors that seem to help youth from similarly disadvantaged backgrounds to attain greater success in life: family, community institutions (especially churches), and schools (including counseling and mentoring programs).

In this book's fourth chapter, "Family Background, Church Attendance, and School Achievement," Linda Datcher Loury, a professor of economics at Tufts University, explores the impact of family and church on achievement. Analyzing the ETS-Head Start Longitudinal Study, a large national data set, Datcher Loury found that parental attitudes and behaviors affected children's school readiness at age 5 and school achievement at age 12. She found that when mothers read to their children several times a week, participated in groups such as the PTA, and had (and expressed) high educational expectations for them, the children, in turn, had higher reading and math test scores. Higher reading scores were also associated with the presence of puzzles, paints, books, encyclopedias, records, and musical instruments in the home. Datcher Loury also analyzed the High School and Beyond Sophomore and Senior Cohorts and found that regular church attendance during the high school years was associated with increased years of schooling for black and white females (but not males).

Thus, according to Datcher Loury, youth whose backgrounds are similar in terms of parental education, family income, and family structure experience varying levels of educational success because of the different levels of social capital available to them. The factors leading to greater achievement that she identified tend to derive from the youth's family.

"Listening to Young, Inner-City African American Males," this book's fifth chapter, illuminates the important role of supportive schools, as well as families. In it, Kathryn Taaffe McLearn, an assistant vice president at the Commonwealth Fund, and Shawn LaFrance, a former program officer there, report on what a sample of young black males said helped them succeed in school. In a survey for the Fund, Louis Harris and Associates conducted in-person interviews of low-income males aged 17 to 22 in predominantly black neighborhoods of four large U.S. cities. Half of the males had dropped out of school; the others were either in high school, had graduated, had obtained a GED, or were in college.

According to McLearn and LaFrance, the young men who "succeeded" in school (that is, did not drop out) reported that parental and teacher support were the most important factors that helped them stay in school. The authors identified a number of "protective family characteristics" that were associated with academic success. The successful students said that their parents were more likely to supervise homework and visit teachers; they were also more likely to report that they had a quiet, safe place to study after school. Moreover, they were more likely than dropouts to have grown up with two parents in the home, and less likely to have moved frequently as a child or to report that a parent had a mental health or substance abuse problem.

In addition, the males who succeeded in school were more likely than those who dropped out to rate their teachers as competent; to have participated in a community, school, or church program; and to have had access to a counselor or mentor. They were also more likely to have had a job while in school.

School-Related Interventions

These and other studies suggest that many interventions might reduce disconnectedness. Some could target youth after they have become disconnected, including programs for teen mothers that provide basic education, training, and family planning services. And, as the remaining chapters in this book describe, other interventions could take a preventive approach, especially focusing on school-related programs.

Most youth were still in school through the 11th grade. Thus, up to age 16 or 17, high schools still provide a platform for preventive services aimed at the most troubled youth. We are cautiously optimistic that three school-related interventions—career-oriented education, after-school "safe havens," and efforts at targeting individual deficits—may prevent many disadvantaged youth from dropping out of high school.

Career-Oriented Education

Recent ethnographic studies bolster the widely held view that youth will be more responsible about schooling and other personal behaviors if they have something to look forward to, such as a good job. Elijah Anderson of the University of Pennsylvania, for example, argues that unmarried early motherhood and fatherhood, a common route to long-term disconnectedness, is a response to a perceived lack of life opportunities. In his study of a low-income, predominantly black neighborhood in Philadelphia, he found that youth were involved in a game in which young girls were lured into having sex by the older boys' "vague but convincing" promises of marriage. The girls who went along with this ruse usually ended up "pregnant and abandoned" [Anderson 1993].

Anderson argues that this male "wantonness" is attributable largely to the flight from the inner city of many well-paying, blue-collar jobs and the lack of adequate skills for those jobs that are still available. He concludes, "When a sense of future exists, we will see more responsible behavior, sexual and otherwise" [Anderson 1993]. Many middle-class youth, after all, are also sexually active, but they are much less likely to have children because they know that unwed parenthood will compromise their futures.

A host of factors contribute to inner-city youth unemployment, including the absence of jobs (or of networks to inform youth about existing jobs) and racial discrimination by employers. But the lack of an education and work-related skills are central. Youth who see a concrete connection between what they learn in school and a brighter future may be less likely to drop out. A renewed emphasis on career-oriented education, supplemented by enhanced job-counseling and job-finding services, may help establish this link.

In this book's sixth chapter, "The 'Hallwalkers,'" Hillard Pouncy, a fellow at the University of Pennsylvania, warns that many disadvantaged students see little value in attending classes because they do not connect schooling with their future financial well-being. In the West Philadelphia high school he studied, many of the students were simply not mentally engaged. Instead, they passed the day by walking the halls.

Pouncy argues that career-oriented education can have multiple positive effects on students, citing as an example a study of New York

City's 59 career magnet programs (the city's version of school-to-work programs). The magnet programs were designed to be selective, but because of political opposition to such an "elitist" approach, a compromise was made to admit half of the students by lottery, with one-sixth required to be below average in reading and math skills (measured in the 8th grade).

The lottery had the effect of randomly assigning applicants to either the experimental (magnet) programs or regular high schools. Pouncy reports on a study by Robert Crain and his colleagues at Columbia University, which analyzed the records of 9,200 lotteried students and conducted in-depth interviews with 110 of the youth. Compared with students in standard high schools, students enrolled in the magnet schools exhibited fewer risky behaviors (such as smoking and drinking), took more career-related courses, had higher post-graduation earnings, developed new social networks, improved their language skills, and earned more college credits.[10]

Unfortunately, these findings are not generalizable to the city's entire school population, because only students who actually applied to the program were part of the study. The findings only reflect the program's impact on students who, by applying to the magnet program, are presumably more motivated to do better in school. Nevertheless, as Pouncy concludes, the study illuminates what would happen to the hallwalkers if they entered a selective career magnet school.

In this book's seventh chapter, "Improving Links Between High Schools and Careers," Robert Lerman, director of human resources policy at the Urban Institute, argues, in effect, that the students Pouncy observed in the hallways might be right. He says that schools are failing to provide disadvantaged students with the skills they need to succeed in the labor market. Worse, the schools may weaken young people's motivation to succeed, because, according to Lerman, performing well in school does not automatically translate into a good job.

Lerman asserts that a career-oriented approach to education, one that integrates academics with well-structured work-based learning, is the approach most likely to help disadvantaged young people succeed in school. If students see the connection between what they do in school and their future well-being, they may have a stronger incentive to learn—and stay in school. At the same time, work-based education programs provide valuable job experience, contacts, and references.

According to Lerman, a work-based learning system would appeal to employers, many of whom are critical of the school system for failing to equip students with the skills needed for today's job market. He cites surveys of employers finding that most entry-level jobs require more than basic competencies in math, clear speaking, and writing. For example, one study of employees in 300 large and small businesses in New York State and a survey of 3,000 employers in four metropolitan areas found the following qualities were valued by employers, yet rarely addressed in traditional academic programs: working well as a team member, using information systems, setting priorities, having good personal habits, and reacting constructively to positive or negative feedback.

There is some evidence that even "at-risk" students can be prevented from dropping out of school through career-oriented education. Located outside of Los Angeles, the East San Gabriel Valley School District's Marketing/Merchandising/Apparel Program serves students who are below grade level in basic skills, have a history of poor academic achievement, are two or more years older than other students in the same grade, reside in a low-income household, or come from a family where one or both parents or siblings dropped out of school. The dropout rate in the district is as high as 50% in some schools. Two-thirds of the district students are minorities, and a similar proportion come from single-parent families. More than half have a grade point average under 2.0.

Juniors and seniors participate for three hours each day. They have access to academic and vocational assessment, career guidance, individualized academic remediation, and tutoring. Job skills are taught through a combination of classroom-based and business-based instruction. The companies supporting the program include Macy's, American Airlines, K-Mart Corporation, Safeway Stores, Nordstrom, Hallmark Stores, and B. Dalton Books.

Compared to students with similar academic and socioeconomic backgrounds who did not participate, the students in the program were 41% more likely to graduate from high school (92% versus 65%). About two-thirds of the program group went on to postsecondary education, compared with 44% of the comparison group. After high school, 87% of the program group was employed, 36% more than the comparison group (64%). Finally, students in the program group were twice as likely to have "upwardly mobile" jobs, defined as jobs with some management responsibility or a pay raise in the past year (15% versus 7%) [Floyd, undated]. Although a selection effect undoubtedly boosted these positive statistics, the magnitude of these differences suggests that the program helped large numbers of young people.

Many inner-city students, however, do not have access to career-oriented programs. The U.S. Department of Education's National Assessment of Vocational Education found that while 80% of suburban school districts provided access to vocational schools, only 68% of urban districts and 55% of rural ones did so. The report found that "at least partly because of their greater concentration in suburban areas, [vocational schools] are less accessible to special populations of students [such as single parents], minority students, and, ironically, vocational students" [U.S. Department of Education 1994]. (Because these figures derive from responses to a yes-no question about "access," they do not necessarily reflect the degree of availability within the school districts—or the quality of the programs.)

Our impression is that actual availability is even lower in the inner city. According to the NLSY, for example, only 22% of long-term disconnected males and 30% of females were involved in vocational education clubs through school. In part, this low number reflects the fact that many of the long-term disconnected youth had dropped out of school and therefore could not be involved in any school-related activities. Nevertheless, it also suggests the degree to which career-oriented education may not be available to those who need it most.

How would an expansion of career-oriented schooling be accomplished? In this book's eighth chapter, "Focus High Schools," Paul Hill, director of the Institute for Public Policy at the University of Washington, describes how many urban high schools serving low-income students no longer perform their traditional role: linking young people to the institutions of adult life, such as higher education, the labor market, or particular employers. His solution to the bureaucratic breakdowns and general disarray of many public school systems is to encourage individual schools to develop clear and explicit missions—about the skills their graduates are expected to have acquired and the ways in which they will teach those skills.

Hill studied the outcomes of students in eight New York City high schools: three Catholic schools, two neighborhood comprehensive schools (or standard public schools), two special purpose public schools, and one "last chance" school for those who failed regular high school. He found that, compared to similar students attending neighborhood schools, students in special-purpose schools and parochial schools (what he calls "focus" schools) were more likely to graduate, take the SAT, and score higher on the SAT.

Unlike the comprehensive schools, the focus schools had simple and well-understood goals and control over their teaching methods. Definite goals and consistent programs allowed focus schools to build long-term relationships with families, employers, and institutions of higher education. The comprehensive schools, in contrast, had diffuse missions and programs that were constantly redefined by the actions of the district school board and central office. As a result, they tended to be unstable, have weak relationships with families and employers, and emphasize compliance over student outcomes. Hill concludes that school systems could serve all students better by substituting focus schools for poorly defined comprehensive schools. This requires school boards to enter long-term performance agreements with schools. This also requires giving schools control over their budgets and programs, and allowing students and teachers to choose among schools.

After-School "Safe Havens"

While classes and work experience can engage students during the school day, many disadvantaged youth return to neighborhoods that are teeming with gangs, drugs, and other diversions and that provide little adult supervision. Many grow up in households where, because of a variety of factors, they receive little academic or emotional support. Long-term disconnected youth were twice as likely as those never disconnected to be reared in a single-parent family, twice as likely to have four or more siblings, and three times as likely to have grown up poor. Long-term disconnected youth were only about half as likely as those never disconnected to have had magazines, newspapers, or library cards in their homes.

According to the Carnegie Council report, *A Matter of Time*, 40% of an average adolescent's time is unsupervised, and the peak time for adolescent violence, crime, and sexual activity is during after-school hours, 3:00 P.M. to 6:00 P.M. The same study also found that young people do not want to be left alone; they want regular contact with adults.

This suggests that many youth might benefit from after-school activities that are school based, school linked, or operated through community institutions. School-based activities, such as sports teams, bands, and clubs, are one example. Community centers often offer intramural sports and other team projects. Church-based groups, YMCAs, and Boys and Girls Clubs are other settings that enable students to spend time with their peers while under adult supervision. All such venues can give youth a sense of belonging, as well as a safe place to go after school.

And yet, our analysis of the NLSY indicates that long-term disconnected youth were only about half as likely to have participated in these activities as were youth who had never been disconnected. About one-quarter of long-term disconnected males had participated in an afterschool activity compared with 55% of males who had never been disconnected. For females, the figures were 20% and 46%, respectively. Again, the size of these differences may reflect the fact that long-term disconnected youth became disconnected around age 16 and, having left school, could not participate in activities.

Schools are experimenting with various approaches to engaging students during afternoon hours and long summer breaks. For example, since the mid-1980s, the number of schools that have adopted year-round schedules has increased almost six-fold, from 400 in 14 states to 2,700 in 41 states [Benning 1998]. Other programs seek to fill after-school hours with enriching projects. One, the Quantum Opportunities Program (QOP), engaged students from welfare families most at risk of dropping out in ongoing educational and community service activities.

In this book's ninth chapter, "Extending the Time of Learning," Andrew Hahn, associate dean of the Heller School at Brandeis University, summarizes the findings of this project. The program operated in four cities—Philadelphia, Oklahoma City, San Antonio, and Saginaw, Michigan. Each of the four sites compiled a list of the disadvantaged students (from households receiving some form of public assistance) entering the 9th grade. From this list, 25 students were randomly assigned to participate in QOP and 25 were randomly assigned to the control group.

The participants were provided with four years of intense academic and community services and an adult mentor and a peer group. "Once in QOP, always in QOP" was the program motto. Students could be inactive for periods of time and QOP staff from the community-based organizations that ran QOP never gave up on the students. The students attended plays and concerts, visited museums, and "job shadowed" professionals. They also performed community service projects ranging from tutoring elementary school students to neighborhood cleanup. Students also received small stipends for participating in approved activities, bonus payments for completing segments of the program, and matching funds that were placed in accrual accounts for use in a postsecondary activity.

After two years in the program, QOP students scored higher on tests of academic and functional skills than did those in a control group. In fact, QOP's effects seemed to increase over time. After four years in the program, QOP students were more likely than those in the control group to have graduated from high school, to be enrolled in postsecondary school, and to have received an award in the past year. QOP students were less likely than the control students to have dropped out of high school and to have had a child [Hahn 1994].

While the results of the evaluation are promising, they were largely driven by the enormous success of the Philadelphia site, where program participants performed better than the control group on all of the indicators. The experience of the other sites was more mixed. As is often the case, implementation may have been as important as design to the program's success, and raised questions about how best to replicate the program.

Targeting Deficits of Individual Youth

The youth described in the AEI/Child Trends study had both academic and emotional deficits that likely contributed to their dropping out of school. Other studies have found a connection between academic problems and high-risk behavior. The Manpower Demonstration Research Corporation, for example, designed an intervention for teenage mothers who were also high school dropouts. A baseline interview found that the average young woman, despite being 18 years old, read at the 8th grade level [Quint et al. 1994]. Interventions designed to reduce these deficits may help prevent disconnectedness.

As described above, long-term disconnected youth scored poorly on a test of cognitive skills and academic ability in relation to short-term disconnected youth and to those who were never disconnected. The average long-term disconnected male scored in the 24th percentile of the AFQT, while short-term and never-disconnected males scored in the 42nd and 59th percentiles, respectively. (For all three groups, females' scores were similar to the males'.)

The problems these students face should not be ignored. In some communities, math, English, and science classes are "tracked," thus allowing students who are having difficulty in a certain subject to proceed at a slower pace. Some oppose this kind of special treatment for fear it will diminish student self-esteem. For those who need extra assistance, then, schools could have readily available help outside of class. Some examples are tutoring by teachers before and after school, tutoring during set class periods, and resource centers to help students work on academic deficiencies (such as computer labs with programs to improve math or verbal skills). Some schools also use peer tutoring.

Long-term disconnected youth were also more likely to suffer from emotional deficits. Psychologists have found that youth who do not feel good about themselves are more susceptible to the pressure of their peers to engage in risky activities, such as drug use and unprotected sex [Benoit 1996]. The NLSY measured this variable with the Rosenberg Self-esteem Scale, which was administered to the youth at ages 15 to 17. Only about 40% of long-term disconnected males and females scored above the mean, compared with 60% of those never disconnected.

Mentoring may help in this regard. Regular contact with a successful adult can give a student sorely needed individual attention. Moreover, a caring adult may help that youth chart a path through adolescence by assisting in decisionmaking and goal setting. Many programs recruit adults from the same neighborhoods as the students so that mentors can serve as powerful examples of overcoming obstacles to become successful, working adults.

One mentoring program that has shown positive results is Big Brothers/Big Sisters. Public/Private Ventures evaluated the program in eight cities.[11] Adolescents aged 10 to 16 who signed up for the program were randomly assigned to either a mentor or a waiting list. Youth in the program group met with their mentors at least three times each month for approximately four hours. Half the youth were minorities, more than 90% lived with only one parent, and most came from low-income families.

Eighteen months after they began the program, the youth were reinterviewed. Evaluators found that the youth with mentors fared better than the control group on a number of indicators: they were 46% less likely to initiate drug use (and minority participants were 76% less likely to do so); 27% less likely to initiate drinking; one-third less likely to report hitting someone; and half as likely to skip school days. There were no statistically significant differences in self-concept between the two groups, however [Tierney et al. 1995].

These promising results should be understood within the context of the evaluation, which was based on self-reports of behaviors. It is possible that youth with mentors gave what they perceived to be the socially correct responses to questions. Moreover, on many of the measured behaviors, the base was so small that a large increase did not represent a major shift in behavior.

In this book, we have focused on career-oriented education, after-school "safe havens," and services targeted at individuals. But there are many other approaches to keeping young people in school and on the path to successful futures.

Broader Interventions

As defined by this study, youthful disconnectedness appears to be widespread in our society. About one-third of both males and females who reached adolescence in the 1980s spent at least 26 weeks in one or more calendar years not in school, not working, not in the military, and not married to someone who met at least one of these criteria. But most of these young people were disconnected in two or fewer years and, on average, did not suffer severe personal and economic hardship as young adults.

It is the long-term disconnected who had the most severe problems as adults and who pose the most pressing challenge to social policy.

Until now, however, remedial programs have not been able to reconnect many of these youngsters to the broader society. This is why researchers and policymakers have been eager to find promising approaches to the prevention of disconnection.

This interest in prevention often translates into support for preschool interventions like Head Start. The significance of the work reported in this volume is that it identifies another opportunity for intervention: high school. The majority of youth who became disconnected were in school as late as the 10th or 11th grade. Our basic point is that even as adolescents—whose futures seem so bleak—these young people are still in school, within the reach of preventive intervention.

What about other interventions? In this book's tenth chapter, "Youth Development Programs," Jodie Roth of Teachers College at Columbia University, William Foster of the Center for Addiction and Substance Abuse at Columbia, and their colleagues review the current universe of youth development programs. They note that, on the most basic level, "youth development" programs see young people as resources to be developed, not problems to be managed. Such programs provide young people with access to safe places, challenging experiences, and caring adults on a daily basis. The authors also argue that youth development programs have the potential to help those "out of the mainstream," such as youth in the juvenile justice system and mental health institutions.

The authors found that there are few rigorous studies of such programs, making it difficult to determine what programs, if any, "work." After reviewing 60 evaluations, they identified and analyzed six rigorous studies. All six of the evaluations found positive changes in attitudes and behaviors in areas such as school completion, drug use, and young parenthood. However, no evaluation found positive outcomes for all attitudes and behaviors measured. The authors argue that, while none of the programs had universally positive findings, several general themes stood out. Implementation is important. So, too, is staff commitment to the program, their personal contact with students, and their skill at relating to adolescents. Program duration also seemed to be an important aspect of the design. The authors conclude that, while there is great interest nationally in increasing young people's access to youth development programs, policy makers and practitioners should proceed cautiously. More evaluations are needed before youth development programs can be deemed successful for diverse populations and communities.

In the Epilogue, Hugh Price, president of the Urban League, calls for preventive interventions based on strong relationships between youth and adults. He warns against the "get tough" policies currently in vogue, arguing that society will not be able to prosecute or jail its way out of teen crime and behavior problems.

Price argues that youth development programs can have beneficial effects beyond providing students with places to go during the afternoon. When cities become healthier environments for young people, they also become safer and more attractive places for adults, commuters, shoppers, tourists, and employers. Youth development programs, he asserts, can be cost-effective and humane public investments.

America's Disconnected Youth: Toward a Preventive Strategy emphasizes the importance of educational and youth programs—and their potential. But it is not meant to serve as a detailed blueprint for expanding services. There are too many unanswered questions. We hope that future research will help determine which ideas and strategies are most promising.

Instead, this book makes one overarching point, made repeatedly by all of the authors: Even as late as adolescence, at-risk youth—whose futures seem so bleak—are still in school, and still within the reach of preventive intervention. We need not—and should not—give up on them.

References

Achatz, M., & MacAllum, C. (1994). *Young unwed fathers: Report from the field*. Philadelphia: Public/Private Ventures.

Anderson, E. (1993, December 31). Abolish welfare, And then what? *Washington Post*, p. A21.

Benning, V. (1998, April 20). In Fairfax, year-round classes. *Washington Post*, pp. A1, A8.

Benoit, M. (1996). *Intrinsic psychological issues in teen pregnancy*. Paper presented at a conference at the American Enterprise Institute, Washington, DC, October 29-30.

Besharov, D., & Gardiner, K. (1997). Preventing youthful disconnectedness. *Children and Youth Services Review, 19*(3), 1-18.

Cameron, S., & Heckman, J. (1993). The non-equivalence of high school equivalence. *Journal of Labor Economics*, 11, 1 (Part 1, January).

Floyd, R. (undated). Program effectiveness panel submission. Unpublished paper, West Coven, CA, East San Gabriel Valley Regional Occupational Program.

Hahn, A. (1994). *Evaluation of the Quantum Opportunities Program (QOP): Did the program work? Executive summary*. Waltham, MA: Brandeis University.

Quint, J., Polit, D., Bos, H., & Cave, G. (1994). *New chance: Interim findings on a comprehensive program for disadvantaged young mothers and their children*. New York: Manpower Demonstration Research Corporation.

Tierney, J., Grossman, J.B., & Resch, N. (1995). *Making a difference: An impact study of Big Brothers/Big Sisters*. Philadelphia: Public/Private Ventures.

U.S. Bureau of the Census. (1992). *Money income of households, families, and persons in the United States: 1991*. Washington, DC: U.S. Government Printing Office.

U.S. Department of Education. (1994). *National assessment of vocational education: Interim report to Congress*. Washington, DC: U.S. Government Printing Office.

U.S. Department of Education. (1993). *Dropout rates in the United States: 1992*. Washington, DC: U.S. Government Printing Office.

U.S. Department of Health and Human Services [DHHS], National Center for Health Statistics. (1998). *Monthly vital statistics report, 46*, 11S (June 30).

Notes

1   As it turned out, considering marriage to be a form of connection did change our basic findings; all but about 7% of married women were connected through a second activity, such as their own work.

2   All the results presented are statistically significant at the .01, .05, or .10 level.

3   Adult outcomes were measured in 1990 and 1991 when the youth were aged 25-27 or 26-28.

4   Measured in 1991.

5   See, for example, Cameron and Heckman [1993].

6   These characteristics were measured in 1979 when the youth were aged 14 to 16.

7   The U.S. Department of Education [1993, pp. 16-17] found that low-income students make up a disproportionate share of drop-outs: students with family incomes in the bottom 20% of the distribution accounted for 42% of all dropouts. Middle-income students (20% to 80% of all family incomes) represented 53% of all dropouts. Thirty-eight percent of all dropouts were from central cities, 40% from suburbs, and 21% from nonmetropolitan areas.

8   Because of the age of the respondent and the nature of the test, the AFQT is a measure of learned knowledge as well as IQ.

9   We recognize the possibility of "right-censored" data, since our observation period ends at age 23. For the majority of discon-nected youth, however, disconnectedness began before age 20.

10 The study's findings were not universally positive: Low-skilled students in magnet schools were more likely than those attending regular high schools to drop out.

11 Philadelphia, Rochester, Minneapolis, Columbus, Wichita, Kansas City, Houston, San Antonio, and Phoenix were selected for geographical diversity and because their caseloads were sufficiently large.

1. The Plight of the Inner-City Black Male

Williiam Julius Wilson*

The social deterioration of ghetto neighborhoods is the central concern to policymakers and residents alike. As a representative from the media put it, the ghetto has gone "from bad to worse" [Shapiro 1987, p. 18]. Few observers of the urban scene in the late 1960s anticipated the extensive breakdown of social institutions and the sharp rise in rates of social dislocation that have since swept the ghettos and spread to other neighborhoods that were once stable. For example, in the neighborhood of Woodlawn, located on the South Side of Chicago, there were more than 800 commercial and industrial establishments in 1950. Today, it is estimated that only about a hundred are left, many of them represented by "tiny catering places, barber shops, and thrift stores with no more than one or two employees" [Wacquant 1991, p. 16]. A resident of Woodlawn who had left the neighborhood as a child described how she felt upon her return about the changes that had occurred: "I was just really appalled. When I walked down Sixty-third Street when I was younger, everything that you wanted was there. But now, coming back as an adult with my child, those resources are just gone, completely. . ."

The most fundamental difference between today's inner-city neighborhoods and those studied in the past is the much higher levels of joblessness. Indeed, there is a new poverty in our nation's metropolises that has consequences for a range of issues related to the quality of life in urban areas, including race relations. Neighborhoods plagued by high levels of joblessness are more likely to experience low levels of

---

* Several paragraphs, some rewritten, are integrated into this chapter from Wilson [1996].

social organization, ranging from crime, gang violence, and drug trafficking to family breakups and problems in the organization of family life.

By "the new urban poverty," I mean poor, segregated neighborhoods in which a substantial majority of individual adults are either unemployed or have dropped out of the labor force altogether. For example, in 1990 only one in three adults ages 16 and over in the 12 Chicago community areas with ghetto poverty rates (in which at least 40% are poor) held a job in a typical week of the year. Each of these community areas, located in the South and West Sides of the city, is overwhelmingly black.

Black Men and the Labor Market

Black males have been maligned in recent years. The negative and worsening image of these men exacerbates racial hostility, because it lends itself to overgeneralization about the entire African American community. Years ago, when black males sought jobs, employers mainly checked their strength and stamina. Industries that involved strenuous work readily employed black men.

Data show that 57% of Chicago's employed inner-city black fathers (aged 15 and over and without undergraduate degrees) born between 1950 and 1955 worked in manufacturing and construction industries in 1974. By 1987 that figure had plummeted to 31%. Of those born between 1956 and 1960, 52% worked in these industries as late as 1978. By 1987 that figure had declined to 28%. No other male ethnic group in Chicago's inner cities experienced such an overall steep decline in manufacturing employment [Krogh 1993].

These employment changes have recently accompanied the loss of traditional manufacturing and other blue-collar jobs in Chicago. As a result, young black males have turned increasingly to the low-wage service sector and laboring jobs for employment, or have gone jobless. But, an economic structural argument does not account for the greater success of the Hispanics and whites in holding on to these jobs as they declined or in finding other employment when their industries shut down. Hispanic males, for example, have considerably less formal education than black males, but they have lost manufacturing jobs at a slower rate and when they have been displaced, they have found other employment more quickly [Krogh 1993].

However, although Hispanics and blacks "face the same industrial mix and broad labor market conditions, the immediate social environments in which the two groups cluster are not the same" [Van Haitsma 1991, p. 2]. The neighborhoods, households, and social networks of blacks and Hispanics differ in ways that distinctly affect employment and labor force participation. Black neighborhoods have a greater effect on their residents because they are so heavily impoverished. Unlike blacks in Chicago, Hispanics, especially Mexicans, seldom reside in neighborhoods with poverty rates that reach 40% and higher. For example, in 1980 one-fifth of Chicago's blacks but only 2% of its Hispanic immigrants resided in census tracts with poverty rates of at least 40%. Blacks are not only disproportionately concentrated in these extreme poverty neighborhoods, they are also disproportionately concentrated in neighborhoods with rates of poverty that exceed 30%. Whereas 21% of African Americans lived in census tract in Chicago with poverty rates of 30 to 39%, less than 8% of the Hispanic immigrant population resided in such areas [Van Haitsma 1992].

The highly impoverished black neighborhoods are characterized by a lack of access to resources provided by stable working residents, including informal job networks and stable support of neighborhood institutions. In the Chicago black ghetto neighborhoods that we studied, social contacts were far more successful in helping residents gain informal work to help make ends meet than in obtaining steady employment. Networks existed but generally lacked the capacity to elevate residents into the formal labor market [Pedder 1991].

For example, black men and women in our sample are less likely to report that they received help from a friend in obtaining their current job. Also both black males and females use the public transit system more often than Hispanics, who rely more heavily on car pooling. "Both car pooling and having obtained a job with the help of a friend, are indications that Hispanic workers often work with friends" [Van Haitsma 1991, p. 8].

The absence of effective informal job networks and the availability of many illegal activities increase nonmainstream behavior such as hustling. In other words, there are more hurdles in the path to the formal labor market, and pressures to pursue alternative modes of subsistence, including welfare, informal activity, drug dealing, and other illegal practices, increase.

Does the interpretation of these ethnic differences by agents of mainstream society influence decisions that affect black male employment? An answer to this question explicitly addresses the meaning and significance of race.

This short chapter is based on the following:

- a random survey of 2,495 black, Hispanic, and white households in Chicago's inner-city neighborhoods conducted in 1987 and 1988;
- a second survey of a subsample of 175 respondents from the larger survey who were reinterviewed in 1988 solely with open-ended questions on their perceptions of the opportunity structure and life chances;
- a survey of a stratified random sample of 185 employers, designed to reflect the distribution of employment across industry and firm size in the Chicago metropolitan area, completed in 1988; and
- comprehensive ethnographic research, including participant observation research and life-history interviews, conducted by 10 of my research assistants in 1987 and 1988 in a sample of the inner-city neighborhoods.

Our research project is called the Chicago Urban Poverty and Family Life Study (UPFLS). It covered a wide range of issues, including the experiences of families and women in poverty. This chapter presents and interprets our findings on the declining status of the inner-city black male.*

---

* A fuller discussion of the findings from this project can be found in Wilson [1996].

As one inner-city manufacturer from our study put it, "When we hear other employers talk, they'll go after primarily the Hispanic and Oriental first, those two, and, I'll qualify that even further, the Hispanic Mexican, and any Oriental, and after that, that's pretty much it, that's pretty much where they like to draw the line, right there." As revealed in Table 1-1, interviews of a representative sample of Chicago-area employers by our research team show that many consider inner-city black males to be either uneducated, unstable, uncooperative or dishonest. For example, a suburban drug store manager said:

> It's unfortunate but, in my business I think overall [black men] tend to be known to be dishonest. I think that's too bad but that's the image they have. (Interviewer: So you think it's an image problem?) Yeah, a dishonest, an image problem of being dishonest men and lazy. They're known to be lazy. (There are laughs.) I hate to tell you, but. . . It's all an image though. Whether they are or not, I don't know, but, it's an image that is perceived. (Interviewer: I see. How do you think that image was developed?) Go look in the jails. (Store manager laughs.)

Concerns about theft prompted a suburban employer of an electrical services firm to offer this unique explanation of why he would not hire inner-city ghetto black males:

> If you're in a white neighborhood . . . and you have a manufacturing firm and a ghetto person comes there to apply, it doesn't make any difference what color his skin is . . . if you know that's where he's from you know several things. One is that if you give him a job there, he's going to be unbelievably pressured to give information to his peer group in the ghetto... about the security system, the comings and goings of what's of value there that we could rip off. He's not a crook. He wants no part of it. But he lives in an area where he may be physically in danger of his life if he doesn't provide the information to the people that live around him. As a

Table 1-1. Observations as to Why Inner-City Black Males Cannot Find or Retain Jobs Easily
Frequency (%) of Responses by Employers' Profession

Rational	Customer Service	Clerical	Craft	Blue-Collar	All Employers
Lack of jobs	9.0	7.1	12.5	17.6	11.7
Lack of basic skills	44.5	37.5	37.5	36.8	38.5
Lack of work ethic	25.0	48.0	25.0	52.9	36.9
Lack of dependability	13.6	14.3	12.5	22.0	16.8
Bad attitude	15.9	16.1	25.0	19.1	17.3
Lack of inter-personal skills	18.2	10.7	0	3.0	8.9
Racial discrimination	15.9	14.3	0	13.2	13.4
Unweighted N	44	56	8	68	179

Source: Data from the 1988 employer survey conducted as part of the Urban Poverty and Family Life Study, Chicago

manager, I know that. And I'm not going to hire him because of that. I'm not discriminating against him because he's black, I'm discriminating against him because he has a problem that he's going to bring [it] to me. Now the fact that he is black and it happens that the people around him are black is only coincidental. In Warsaw they were Jews. They had the same problem.

A president of an inner-city manufacturing firm expressed a different concern about employing black males from certain inner-city neighborhoods.

> If somebody gave me their address, uh, Cabrini Green I might unavoidably have some concerns. (Interviewer: What would your concerns be?) That the poor guy probably would be frequently unable to get to work and . . . I probably would watch him more carefully even if it wasn't fair, than I would with somebody else. I know what I should do though is recognize that here's a guy that is trying to get out of his situation and probably will work harder than somebody else who's already out of there and he might be the best one around here. But I, I think I would have to struggle accepting that premise at the beginning.

Other employers expressed reservations about inner-city black men in terms of work-related skills. They "just don't have the language skills," states a suburban employer. A president of an inner-city advertising agency highlighted the problem of spelling:

> I needed a temporary a couple months ago, and they sent me a black man. And I dictated a letter to him, he took shorthand, which was good. Something like "Dear Mr. So and So, I am writing to ask about how your business is doing." And then he typed the letter, and a good while later, now not because he was black, I don't know why it took so long. But I read the letter, and it's "I am writing to ax about your business." Now you hear about them speaking a different language and all that, and they say ax for ask. Well, I don't care about that, but I didn't say *ax*, I said *ask*.

Given such attitudes, the lack of black access to the informal job networks is a particular problem for black males, as revealed in the following comments by an employer:

> All of a sudden, they take a look at a guy, and unless he's got an in, the reason why I hired this black kid the

last time is cause my neighbor said to me, yeah, I used him for a few [days], he's good, and I said, you know what, I'm going to take a chance, but it was a recommendation. But other than that, I've got a walk-in, and, who knows? And I think that for the most part, a guy sees a black man, he's a bit hesitant, because I don't know.

How and why have such attitudes developed? The success that black men had in obtaining manufacturing and other blue-collar jobs in previous years suggests that these strong negative views have only recently emerged. Our data show that, of the employed men in the 1941-55 age cohort from poor Chicago neighborhoods, the proportion of blacks in manufacturing and construction was only slightly below that of whites and exceeded that of Hispanics in 1974. Also the proportion from the 1956-69 birth cohort was considerably above that of whites and only slightly below that of Hispanics in 1974 [Krogh 1993].

The deterioration of the socioeconomic status of black men may be associated with increases in these negative perceptions. Are these perceptions merely stereotypical or do they have any basis in fact? Data from our large survey show that social context variables (neighborhoods, social networks, and households) accounted for substantially more of the employment gap among men than the attitude variables [Van Haitsma 1991]. Also, data from the survey reveal that black men have a lower "reservation wage" than men of the other ethnic groups. Whereas white jobless fathers expected more than $9 per hour as a requirement for working, jobless black fathers were willing to work for less than $6.00. The reservation wage of Hispanic (Mexican) jobless fathers was $6.20 [Tienda & Stier 1991].

But, surveys are not the best way to get at underlying attitudes and values. Accordingly, to gain a better grasp of values and attitudes, our project included ethnographic research that involved establishing long-term contacts and interviews with residents from several neighborhoods. Analysis of the ethnographic data reveals identifiable and consistent patterns of ethnic group beliefs. Consider our findings on the comparisons between black men and Hispanic men in the inner city. Black men are more hostile than the Hispanic men about the low-paying jobs they hold, less willing to be flexible in taking assignments or tasks not considered part of their job, and less willing to work as hard for the same low wages. These contrasts are sharp because many Hispanics interviewed are recent immigrants.

There are "several important reasons why immigrants, particularly third world immigrants, will tolerate harsher conditions, lower pay, few upward trajectories, and other job-related characteristics that deter native workers, and thereby exhibit a better 'work ethic' than others" [Aponte 1991, p. 41]. Two of these reasons were uncovered in our ethnographic data. Immigrants are harder workers because they "come from areas of intense poverty and that even boring, hard, dead-end jobs look, by contrast, good to them" [Taub 1991, p. 14]. They also fear being deported if they do not find employment.

The inner-city black men strongly feel that they are victims of discrimination. They complained that they get assigned the most heavy or most dirty work on the job, are overworked, and are paid less than nonblacks. The immigrant Hispanics also report that they feel exploited, but they tend to express the view that this is to be expected because of the nature of the job. Richard Taub, a researcher on our project, argues that the inner-city black men have a greater sense of "honor" and often see the work, pay, and treatment from bosses as insulting and degrading. Accordingly, a heightened sensitivity to exploitation increases anger and a tendency to "just walk off the job."

One cannot understand these attitudes, and how they developed, without considering the growing exclusion of black men from higher paying blue-collar jobs in manufacturing and other industries and the increasing confinement to low-paying service and laboring jobs. Many low-paying jobs have predictably low retention rates. There was a respondent in our employer survey who reported turnover rates that exceeded 50% in his firm. When asked if he had considered doing anything about this problem, the employer acknowledged a rational decision to tolerate a high turnover rather than increasing the starting salary and improving working conditions to attract higher caliber workers. He stated: "Our practice has been that we'll keep hiring and, hopefully, one or two of them are going to wind up being good." As Kathryn Neckerman, a member of our research team, points out, "This employer, and others like him, can afford such high turnover because the work is simple and can be taught in a couple of days. On average, jobs paying under $5 or $6 an hour were characterized by high quit rates. In higher paying jobs, by contrast, the proportion of employees resigning fell to less than 20% per year" [Neckerman 1993, p. 8]. Yet, our data show that the number of inner-city black males in the higher paying positions has sharply declined. Increasingly displaced from manufacturing industries, their options are more confined to low paying service work. Turnover rates of 50 to 100% are common in low-skilled service jobs in Chicago.

Thus the attitudes that many inner-city black males express about their jobs and job prospects reflect their plummeting position in a changing labor market. The more they complain and manifest their dissatisfaction, the less desirable they seem to employers. They therefore experience greater discrimination when they seek employment and clash more often with supervisors when they find employment. For all these reasons, it is important to link attitudinal and other cultural traits with structural realities.

The restructuring of the economy will continue to compound the negative effects of the perceptions of inner-city black males. Because of the increasing shift to service industries, employers have a greater need for workers who can effectively serve and relate to the consumer, Black males are not perceived to have such qualities. Their attitudes and actions, combined with erratic work histories in high turnover jobs, create the widely shared perception that they are undesirable workers. The perception then becomes the basis for employer discrimination that sharply increases when the economy is weak and employers can therefore selectively choose from a surplus labor force. This discrimination gradually grows over the long term, not only because employers are turning more to the expanding immigrant and female labor force, but also because the number of jobs that require contact with the public continue to climb.

In summary, the issue of race cannot simply be reduced to discrimination. Although our data suggest that inner-city black males have experienced increased employer rejection since the mid-1970s, the reasons include a complex web of interrelated factors including those that are race-specific as well as those that are race-neutral.

Education

The loss of traditional manufacturing and other blue-collar jobs in Chicago resulted in increased joblessness among inner-city black males and a concentration in low-wage, high-turnover laborer and service-sector jobs. Embedded in ghetto neighborhoods, networks, and households that are not conducive to employment, inner-city black males fall further behind their white and their Hispanic male counterparts, especially when the labor market is slack. Hispanics "continue to funnel into manufacturing because employers prefer [them] over blacks, and they like to hire by referrals from current employees, which Hispanics can readily furnish, being already embedded in migration networks" [Krogh 1993, p. 12]. Inner-city black men grow bitter about and resent their employment prospects and often manifest or express these feelings in their harsh, often dehumanizing, low-wage work settings.

The ways in which people adapt to the growing problem of long-term joblessness in such neighborhoods are influenced not only by the constraints they face and the opportunities they have, but also by the repeated ways they have responded to such problems in the past. Thus, in a neighborhood with a paucity of regularly employed families and with the overwhelming majority of families having spells of long-term joblessness, people experience a social isolation that excludes them from the job network system that permeates other neighborhoods and that is so important in learning about or being recommended for jobs that become available in various parts of the city. And as the prospects for employment diminish, other alternatives such as welfare and the underground economy are not only increasingly relied on, they come to be seen as a way of life.

The net effect is that joblessness, as a way of life, takes on a different social meaning; the relationship between schooling and postschool employment takes on a different meaning. The development of cognitive, linguistic, and other educational and job-related skills necessary for the world of work in the mainstream economy is thereby adversely affected. In such neighborhoods, therefore, teachers become frustrated and do not teach children to learn. A vicious cycle is perpetuated through the family, through the community, and through the schools. The consequences are dramatically revealed when figures on educational attainment in the inner-city are released. For example, of the 39,500 students who enrolled in the ninth grade of Chicago's public schools in 1980, and who would have normally graduated from high school four years later in the spring of 1984, only 18,500 (or 47%) graduated; of these, only 6,000 were capable of reading at or above the national twelfth-grade level [Wilson 1987, pp. 57-58].

There is a growing recognition that proposed solutions to the problems of jobs and wages in any of the major industrial democracies cannot ignore developments in the highly integrated global marketplace. My framework for long-term solutions outlines two types of relationships in an effort to address the issues of generating good jobs and combating growing wage inequality among workers—namely, the relationship between employment and education and family support systems and, in the metropolitan context, the relationship between the cities and the suburbs. Each framework involves the integration of programs that involve both the public sector and the private sector. I will address education here.

The United States can learn from industrial democracies, such as Japan and Germany. These countries have developed policies designed to increase the number of workers and "higher order thinking skills," including policies that require young people to meet high performance standards before they can graduate from secondary schools and that hold each school responsible for meeting these national standards. As Ray Marshall points out, "Standards are important because they provide incentives for students, teachers and other school personnel; information to employers and postsecondary institutions; and a means for policy makers and the public to evaluate schools" [Marshall 1994, pp. 6-7]. Students who meet high standards are not only prepared for work, they are ready for technical training and other kinds of postsecondary education. Currently there are no national standards for secondary students or schools in the United States.

Recent research on the nationwide distribution of science and mathematics opportunities indicates that low-income, minority, and inner-city students are in school environments that are not as conductive to learning because of less qualified teachers, fewer material resources, less engaging activities for learning in the classroom, and considerably less exposure to good training and knowledge in mathematics and science. The problem of finding qualified teachers is particularly acute.

A system of national performance standards should include the kind of support that would enable schools in disadvantaged neighborhoods to meet the standards that are set. State governments, with federal support, not only would have to create equity in local school funding and give birth to programs that would foster teacher development (through scholarships and forgivable loans for teacher education to attract more high-quality teachers, through increased supports for teacher training in schools of education, and through reforms in teacher certification and licensing), but would also have to ensure that highly qualified teachers are distributed in local school districts in ways that provide all students with access to excellent instruction.

One important area that could be addressed in programs to equalize resources in the public schools is the availability of computer facilities. Since two-thirds of all new jobs will require the use of computers, all schools should require that students become competent in the use of computers. According to the U.S. Bureau of the Census, only 35% of black youths ages 3 to 17 use a computer at school. Half of their white counterparts have access to in-school computers [Weaver 1995].

Every effort should be made to enlist the support and involvement of the private sector in this national effort. Corporations, local businesses, civic clubs, community centers, churches, and community-based organizations should be encouraged to work with the schools to enhance computer-competency training. Some examples of private-sector involvement in such endeavors should be touted to spur others on. For example, Frank C. Weaver, director of the Office of Commercial Space Transportation at the U.S. Department of Transportation, reported:

> Bell Atlantic and Tele-Communications, Inc. announced in 1994 that they would provide free linkage to the information super-highways for 26,000 elementary and secondary schools in areas served by the two companies. Under the plan, known as the Basic Education Connection (BEC), the school would receive free educational cable television programming and free access to certain data and online services, such as access to the Internet. [Weaver 1995, p. 7]

A step toward the development of national performance standards was taken in the spring of 1994 when Congress passed the Goals 2000: Educate America Act. This act identified a number of goals to be achieved by the year 2000, ranging from student-demonstrated competence in challenging subjects (science, English, mathematics, geography, and history) to the professional development of teachers. Congress appropriated $125 million for Goals 2000 in 1994 and $700 million for 1995. The act encourages states to apply for grants so that their schools can participate in educational improvements outlined in the legislation.

The learning system in other industrial democracies has also been strengthened by family policies to support children. Among industrialized countries, the United States is alone in having no universal preschool, child-support, or parental leave programs. "The absence of such policies makes many of our families, particularly low-income families, very poor learning systems," states Ray Marshall [Marshall 1994, p. 7]. The family structure has undergone fundamental changes in the last several decades. There has been a sharp increase in single-parent families, and many of them are trapped in persistent poverty. Also, in many "intact" families, both the husband and wife must work outside the home to make ends meet. The absence of widely available high-quality preschool and child-support assurance programs places additional stress on these families and hampers their ability to provide a learning environment that prepares children for school and reinforces the learning process.

School-to-Work

The combination of a system of national performance standards in public schools and family policies to reinforce the learning system would greatly facilitate the transition from school to work in the United States. "America has the worst school-to-work transition process of any industrialized nation," states Ray Marshall [Marshall 1994, p. 3]. "Put simply, we have no systematic process to assist high school graduates to move smoothly from school into employment." The focus of U.S. secondary schools and counseling programs is to encourage young people to enter college and obtain a degree. But high school graduates who are not college-bound represent nearly one-half of each graduating class. Thus, they "are left to sink or swim—without advice or career counseling and without any job placement assistance."

Unlike employers in Germany and Japan, employers in the United States who have jobs that offer good wages, career potential, and attractive benefits usually do not hire workers immediately out of high school. As Marshall points out, "Only a handful of the Fortune 500 firms hire fresh high school graduates for entry level jobs offering career opportunities" [Marshall 1994, p. 9]. The larger firms in America do eventually hire high school graduates, but normally not until they have reached their mid-20s, have accumulated some work experience, and have "matured and settled down." Even the "average starting apprentice in the United States is in his/her late twenties. This delay in hiring for career-track jobs results in many youths spending five or six years floundering in jobs that offer neither learning nor advancement opportunities."

The delay in hiring youth has a number of critical consequences for school-to-work transition in the United States:

- It gives young people in Germany and Japan a five-to-ten-year head start in obtaining access to crucial occupational skills training.
- It removes our best corporations and their important learning systems from involvement in the process of molding young workers.
- It eliminates a natural communication network for feeding employer information to schools about the changing skills required in the workplace.
- Most importantly, it disconnects achievements in school from rewards in the workplace, thereby undermining the incentive for academic success [Marshall 1994].

The problem of school-to-work transition confronts young people of all ethnic and racial backgrounds, but it is especially serious for black youths. According to a recent report by the U.S. Bureau of Labor Statistics, only 42% of black youth who had not enrolled in college had jobs in October after graduating from high school a few months earlier in June, compared with 69% of their white counterparts [U.S. Bureau of Labor Statistics 1994]. The inadequate system of school-to-work transition has also contributed significantly to the growing wage gap between those with high school diplomas and those with college training. In the 1950s and 1960s, when school-to-work transition was compatible with the mass production system, the average earnings of college graduates was only about 20% higher than those of high school graduates. By 1979, it had increased to 49%, and then rapidly grew to 83% by 1992.

Our research reveals that social structural factors, including economic restructuring, are important for understanding the experiences of inner-city black men, but there is a good deal that such factors do not explain. Race is clearly an important variable in the social outcomes of these men, but determination of the meaning and significance of race in certain situations depends on knowledge of how it intersects with other factors. Cultural factors, including group attitudes and orientations do play a role in the outcomes of the inner-city poor, but any adequate explanation of their influence has to consider how they have been shaped by structural and racial variables. Effective public policies must take all of these factors into account.

The long-term solutions that I have advanced would reduce the likelihood that a new generation of jobless workers would be produced from the youngsters now in school and preschool. We must break the cycle of joblessness and improve the youngsters' preparation for the new labor market in the global economy.

References

Aponte. (1991). Ethnicity and male employment in the inner city. Paper presented at the Chicago Urban Poverty and Family Life Conference, October 10-12, Chicago, IL.

Krogh, M. (1993). *A description of the work histories of fathers living in the inner city of Chicago*. Working Paper. Center for the Study of Urban Inequality, University of Chicago.

Marshall, R. (1994). School to work processes in the United States. Paper presented at the Carnegie Corporation/Johann Jakobs Foundation, November 3-5, Marbach Castle, Germany.

Neckerman. (1993). What getting ahead means to employers and inner-city workers. Revised version of paper presented at the Chicago Urban Poverty and Family Life Conference, October 10-12, Chicago, IL.

Pedder, S. (1991.) *Social isolation and the labor market: Black Americans in Chicago*. Paper presented at the Chicago Urban Poverty and Family Life Conference, October 10-12, Chicago, IL.

Shapiro, W. (August 24, 1987). The ghetto: From bad to worse. *Time*, 18-19.

Taub, R. (1991). *Differing conceptions of honor and orientations toward work and marriage among low-income African-Americans and Hispanic-Americans.* Paper presented at the Chicago Urban Poverty and Family Life Conference, October 10-12, Chicago, IL.

Tienda, M., & Stier, H. (1991). *Making a livin': Color and opportunity in the inner city.* Paper presented at the Chicago Urban Poverty and Family Life Conference, October 10-12, Chicago, IL.

U.S. Bureau of Labor Statistics. (May 1994). College enrollment of 1993 high school graduates. In *U.S. Department of Labor News Release,* No. 94-252. Washington, DC: Author.

Van Haitsma, M. (1991). *Attitudes, social context and labor force attachment: Blacks and immigrant Hispanics in Chicago poverty areas.* Paper presented at the annual meeting of the Social Science History Association, November 5-8, Chicago, IL.

Van Haitsma, M. (1992). *The social context of nonemployment: Blacks and immigrant Hispanics in Chicago poverty areas.* Paper presented at the annual meetings of the Social Science History Association, November 5-8, Chicago, IL.

Wacquant, L. (1991). The specificity of ghetto poverty: A comparison of race, class, and urban exclusion in Chicago's black and the Parisian red belt. Paper presented at the Chicago Urban Poverty and Family Life Conference, October 10-12, Chicago, IL.

Weaver, F. C. (1995, May). Preparing our youth for the information age: Schools should provide the competency skills Black youth will need to exploit the interactive telecommunication systems in the future. *Focus, 23*(5), 5.

Wilson, W. J. (1996). *When work disappears: The world of the new urban poor.* New York: Alfred A. Knopf.

Wilson, W. J. (1987). *The truly disadvantaged: The inner city, the underclass, and public policy.* Chicago: The University of Chicago Press.

2. Teen Sexuality Among Inner-City White Youth

Patricia Stern

The classroom is quiet. First graders in a predominantly white, inner-city public elementary school raise their hands with excitement and impatience to answer their teacher. She asks, "What number do you subtract from eight to get four?" Looking out at her students around the room, the teacher calls on a boy in the back row. He shouts, "Four!" "Good," she replies with encouragement and direction, "now fill in your petal." They are solving problems together to complete a number flower the teacher has drawn on the board. At the nearby local Catholic school, other first graders are gathered together quietly in a group for an interactive math lesson. The teacher asks the children to identify patterns, first using the calendar and then colorful shapes lining the classroom walls. She smiles at the eagerness of her young volunteers who squirm with anticipation to show her what they know.

Similar scenes are taking place in the other grades in these elementary schools in Milton, a traditionally white, working-class, and increasingly poor neighborhood of Philadelphia.[1] Both of these schools operate in clean, well-maintained facilities. They are bright places. Children's artwork covers the hallways. Classrooms are orderly and colorfully decorated with maps, posters, and thematic materials. Reading books are displayed and available for students to browse at all times. Every classroom from first to eighth grades at the Catholic school has four computers that children use for daily math and reading exercises. There is a computer lab at the public school as well.

Throughout the country, we see children thriving in similar elementary school environments. In these settings, they are excited about learning and responsive to adults who offer nurturing and guidance. However, 10 years down the line, we see a very different picture of youth in high schools, particularly in working-class and poor neighborhoods. For example, the elementary school students in Milton described above live in a community where approximately 40% of the adults in the area have not completed high school; less than 10% have a bachelor's degree or other postsecondary training.[2] What happens between the elementary school and high school years, that young people no longer perceive school to be a place for growth, engagement, and opportunity? Do schools themselves have less to offer these youth to help prepare them for adulthood today?

This chapter explores teen sexuality, pregnancy, and opportunity among white teenagers in a depressed industrial area of Philadelphia. The study is based on a series of interviews conducted in 1993 and 1994 with white youth ages 14 to 19 in the broader Milton area. (See box on p. 51 for interview profiles.) In considering why youth seem to become disconnected from educational institutions as they get older, I focused on the powerful influence of local peer groups. The search for status and respect increasingly takes place in these peer groups and outside of the world of school and adults. My findings suggest that teen sexuality assumes a central role in this search for status and respect in the absence of, or sometimes competing with, activities available through school programs or employment experiences.

This study is not simply a report about the high rates of sexual activity and pregnancy among youth in an inner-city, white neighborhood. It also describes how the social organization of teen sexuality in Milton can deeply affect the lives and sense of future of adolescents. Several themes run through this chapter. First, the peer culture reflects sex roles that are rooted in traditional working-class and Catholic culture. Sexual behavior, pregnancy, and parenthood are all influenced by neighborhood norms. Second, youth often describe their relationships with adults in terms of their difficulties with parents and unstable home lives. Third, the depressed and unsafe conditions in the neighborhood, due to declining employment and increasing drug trade, affect the young

Focus Group I: Milton High School Dropout Prevention Program

	Nine girls	Four boys
Ages:	15-18	5-18
Area:	White and White/Puerto Rican	
Religion:	Catholic and Fundamentalist Christian	

Focus Group II: Comstock Community Center Youth Program

	Two girls	Two boys
Ages:	16 and 18	14 and 16
Area:	White and White/Puerto Rican	
Religion:	Catholic and Protestant	

Small Group and Individual Interview: Riverside Neighborhood

	Three girls	One boy
Ages:	14, 15	15
Area	All White	All White
Religion:	Protestant and Catholic	Catholic

Small Group Interview: Comstock Community Center

	Patrick	Brian
Ages:	17	20
Area:	White/Puerto Rican	White
Religion:	Catholic	Catholic (Atheist)

Interview Interviews: Comstock Community Center

	Annie	Maggie
Ages:	18	17
Area	White	White/Puerto Rican
Religion:	Catholic	Protestant

people's dreams and their perceptions of career and marriage opportunities. Finally, young women who have educational and career aspirations often have difficulty negotiating the terrain of sexuality in this culture.

Not surprisingly, these teens consistently expressed the desire to have caring adults in their lives and detailed the many ways in which they feel their parents and teachers fail them. They also revealed a concern for the lack of control they feel over their lives, or that "things just happen, and you can't spend your life regretting them."

In my subsequent ethnographic research during the past three years in a smaller neighborhood within Milton, however, I have learned more about the difficulties facing adults and parents in these times of rapid economic and social change. I have encountered many parents who express anger and resignation about what they perceive as a lack of respect from young people and a lack of control over raising their children.[3] The adults I have spoken with feel undermined by cultural changes in parenting norms over the past few decades. In particular, many resent child welfare legislation, social service agencies, and even the Catholic Church for condemning corporal punishment and for prosecuting parents. They say that these institutions fail to support, or sometimes directly challenge, parents' authority and discretion to discipline their children.

In addition, the decline of the local job base adds financial insecurity and disorientation to parental and gender roles in these families. Among other problems, there seems to be a particular strain on men of all ages who seek to support families at a time when blue-collar occupations traditional to the neighborhood are disappearing. While men were the sole or the main breadwinners a generation ago, women often play this role today. Even in a two-parent family where both adults work, a mother's financial contribution is likely to be co-supporting rather than supplementing the family income.

I would like to emphasize two final points, based on my subsequent research, that put the voices of these youth in my initial study in a broader context. Youth across America today from myriad socioeconomic, racial and ethnic, religious, and geographic backgrounds engage in early and risky sexual behavior. I think it is important to focus on how neighborhood norms in Milton affected teens' response to the consequences of their sexual activity. This includes both prevention strategies (i.e. being sexually active and not using birth control) and how they face and actually handle pregnancies (i.e. forgoing possible alternatives to keeping a child, like abortion or adoption). Most importantly, this study seeks to explain how these teens connect sexual activity, pregnancy, and opportunity with ideas about how school or work experience during their teen years will affect their adult lives.

It is important to appreciate the cultural norms and meanings in having children at a young age in this white working-class and largely Catholic neighborhood. Regardless of how young the parents might be, members of their extended families, and often neighbors, come together around a baby and generally participate in taking care of young children. If a 16-year-old young woman gets pregnant, her parents might be upset initially but would ultimately accept and most likely help raise the baby in their home. Her peer group would probably gossip about her pregnancy, but eventually she would receive positive attention and status for having a baby.

The final point is that white youth in this neighborhood often are not exposed, encouraged, or connected to career development paths that would offer compelling alternatives to starting a family at a young age. Many do not perceive alternatives to hanging out with their peers on the corner and/or getting involved with a growing informal or underground economy. While there are exceptions, many youth in Milton lack as role models adults who have made their way through the educational system or who see education beyond high school as relevant to future employment.[4] Thus, pursuing formal higher education and even involvement in high school activities compete with what youth themselves perceive as more culturally acceptable, emotionally fulfilling, or lucrative pursuits.

Research on urban poor white youth and their experiences of sexuality and family life has received relatively little attention from American scholars and policymakers compared with economically marginal urban black and Latino youth. This study offers an ethnographic portrait of white youth in an urban white ethnic neighborhood of Philadelphia. It seeks to represent their understanding of sexuality and pregnancy as expressed in the meanings in and consequences of sexual attitudes and practices that shape their everyday lives and future aspirations. This account is based on interviews with white working-class and economically marginal teens residing within this white ethnic neighborhood.

For all its glamour and allure, teen sexuality operates powerfully as a medium of exchange and a mechanism of control for the white youth in this community. In its most reduced formula, girls have sex for love; boys establish status through sexual conquest. In their more complex manifestations, sexual attitudes and practices among these urban white teens reflect contradictions arising out of conflicting messages about forging an adult identity amidst shifting social norms, collapsing community institutions, and a failing local economy. Control over sexuality for teens in this neighborhood has public dimensions in the larger peer group, as well as private ramifications for relationships between boys and girls. For young women, intercourse is a particularly significant site of struggle for control over their bodies and their futures in a peer culture where unprotected sex is a pledge of intimacy. This paper will focus on complex attitudes toward and experiences of sexuality, pregnancy, and sense of future which illustrate important connections between teen sexuality and life options of inner city white youth.

Teen Pregnancy and Community Studies

Ethnographic studies of black and Latino youth have examined teen sexuality, pregnancy, and motherhood through detailed accounts of negotiation of normative structures and socioeconomic constraints that contour concepts of masculinity and femininity and sanctions on illegitimacy in urban communities [Anderson 1990; Horowitz 1983; Fine 1992]. In his representation of sex codes in an African American neighborhood of Philadelphia, Elijah Anderson views patterns of teen sexuality and increasing unwed parenthood among urban black youth as a cultural response to complex barriers of poverty and racial discrimination in American society. Ruth Horowitz's symbolic interactionist analysis of teen sexuality, pregnancy, and female identity demonstrates the social construction and management of passion, virginity, and motherhood in a Chicano neighborhood in Chicago. Michelle Fine also explores the social control of female sexuality in her work with African American and Latina girls in the Philadelphia public schools.

Ethnographic and interview studies of white working-class life have captured the values and orientations, difficulties and fears distinctive of lower income white ethnic communities [Gitlin 1970; Binzen 1970; Kornblum 1974; Rubin 1976; Rieder 1985; MacLeod 1987; Newman 1988]. These accounts document the impact of industrial decline and racial and ethnic competition for jobs and turf on blue-collar communities and the consciousness of working-class whites. In her book, *Worlds of Pain*, Lillian Rubin depicted the wounding experiences of poverty, abuse, neglect, and frustration in American working-class family life. Jay MacLeod dramatized the depressed aspirations and future prospects of urban white male youth in his comparative study of black and white teens in a low-income community.

White adults and teenagers from a range of socioeconomic backgrounds have been studied in aggregate survey research on pregnancy, contraception, and abortion [Luker 1975; Zelnik et al. 1981; Loewenstein & Furstenberg 1991; Nathanson 1991]. Survey studies on contraceptive decisionmaking have examined the social dimensions of individual sexual attitudes and behavior. In her analysis of female sexuality and heterosexual relations, Luker identifies social costs of contraception and benefits of pregnancy influencing individual contraceptive decisionmaking. Constance Nathanson defines the decision to contracept as a continually negotiated event that is processual, circumstantial, and intimately linked to relationships. Other survey research on teenage sexuality and contraception has addressed teen pregnancy from a public health perspective. These studies have attempted to locate variables most conducive to policy intervention, such as the increasing availability of birth control.[5]

Teen sexuality among inner-city white teens has not been specifically addressed in survey research on adolescents. Nor have the meanings in and consequences of teenage sexuality and pregnancy in poor white communities been adequately documented by ethnographers of urban culture. Anderson and Horowitz analyze teen sexuality, pregnancy, and family life among black and Latino teens in terms of minority youth experiences of segregation, discrimination, and alienation from mainstream America [Anderson 1990; Horowitz 1983]. However, white working-class marginality and its impact on teen sexuality has not been examined in the context of increasing contradictions and hardships in urban white ethnic culture.

In his book, *Whitetown, U.S.A.*, Peter Binzen captures the difficult experience of white ethnic immigrants and their descendants who inhabit segregated urban enclaves and remain outside of white middle-class America [Binzen 1970]. These "havelittles," usually of Roman Catholic and Evangelical Protestant persuasions, lack the power and affluence offered by the American WASP establishment [Binzen 1970, p. 12]. They have lost economic benefits once provided by urban political machines that traded patronage for "Whitetown" political support. Underlying economic constraints and anxieties of white working-class families have fueled provincial and prejudiced white ethnic attitudes toward other races. Stereotypes of poor white bigotry toward and competition with African Americans and other minority groups reflect genuine white working-class fears and frustrations about job security and home equity.

In previous periods of American prosperity, economic benefits did not trickle down into "Whitetown" neighborhoods. The promise of the "American Dream" is all but extinct for white working-class families as modest employment benefits and savings have been eroded by more recent global economic problems and local restructuring of production. While "Whitetowners" have been notoriously patriotic and disproportionately represented in American military service, urban white ethnics are resentful of economic policies and programs provided by the Federal Government designed specifically to help minorities [Binzen 1970, p. 79-113]. Thus, adults and youth in "Whitetown" neighborhoods experience a peculiar form of alienation as economically and socially disenfranchised majority citizens.

This study seeks to represent the social organization of teen sexuality among white youth in a lower-income white ethnic neighborhood. It offers an understanding of teen sexuality as it is interpreted and practiced through the norms, orientations, and behaviors of young men and women in the context of confusing and grim economic and social realities. This account comes out of discussions with urban white teens about their own sexual negotiations, as well as their renderings of their white peer group with respect to sexual relations, pregnancy, and future aspirations.

Sexuality is a crucial terrain in which youth in this community search for self-esteem, manhood and womanhood, and adult independence. For many of these teens, pregnancies at an early age hold promises of enhanced status and emotional fulfillment that are not perceived to be available or attainable through educational or occupational achievement. For others, pregnancy is a constant threat to an alternative vision of upward mobility through investment in academic or vocational training. Even for the most ambitious and aware, however, teen pregnancies and problems associated with poverty, violence, and drug culture in this white working-class and economically marginal neighborhood often derail plans for a different and better future.

Data and Methods

This study is based on two focus groups and small group and individual interviews with youth in the Milton neighborhood of Philadelphia. The teens interviewed in the two focus groups are participating in a public high school dropout prevention program and a community center youth program. Eight teens interviewed individually and in small groups were referred through participants at the community center, but are not currently involved in the youth program. In the two focus groups, boys and girls were interviewed both together and in separate groups to investigate "male" and "female" perspectives. Youth in these groups constructed a general portrait of teen sexuality in Milton primarily through the trading of accounts of peer group, familial, and neighborhood problems. Individual and small group interviews featured more complex renderings of peer culture, relationships with parents, and male and female sexuality.

In the first focus group of 13 students at Milton High School, many of the teens had dropped out of school for several years and had joined this program to accelerate their completion of graduation requirements. In the second focus group, four youth at the Comstock Community Center Program attending public, vocational, and Catholic schools in the neighborhood participate voluntarily in activities and socializing with staff and other teens (see box on page 51 for interview profiles). As a result, these findings reflect the views of particularly aware and motivated young people who have sought out assistance and adult guidance. Their personal experiences and their representation of more prevalent heterosexual attitudes and practices of their peers will be presented here.

This historically white working-class neighborhood is in the midst of ethnic and racial transition with an influx of Latino, African American, and Asian residents in recent decades. The neighborhood is divided into white enclaves, mixed sections, and predominantly Latino areas. Youth from these focus groups live in white or mixed sections of the community. Within this sample, three girls and one boy currently reside in a slightly more homogeneous, affluent, and stable white neighborhood that is contiguous with Milton. Their views on teen sexuality among urban white youth are included in this study as they relate to experiences of teens interviewed from Milton.

The Milton Neighborhood

The Milton neighborhood in Philadelphia has traditionally been a white working-class community supported primarily by the textile and shipping industries [Binzen 1970]. Its first major period of development occurred by the 1830s with the influx of Irish and German immigrants into Milton. The neighborhood continued to expand with subsequent waves of Poles, Italians, Ukrainians, and Jews settling in various sections of Philadelphia in the late nineteenth and early twentieth centuries. Today, Milton is an inner-city community of 35,700 residents. It is still largely a white-ethnic neighborhood with 32% of its residents reporting Irish ancestry, as well as 24% of German, 11.4% of Polish, and 8% of Italian descent.[6] According to the 1990 Census, the Milton neighborhood is 94% white.[7] Evidence of Puerto Rican, Asian, and African American migration into the neighborhood is seen primarily in three census tracts on the western edge that contain white populations of 85%, 91%, and 93%. Non-white residents are highly visible in Milton and white residents frequently attribute social and economic problems to the increasing Hispanic and Asian presence in the neighborhood over the past 10 years. However, the 1990 Census shows that the non-white population in Milton consisted of 3% Hispanic, 2% Asian, and 1% African American residents.[8]

Milton's local economy flourished into the twentieth century until its factories and banks shut down during the Great Depression in the 1930s. The business climate and local economy was revived again by wartime industries during World War II.[9] By the 1950s, however, many residents moved out of the already deteriorating neighborhood as part of the postwar suburbanization movement fueled by the federal government which offered such incentives as affordable housing mortgages and a new highway system. This trend of white out-migration has intensified in the past decade with continued ethnic and racial changes and intergroup violence.[10]

Along with its declining population, Milton has also lost most of its industrial base in the last couple of decades [Loeb 1992]. Businesses and smaller industries that remain encounter serious problems with theft and vandalism. The neighborhood economy has also been hit hard by the national recession, as well as by long-term disinvestment and neglect from public and private financial and development institutions. Within this depressed climate, Asian and Puerto Rican immigrants have established viable business strips in the neighborhood. In addition, a thriving interstate drug trade conducted in Milton provides an alternative local economy and source of employment for neighborhood residents, as well as a disincentive for legitimate business to locate in the area.

Social Profile

The social boundaries of the Milton neighborhood are strikingly elusive. Attempts at boundary definitions reveal the embattled history of this "Whitetown." As economic and physical conditions have deteriorated and ethnic and racial succession have coincided with recent decline, white ethnic residents of Milton have sought to both separate themselves from non-white newcomers and uphold values and homogeneity of the old neighborhood. Some whites make distinctions between white Milton and Puerto Rican "West Milton"; others claim specific white subsections of the area as their place of residence. The name "Milton" itself evokes a multitude of images with widely differing meanings. To most outsiders, Milton signals danger and decay. White residents of nearby more affluent and stable communities extend the geographical designation of "Milton" to label pockets where social problems abound. Yet, elderly whites who have chosen to remain in Milton or who cannot afford to leave nevertheless cling to nostalgic memories of working-class decency and solidarity.

Teens in this study describe Milton as an increasingly dirty, violent, and alienating place for white youth. They have experienced the destabilizing impact of neighborhood economic changes as their fathers and mothers have lost their jobs to layoffs or injuries and have lacked skills to reenter the market. According to the 1990 Census, the neighborhood median family income in Milton was $25,500. However, family incomes in the community ranged from $19,000 in the census tract with the highest percentage of minority and immigrant residents to $30,500 in a nearly all-white census tract. In addition, 46% of the adult population in Milton attained a high school degree in 1990. Less than 5% of adults in the neighborhood had obtained a B.A. degree or advanced training [U.S. Census 1990].

The urban white teens in this study live in a variety of family arrangements, including single-parent and two parent homes with working adults and adults on welfare or disability. The percentage of female headed families reported in Milton's six census tracts in 1990 range from 18% to 40%. On average, 21% of the residents in Milton reported living below the poverty line, from 33% in the poorest census tract to 13% in the most affluent. The neighborhood percentage of children under 18 years old living below the poverty line was 18% in 1990.

White teens in Milton go to an array of public, vocational, and Catholic schools throughout Philadelphia. In the interviews with white youth, teens did not identify a "neighborhood" high school in Milton. Moreover, they stressed that there are few public schools with a sizable population of white students. As Puerto Ricans, Asians, and African Americans have entered the Milton community, white parents have routed their children to Catholic schools or select magnet schools within the public school system. In 1990, 43% of children under 18 in Milton went to private schools, ranging from 23% to 55% among the six census tracts.

According to the youth in this study, pregnant white teenage girls are a common sight at school and around the neighborhood. The City of Philadelphia Department of Public Health reports that there were 620 live births to white mothers in Milton in 1990; 334 of these births were to unmarried white mothers.[11] In 1990, there were a total of 23 births to 16-year-old girls and 95 births to 17- to 19-year-olds of all races reported in the six census tracts.[12] On average, 95% of the births to unmarried mothers in Milton that year were to white women. In the three western census tracts of Milton in which an average of 10% of the residents are non-white, 11% of the total births were to unmarried mothers of other races. Thus, it appears from the 1990 Census data that unmarried white women in this working-class and economically marginal neighborhood are having babies with the same frequency as their African American and Latina counterparts.[13] The following ethnographic analysis will explore the social organization of teen sexuality and pregnancy and its cultural meanings for white youth in Milton in the economic and social context described above.

Teen Sexuality

Preliminary findings from focus group discussions and interviews indicate that there is a high rate of sexual activity and pregnancy among urban white youth. Knowledge about contraception and fertility is incomplete or erroneous; birth control is used inconsistently and often ineffectively. Many teens in this study expressed fears about venereal diseases and AIDS, but not about pregnancy. Pregnancy seems to be taken for granted or even a desirable outcome of sexual relations. Abortion is viewed as an unacceptable way of managing pregnancy, but remains for some an available though stigmatized alternative to parenthood. Many young women expect babies to be a reliable source of love and means to independence from their own families. Many are frustrated, however, by the demands of teen motherhood that disrupt educational, socializing, and dating possibilities and rely on mothers or in-laws to assume responsibility for child-care. While some boys demonstrate desire and ability to provide for a baby, many are not interested in or prepared for fatherhood.

Peer Culture: A Game of Control

Dating is considered an old-fashioned term for amorous activity between boys and girls in Milton. According to the youth interviewed, the art of romance is a thing of the past. "Going out" or "being with someone" for these white youth means spending time and being sexually involved with one person. In discussions with teens in this study about sexuality, the issue of control emerged as a central theme in sexual relations among inner-city white youth. Teens in the two focus groups vividly portrayed social-sexual struggles for control between boys and girls. Flirting and "playing on" (cheating on) a boyfriend or girlfriend are main devices for getting respect from peers or exercising power in a relationship. Girls get pregnant to try to "hold" boyfriends or to get revenge for infidelity. Boys "get girls pregnant" to keep them from "being with" other guys.

Peer pressure to "be a man" among urban white boys involves being in control of girls and being in control of relations with girls in front of other guys. Boys tell girlfriends what to wear, who to talk to, and how to walk to limit their attractiveness and availability to other guys. Boys establish themselves "as men" and derive self-esteem through ongoing interactions with other guys that evolve into what is known as "the talk." In this forum, boys present exaggerated or fictitious versions of sexual exploits or bad treatment of girls, "to make themselves look good, to be accepted, to fit in." Youth in these focus groups claimed that some young men participate in "the talk" publicly, but demonstrate respect and love toward girlfriends in private. Several boys in this study who did not consider themselves part of dominant male "in-groups" reported that they discuss girls, sex, and relationships independently with close male friends.

According to female teens in the two focus groups, girls do talk about sex publicly but do not have a common set of standards to judge behavior or an equivalent public forum for sharing sexual information. They confide in and advise their closest friends about problems and suggestions with relationships, but distrust other young women with intimate sexual details. Annie, an 18-year-old attending Bruckner Vocational High School, warned of the dangers of the rumor mill for teen girls in Milton:

> Somebody could go off and tell whoever and the story gets blown out of proportion, mixed around…I always watch who I talk to. I make sure that person won't say anything unless I want them to…people get hurt…it can bring down my reputation as a person.

Maggie, a 17-year-old friend of Annie's also at Bruckner Vocational High School, revealed in an individual interview that young women also "brag" about sexual activity. She pointed out, "A girl will talk about sex to be accepted…she'll act like she's done things I can't imagine porn stars doing so she's thought of as 'experienced.' I guess they just want people to like her, and they think 'talking sex' will get her friends." Both boys and girls interviewed in the study reported that, while everybody talks about casual sexual encounters, girls who talk about sex in the wider female peer group tend to include details about intimate relationships with steady boyfriends.

Young women in this urban white neighborhood are acutely aware of the double standard operating in the peer group, but feel powerless to challenge the accepted norm: Boys are rewarded socially for having sex with many girls; girls get a bad reputation for having sex with many guys. Patrick and Brian (two friends ages 17 and 20, respectively, both employed and not currently attending school) articulated these social rules clearly in an interview together:

> B: For a guy, its like, its great if he sleeps with a lot of women, but if a girl does it they're looked at as a hooker, a sleaze...

> P: If a guy knows a girl likes to have sex, they would want to have sex with her. She's "easy..."

> Interviewer: Would you go steady with such a girl?

> P: Only stupid ones, if they didn't "know about her" probably...

> Interviewer: Would you trust her?

> B: No, if I was goin' with her and I didn't "know about her" and I found out, I wouldn't trust her. I would probably break up with her.

Thus, for boys in Milton, knowing a girl's record is key to defining a sexual relationship in which trust and reputation are constantly on the line.

Young women internalize this standard with its conflicting expectations for what is "desirable" to men as they attempt to construct guidelines for their own sexual behavior. Ironically, in a peer culture where sex is accepted and prevalent, teen women who engage in diverse sexual practices with multiple partners are nevertheless labeled "bad." This labeling process is subtle, yet powerful, as Annie explained in her interview: "A lot of girls I know just go out and have one-night stands.

That's not so much considered wrong but a lot of other girls I know get the impression that if you go on a one-night stand, you are a 'slut' and that's what it is considered."[14] Not only do boys judge girls on their sexual behavior, girls judge one another. Although they expressed approval of young women who are open about their sexuality, girls in the focus groups criticized promiscuous girls who get pregnant but cannot establish paternity as "careless and stupid."

One area where girls interviewed in focus groups did describe resistance to peer culture and the gendered power relations created and enforced by it was on the subject of clothing. Boys and girls in the two groups argued over whether girls should wear bodysuits to school.[15] In these interviews, the boys insisted that it was "unfair" for a girl who had a boyfriend to wear a bodysuit to school, because she was intentionally attracting other guys. The girls in the groups argued that a young woman should wear whatever she wanted, and that her boyfriend should trust her. In this peer group, the fashionable form-fitting bodysuit has become a symbol of uncontrolled female sexuality. The multiple and conflicting meanings surrounding it have to do with who has or should have the authority to control it.

Teen Gender Roles: "It's a guy thing/girl thing"

Sexual norms in Milton's white teen culture are organized around conflicting social ideas about what it is to be a man or a woman. Dominant definitions of masculinity and femininity are taken for granted by teens as normal. The double standard operating in this peer group, which constrains teen women socially and sexually is defined, redefined, and legitimated through daily interactions.[16] In their renderings of social-sexual relations, white youth in these interviews appeal to nature. Guys are naturally sexual. They need and want sex. Girls naturally love "love" and equate sexual pleasure with affection. All of the girls interviewed regarded men, as a group, as "pigs" who always want sex and power and who deny girls sexual gratification and emotional attention.

Boys interviewed did not have an equivalent category for girls. In his comparison between male and female sexuality, one boy described his own sexual experience in natural terms but stumbled on the contradictions inherent in his sexual encounters with young women:

> I know that it's hard for a guy to not have sex…it's weird, like, as soon as a guy gets to a point, without even knowing, without hearing anything about sex, he automatically knows what to do…it is a natural thing with guys. I think women are different. Well, I think some women like sex, you know, a lot of women do. But they [most women] are uptight about it.

Most boys in these interviews for whom sex seems instinctual did not make a link between peer pressures on women to be "good" and constrained female sexuality. Many boys perceive girls' sexual reluctance or unwillingness to have sex as an innate lack of desire, rather than a response to social limitations and contradictory expectations. One boy commented, "A lot of girls I know…they just lay there. You got to do everything for them and they get all the enjoyment…they don't let you really explore your body. They're boring…you have to tell them what to do." Many girls in Milton who have been socialized not to enjoy sex or "give it up" are confused and resentful when asked by their boyfriends to engage in oral and anal sex. They fear that they will lose his respect and the privileges intendant in the "girlfriend" status.[17] Nevertheless, in describing specific practices in their sexual relations with men and their own pursuits of sexual satisfaction, the young women interviewed in the two focus groups also spoke of adjusting their modes of femininity in response to "what the situation calls for."

As frustration and resentment build between boys and girls, control and abuse are frequently part of the experience of sexuality for teens in Milton. Based on their own encounters with guys, many girls interviewed accept the notion that male sexuality is naturally unbounded and potentially dangerous. Maggie expressed concerns about women being the victims of male sexual instincts and cravings, as she notes, "Boys can't always know how to control themselves…girls have to be careful, even though guys shouldn't touch 'em." Female victimization at the hands of uncontrolled male sexuality is a common "definition of the situation" [Goffman 1974] which precludes the experience of a female sexuality free of fear and guilt. Many girls in these interviews described their experience of sexuality in these terms.[18]

Often girls see peer games of flirting and control as natural and unchangeable, yet acknowledge that these are collective practices in their peer culture. Annie recounted the agreed-upon rules for sex and the female role in this teen mating ritual as "a girl thing": "It's a girl thing … You have to tease, you go out with someone. And however many years, months, hours, or minutes determines when youse gonna have sex or when youse gonna talk about it."

From discussions with white teens in Milton, there is evidence that teens in this community recognize that these rules are actually negotiated. Many youth are trying to construct new patterns for sexual relations based on notions of gender equality gleaned from wider society. In contrast to assessments of the "nature" of men and women, a number of teens also depicted alternative attitudes toward and practices of sexuality in heterosexual relationships. Some girls just want sex for physical gratification and seek abortions for unwanted pregnancies; some boys want loving sexual relationships with girls and will support a child they fathered. While they feel trapped by the double standard, the girls in this study also claim that women "have the right" to independence and respect in sexual and familial relationships and in the workplace.[19]

The Search for Adulthood: Love and Independence

For urban white youth in this neighborhood, the search for adulthood and self-esteem is carried out intensively in the terrain of sexuality. Many girls have sex for love, as one teen at Comstock Community Center observed: "A girl will like a guy for a long time…she'll do sex to get his attention…She has no self-esteem. She thinks she is getting attention from the guy. She feels love, even if it is for only two hours—

she thinks it's worth it." Many boys have sex without this emotional attachment, as one boy explained, "If it is out there waiting for him, he'll take it." Other young men prefer intercourse in the context of an intimate relationship.

Teens in Milton adopt birth control practices according to the type and seriousness of their sexual relationships. Many boys use condoms during casual sexual encounters. A smaller number of girls obtain the pill, sponge, diaphragm, and other contraceptives from doctors and clinics. However, youth involved in steady relationships tend not to use contraception with the exception of the withdrawal and rhythm methods. Condom use among teens in this neighborhood is often motivated by fear of sexually transmitted diseases and AIDS rather than desire to prevent pregnancy. Conventional wisdom on "protection" for boys is generally based on reputation and achieved status of girls. As several boys put it, "You don't have to worry about disease if you have known a girl long enough."

For many of these youth, birth control is expensive and difficult to obtain. Asking parents to contribute to contraception requires teens to reveal and even discuss their sexual activities. Because many youth in this community avoid the topic of sex completely with parents, they feel they cannot afford the emotional and financial costs of birth control. "The money has to come from somewhere," commented Annie, "and parents want to know where it is going." Several teens cited abstinence as the only way to be "one hundred percent safe," but reject it as a reasonable approach to the attractions and demands of teen sexuality.

Patterns of contraception use and nonuse among teens in Milton cannot be explained fully by ignorance, lack of access, discomfort, and financial burdens involved with birth control. Attitudes about contraception among urban white youth are deeply rooted in local cultural understandings of sexuality and gender relations.[20] Peer pressure promoting unprotected sex is reinforced by the privileged image of sex as a "natural" act. Condoms are considered "unnatural" and uncomfortable by many girls as well as boys. According to some teens in these interviews, some boys advance a justification for not wearing condoms that if they get AIDS "out of pleasure," it is not a problem. The most common reason for not using birth control among these youth is that unprotected sex is a pledge of intimacy and trust that elevates "fucking" to "making love." While this system serves to satisfy male desires not to use condoms and female wishes to feel loved, teens in this study do believe in "natural sex" as an expression of romantic love and commitment. Many teens in this study imbued steady relationships with a sanctity that sharply contrasted with their matter-of-fact portrayal of rampant casual sex.

Individual responses to and conventional wisdom about particular forms of contraception reveal difficulties teens have in managing adult responsibilities entailed in sexual activity. Several of the girls interviewed voiced concerns about unpleasant or dangerous side effects of the birth control pill. Referring to the pill as "birth control," Annie explained another reason why oral contraception is not a reliable or desirable method for teen girls:

> A lot of my girlfriends are on birth control…and have had side effects, and a lot of others haven't but don't like it because…I mean, you forget. It's like, when you have to take your vitamins, you don't remember to take them everyday. You just take them whenever you see them or whenever you remember to take them. I mean, a lot of people don't remember.

Annie's juxtaposition of birth control pills with vitamins suggests that many teen girls have not integrated sexual activity into an adult conception of their bodies and their futures. This dissociation of sexuality from responsible consideration of its physical and emotional impact often leads young women in this neighborhood who are concerned about future plans to stop having sex.

While boys and girls struggle with one another for authority and power in sexual relationships, they are remarkably passive about sex and its consequences. According to the youth in this study, sex and pregnancy are not in their control. One girl at Milton High School said, "At this school, it's [pregnancy] is like an epidemic." Sex "just happens" at any possible time or place. White teens in Milton have sex in their parents' homes, at school, in cars, in abandoned buildings. In the heat of the moment, contraception is not important. Pregnancy is not a concern that significantly influences sexual behavior. For teens in this neighborhood, pregnancy is a normal risk involved in sexual activity. As one outspoken young woman put it, "You lay, you play, you pay." Youth in these discussions who claim to use contraception condone accidental pregnancies due to contraceptive failures. Whether such failures occur due to technical problems like condom breakage or inconsistent or improper use of contraception like forgetting to take the pill or lying about being on it, all of the youth interviewed insisted that "accidents happen, people make mistakes."

Because of conflicting feelings about the meanings and responsibilities involved in regular and effective contraceptive use, youth in this study justified the high rate of young pregnancies in Milton with a set of explanations generated and sanctioned within teen peer culture.[21] Although they admitted that many of these "mistakes" are due to unprotected sex, most of the girls interviewed emphasized the importance of not regretting their actions. It is a survival mechanism, as Annie points out, "Whatever happens happens, and it's not always like what you wanted to do, but you have to live with that for the rest of your life. You can't go around and regret what you did because if you didn't want to do it, you shouldn't have done it." As they presented the difficulties of teen parenthood, young mothers interviewed always stressed how much they love their babies. These contradictory attitudes toward control over sexuality and its consequences are complicated further by the fact that many of these youth admit freely that they are, themselves, the "mistakes" of teen parents.

Like their own parents, many white teens in Milton regard pregnancy and children as a source of love and a means to independence. However, an increasing breakdown in the social organization of the neighborhood today limits opportunities to realize these goals that were more available for previous generations.[22] Youth in this study made it clear that pregnancy and children often fail to satisfy either need, as one boy in the Milton high school dropout prevention program explained:

> It makes them [kids] feel like they are an adult, they are so insecure about themselves...they have to feel like they can handle the world. If they have a kid, then they're grown and they don't have to listen to their parents anymore. But it doesn't work that way, because once they do it, they're gonna be going back to their parents because they need help.

For most girls in this white working-class and economically marginal neighborhood, receiving welfare is not a major incentive for pregnancy. One 16-year-old girl explained that more often, young women have babies "to fill up their emotional needs that other adults leave." Youth in these interviews described childlike images of babies held by teen girls. In her reflections on the prevalence of teen pregnancy, Annie captured a seductive and wishful fantasy of having babies commonly expressed by girls in Milton:

> A lot of girls feel that they don't have anybody, that they need somebody to love. They're in broken homes, broken relationships with parents, ex-boyfriends, and friends. So, they decide that they want to get pregnant. And they just think it's like taking care of a *baby doll*, which it isn't.

A 17-year-old mother at Milton High School described this retreat to childhood from a veteran perspective, "Girls want babies because they think they're cute...they want to put little dresses on them and push a coach [stroller] around...but they don't have to live with them." Pregnant girls in Milton soon realize that having a baby affects their education, social life, and dating prospects. Teen mothers interviewed in this study rely heavily on their own mothers and in-laws for child care.

While teens tend not to take responsibility for contraception, they do face the consequences of pregnancy more actively. Peer pressure for boys to stay with pregnant girls and the babies they fathered is common among white teens in this neighborhood. The male peer group expects a guy "to do something," even in the infrequent case of raising money for an abortion. Many guys in their late teens and early twenties are involved with their children, as Brian reported, "A lot of my friends do stay [with girls they get pregnant]. Even if they broke up, they still support the kid, still see the kid, they have visitation rights."

Many teen boys who embrace fatherhood view their children as a natural extension of themselves. A 16-year-old boy at Milton High School whose girlfriend at the time of the focus group thought she was pregnant said, "Some guys will stay. It is their progeny, and they have feelings for it ... if my girlfriend is pregnant, it would be perfect. We would have the baby, and I would find a job." One girl at Milton High School said that many guys imagine their babies to be male and some urge pregnant girlfriends to "stay healthy," presumably for their sons. Paternal claims over babies can be difficult for a teen mother. When couples with babies break up, teen fathers sometimes compete with mothers for control over the child. One 17-year-old mother pointed out that the father of her baby buys expensive athletic shoes and clothes for the child while she barely affords to provide basic items like diapers. While she is irritated by her ex-boyfriend's behavior, this young mother worries most about the divisive effect his "spoiling" might have on her relationship with their child.

Many white teen fathers in this neighborhood try to find employment to support a baby and ask girlfriends or wives to work to avoid welfare.[23] It is a question of pride for young men in Milton, according to Brian:

> B: A lot of my friends who have babies don't like to be on it [welfare] …The guy I live with, before they got married, she went on welfare. He didn't want her to be on welfare. Too much pride, I guess. So they got off of it. Same with my cousin. He didn't want her to be on welfare, so she had to work.

Men, women, and families do receive welfare in Milton; some people in the neighborhood remain on welfare their whole lives. Nevertheless, in this "Whitetown," teens draw clear lines between the deserving and undeserving poor. Welfare is seen as a temporary solution to real problems experienced by people in an economically devastated working-class neighborhood. Maggie conveyed this view of welfare voiced by many teens in this study: "They [people] just need help at this time …it's not like they've been on it for their whole lives or will be on it for the rest of their lives. Its just sometimes you need a little extra help and welfare is there for you."[24]

In Milton, male peer groups exert a major influence on a young man's response to fathering a child. While many stay, other white guys do leave pregnant girlfriends without financial assistance or personal support. Responsible fatherhood requires lifestyle changes, and many of these young fathers are not willing or equipped for such changes. Brian observes disruptions in the lives of his friends who are in their early twenties:

> They [young fathers] don't have a life anymore. I mean, they have a life, but, they stay in a lot more…They don't have as many friends as they used to…they work harder, can't go to school…But, they're not ready. They are not ready at all. They try hard, but they're not ready.

Boys interviewed at Milton High School acknowledged that it is easier for guys to shirk responsibility for their babies, as one 16-year-old boy admitted, "We can roll [take off]." Annie expressed her disapproval of this male behavior, remarking, "Guys in the neighborhood don't care. They'll say, 'I knocked her up,' but they don't have jobs; they cheat on girlfriends." Commenting on an increasing number of sexual relationships between Puerto Rican boys and white girls in Milton, teens in this study observed that Puerto Rican guys in the neighborhood usually abandon pregnant white girlfriends.[25] In his interview, Patrick observed, "White guys have a better chance of staying than Hispanics. They get them [white girls] pregnant and leave, then go back to them to have more sex." Maggie pointed out another aspect of the dynamic between white girls and Puerto Rican boys, as she remarked incredulously, "Puerto Rican guys just leave [a pregnant white girl]. It's like, they disappear off the face of the earth!…White girls fall for Puerto Rican guys. They keep going back, getting pregnant with them again."

While teen pregnancy is accepted and common among urban white youth in this area, abortion is viewed as an unacceptable response to pregnancy except in the cases of incest, rape, or medical emergencies. Youth in this study condemned teens who have abortions because they feel unprepared for parenthood or want to avoid the sanctions of their own parents. To many of them, abortion is murder. One 17-year-old mother with a 2-year-old daughter commented on her decision to continue her pregnancy: "I knew I did not want an abortion. I knew it from the start because I don't believe in it. The baby didn't ask to be put there…So why should you kill the child before it even has a chance to come out and live?" Another young man emphasized the responsibility involved in sexual relationships that result in pregnancy, "Whatever happens, it is both of our faults. I am not going to kill someone else for something we did." Maggie reported that her female peer group rallies around a pregnant friend. Her description of this "help" revealed a coercive dimension to female peer involvement with pregnancies, as Maggie noted, "My friends wouldn't allow me to have an abortion. They would help them [pregnant girls] keep their babies in any way they could. Maybe they would help arrange an adoption."

The Search for Adults: "Being There"

Family life in Milton is often unpredictable and sometimes disruptive. While some teens in this study described positive and trusting relationships with parents, others reported mental, physical, and substance abuse by adults in the household. Divorce is common. Mothers bring boyfriends into the home, often putting the man's needs before those of her children. According to these youth, many mothers stay with men (husbands or lovers) who physically and emotionally abuse them because they are afraid to be alone. Some of these teens disapprove of their mother's neglect and mistreatment of their children but attribute it to low self-esteem.[26] Living with both a mother and a father, however, is not always an advantage in this white ethnic neighborhood. One teen described her situation at home: "My dad is a smart guy, he's a carpenter and all. But he is lazy. He does drugs and abuses my mom …telling her she is fat and ugly, hitting her for no reason…They separated for a while, but she's still with him." Regardless of their situations, many teens in this study believe that "the child should come first" and that the parenting they receive is inadequate.

In a neighborhood where many children live with unmarried and divorced mothers, youth experience confusion about fathers. One young woman reported that she has called four or five of her mother's boyfriends "dad" since her parents divorced. In these discussions with white youth, teens drew a clear distinction between a biological "father" and a present and caring "dad." In his recounting of the men in his mother's life, one boy revealed the painful absence of a father in both senses: "I don't consider my stepfather a father. I consider him a friend. I don't even call my real dad "dad." I just call him by his first name. I don't know why. He was never there for me, I guess."

Several teens in this study have virtually no contact with their biological fathers who live in the same neighborhood. Brian's father had been addicted to heroin and abusing his mother when he left the family a decade ago. In his interview, Brian noted defensively, "I don't even know if my father is dead. He went to the hospital about a year ago when he was on methadone. I haven't heard about him since." Although he hates his father for abandoning the family and hurting his mother, Brian still misses having a "dad." In tenth grade, he gave himself a head injury so he could drop out of a public high school in Milton, because of harassment by Puerto Rican boys. Although he earned a high school equivalency degree since that time, Brian still wonders if this difficult experience would have been different had his father been involved in his life. He commented tentatively, "I had nobody pushing me. I would've finished school if…I would have wanted a father 'there' to straighten me out because I have an attitude."

White teens in this study want their parents to "be there." Several youth described close relationships with parents in which sex, contraception, and dating are discussed openly. One boy commented on his friendly connection with his father: "I love my dad. We joke about sex. Sometimes when I get home, he asks me `Did you get some?' Other times he talks serious with me about using condoms and protecting myself." Many youth, however, described fathers as unapproachable and unforgiving, particularly on the topic of teen sex. Maggie says she never considers talking to her father about her personal life, "No way, he's not there. He's so stupid. He likes my boyfriend but never asks about the relationship. He's just like a little island that sits in his chair. My mom's the boss. She does everything." Some teens in Milton "parent" their own parents. One young woman described this experience with her mother:

> Here I was 18 years old and I wasn't allowed to go out
> to parties and stuff and here she [mother] was every
> weekend staying out all night with her friends...So, I
> felt she was acting 18 and I was acting 37, taking care
> of my brothers, cooking, cleaning, getting my home-
> work done, plus going to school and going to work.

Many of the teens interviewed feel abandoned or rejected by parents who do not offer them affection or guidance. One young mother has realized the consequences of neglect: "Maybe I wouldn't have had my daughter if my mother had talked to me. She could have taught me." While they defend their adolescent right to privacy, a remarkable number of teens in this study felt that parents should talk about sex and contraception with their children. In her interview, Annie again portrayed the complexities in and consequences of children having children as a way to "grow up" in the Milton neighborhood:

> I could blame it [teen pregnancy], I would blame it on
> their parents because that's something it's not their
> [teens] fault, accidents do happen, you know, you got
> to grow up some time...when you become a teenager,
> that's something they [parents] have to deal with. That's
> something they have to talk about and they never faced
> the responsibility to do it, and now they're gonna be mad
> at their children for goin' out and getting pregnant.

Most teens in this study were aware of this cycle of teen pregnancy but view their peer culture in "the nineties" as being fundamentally different from that of their parents. From their descriptions of their parents' histories, it appears that the social organization of the neighborhood provided symbolic, institutional, and economic support for marriage as a resolution of teen pregnancy and illegitimacy. More industrial jobs were available in the neighborhood; more families were involved with the Catholic Church. The high divorce rate and prevalence of abuse among parents in this neighborhood, however, leads today's youth to question the benefits of such rigid social structures. In addition, the bleak economic outlook and dearth of secure jobs discourages teen men, in particular, from taking up traditional roles as providers for young families.

Teens in this study are, nevertheless, attuned to traditional moral codes for sexual conduct. While most of these youth are sexually active, they are concerned about adult "messages" regulating sexuality. Many endorse parental limits on sexuality as "general" guidelines for teens, but do not abide by such rules themselves. Similarly, some youth who are sexually active disapprove of free condom distribution at schools because it "sends out the wrong message…It is better to make sex more difficult to keep people on their toes." Others point out that promotion of condom use conflicts with messages of religious or school authorities advocating abstinence or delaying sex until marriage. There were also a number of teens in this study who recommended more sex education and access to affordable birth control and gynecological care for neighborhood youth.

Most boys and girls in this study do not turn to religion for moral guidance, particularly in the area of sexuality. In this white ethnic urban community, youth come from predominantly Catholic backgrounds. Most teens and their parents do not attend church or consider themselves to be religious, however. When asked if religion is an important factor influencing their attitudes about sex and sexuality, many teens in this study focused on the impracticality and hypocrisy of Catholic doctrine as practiced in their community. Brian and Patrick talked at length about their confusion over and disappointment with Catholicism:

B: I'm an atheist…All my family is Catholic, and you're not supposed to drink and have sex with women if you're not married… My cousins cheat, my aunt is a hooker on "the Ave"…I see every one of them doing it, then there's no way I'm going to believe in that religion anymore.

P: It's true. If they say it says in the Bible (I've never really read the Bible to be honest with you), "It's a sin." Everybody sins…all the time. Everybody. Who waits? People say, "I'll wait until I'm married to have sex." That's like one out of a hundred people! How can people say they are Catholic and believe in God when they sin so much?

Individuals in these discussions, however, revealed remarkable vestiges of Catholic influence on their sexual conduct and approach to family life.[27] Birth control is not used in steady sexual relationships. Norms against abortion are rooted in the sanctity of prenatal life. Acceptance of pregnancy and teenage parenthood by girls and boys suggests the tenacity of traditional family structures. Youth who do not practice Catholicism currently intend to raise children in the Catholic religion. In Milton, Catholic culture still influences social-sexual relations between boys and girls along patriarchal lines. In particular, Catholicism offers a set of definitions about femininity as primarily "selfless" in service of God and the traditional family, which are reflected in various permutations of gender relations throughout the neighborhood.[28]

Searching for a Future: Marriage and Work

Living amidst pressures of poverty and violence that have worsened in their lifetimes, teens in this study nevertheless expressed aspirations of meaningful marriage and employment. According to one boy, most teen marriages in the neighborhood resemble unstable adult marriages characterized by financial worries and poor communication. Maggie defined an ideal marriage against what she considered the less-than-ideal pattern of marital relations in Milton, "An ideal marriage? No fighting, no cheating, respect for each other, honesty, open—talk about everything." Many boys and girls in these interviews described ideal marriages in terms of mutual love and equality in housework, child care, and employment. To several girls in the study, this means getting and giving financial support for both partners' schooling. At the time of her interview, Maggie's boyfriend, whom she intends to marry, is about to enter culinary school. She discussed her plan to support the couple at this point in their relationship:

> I don't mind supporting my husband because it's been the husband supporting the wife for how many years now, since the world began I guess—as long as he contributes, cleans the house, takes care of kids like a woman would do when she was home.

She expects different and better treatment from her boyfriend than she has known in her family and community.

Many teens in this study also have higher occupational expectations than those of their parents. While adults in the neighborhood work in factories, offices (as secretaries), in the trades, or collect government checks, these youth want to be teachers, business executives, nurses, and lawyers. The aspirations of the teens interviewed reflect attempts to integrate familiar and available work patterns in the neighborhood with images of professional life portrayed in the media and advertised in wider society. Their dreams of greater material comfort and enjoyable work collide with daily assessments of a decaying local economy and a lucrative drug trade that offers "easy money."

Some young men hold more traditional beliefs that men should do "hard work" and women should be home with the family or work part time. Acknowledging that his views about work and family appear to be old-fashioned, Patrick admitted:

> I'll be honest with you, I'd rather do something hard because then I could say… "Look at what I did." I think men should work harder…I'd like to be working at a

high paying job where you just get paid and you don't
have to worry about stuff…like construction work.

Some teen boys, however, wish to emancipate themselves from the
subordination and frustration of blue-collar jobs that exhausted and
dispirited their parents. Brian currently holds a job doing inventory in
a clothing factory but plans to attend community college to become a
dental technician. While he is one of the few among his friends who
does have what is considered a "good job," Brian wants more out of his
work. He commented, "A good job for a man is not working in a factory or a warehouse. If you're the owner, fine, but if you're just a little
person inside working, no…Unless you're happy doing it. I'm not happy
doin' it." Girls in the study who expressed professional or white-collar
aspirations tended to name feminized fields such as nursing, teaching,
and office management. Most teens in this study viewed education as
necessary to obtain desirable jobs. All of the young mothers in the high
school dropout prevention program returned to school "for their
children's future."

The outlook for white teens in this working-class and economically
marginal neighborhood, however, is grim. All of the youth interviewed
expressed intentions to finish high school. A few said they have considered going to college or seeking advanced or specialized training. Only
one in four students graduate from Milton High School, however; the
dropout rate at Bruckner Vocational High School is not far behind.
College and vocational counseling programs are perceived by students
as inadequate. Both girls and boys abandon education plans to raise
and support babies. Available employment for teens in the area is low-
paying and unattractive service sector work. Dealing drugs in the neighborhood is known to be easier and more lucrative than working "a
hard job." A number of teens interviewed cited Affirmative Action and
other race-based programs as contributing to white unemployment.[29]
One 14-year-old girl remarked, "I think Affirmative Action is so unfair
…My dad applied for a poster job and they didn't take him because
they were looking for minorities…It's just going to drag our race down."

The Search for Pleasure:
Female Sexuality and the Future

The conflict of meanings and experiences involved in teen sexuality and family life in Milton has especially harsh consequences for young women and their future aspirations. The girls in this study expressed contradictory and often competing accounts of reality in terms of the pressures, disappointments, and difficulties they face. In spite of increasing awareness of feminist ideas and claims, traditional working-class family life and Catholic influences on gender relations are reproduced in adolescent female behavior and reinforced in peer group culture. Young women interviewed revealed that they cook, clean, and do errands like their mothers for their own families and their boyfriends. They work in clerical and service jobs to earn extra income for themselves and their families. Many of these girls search for self-esteem in sexual relationships that often result in motherhood at an early age. Thus, even with some exposure to alternative notions of female equality and capability, many young women in Milton envision their future based on the "way things are," most notably, the oppressive power relations in their families.[30]

Virtually all of the teen girls in this study had difficulties discussing female sexuality and pleasure apart from submissive relations with men. Young women in these interviews who ventured to talk about their sexual satisfaction concluded that boys in the neighborhood do not seek to please them sexually through romance, foreplay, or attention to female orgasm. Nor do girls ask their boyfriends for such pleasures. Some young women who expressed interest in their own pleasure referred to common frustrations with sexually inattentive boyfriends and mismatched desires. As one girl put it, "It's rarely ever that youse wants to 'do it' at the same time." Fights over the timing of sex have deeper meanings, however. What these young women complained about the most was that guys just want to have sex. Many girls in Milton equate pleasure in sexual relationships with affectionate and trusting friendship, as one sixteen year-old girl explained, "girls want attention, to share experiences, do stuff together, just to have somebody."

One 18-year-old at Milton High School described her enjoyment of multiple orgasms, taking pride in her freedom to "fake an orgasm when the situation calls for it." Nevertheless, even the sexual pleasure this young woman claims is embedded in peer culture notions of sexuality. She continues to have unprotected sex and reported that she is the only one of her friends who has not gotten pregnant. Reflecting on her sexual history, she smiled with pleasure and with guilt and said, "I'm lucky, I guess."

These girls' responses to sexual relations suggest that working-class culture rooted in Milton's Catholic tradition and its implications for female sexuality and motherhood still influence young women, consciously or unconsciously. The feminine behavior girls know and emulate involves privileging men and children's needs over their own pleasure and self-fulfillment [Weedon 1987, p. 96]. Definitions of femininity and female sexuality common in working-class Catholic culture can be traced in these girls' notion that they have to "pay" for being sexually active. The widespread belief that motherhood promises a reliable source of self-esteem and status for a teenage girl in this white ethnic community may also be rooted in persistent Catholic notions of femininity. To girls who view "natural" and "good" sex as heterosexual and procreative along Catholic lines, the double dilemma of having premarital sex and using contraception can be managed in part by having unprotected sex.[31]

Some teen girls fear that love and the search for love through sexuality makes women desperate and vulnerable. One 17-year-old woman revealed her suspicions about female sexual pleasure and her anxieties about the impact of sex on a woman's life:

> Sometimes I think they're [girls] not really getting pleasure out of sex, but they're using it to hide something that they need to tell somebody…their innermost feelings…and then some day you'll end up flipping out on somebody…probably flipping out on the wrong people…you could end up in the hospital, mentally ill.

Teen girls get negative messages from their teachers about the threat of pregnancy to future aspirations. According to many of these young women, adults at school look down on pregnant girls, as Maggie observed, "Teachers say 'She ruined her life. She's not responsible' because she can't finish her education, because she's pregnant and has to take care of the kid." Young women in these interviews reported that parents in Milton get angry when their daughters get pregnant, but generally incorporate a new grandchild into routines of family life.

For those teen girls in these interviews who articulated aspirations about continued education and meaningful employment, sex and sexuality are fundamentally at odds with their sense of future. Annie talked about how an early pregnancy would destroy her childhood dreams and her family's expectations of her to "be somebody." At the moment, she has ceased sexual activity with her steady boyfriend to ensure her plans to go to community college. On the subject of her own pleasure, Annie commented with slight exasperation:

> Look, I can imagine it [sex] for myself, but as of now, I know it's not what I need, what I want. It is not a priority for me, sex is not a priority. I can see after college…I just think I have to wait…waiting is the best thing for me for it to be pleasurable.

To Maggie, "good sex" takes place between a man and woman who love each other and want to spend their lives together. She explained, "They have to be emotionally strong, not just want each other. They have to 'click' to be able to have sex…when you're with somebody you love, its 'making love.'" She expressed disgust at what she called "perverted sex" practiced by girls with multiple lovers who "ain't got nothing better to do than have sex." Annie described making love as when "you're not worried about making any mistakes." Both of these young women do not believe that they can enjoy sexual pleasure as they define it at this point in their lives without sacrificing their future. They have resolved to forego sexual intimacy for now and expect their boyfriends to accept their determination.

Among all of the girls interviewed in this study, Annie demonstrated the clearest and most effective involvement in school, her job at the community center, and her future education. Yet, Annie struggles harder than many of her female peers to reconcile her chosen identity as a liberated woman with deeply rooted traditional notions of femininity. In this process, she has excluded other possible expressions of female sexuality.[32] Throughout her interview, Annie distinguished her own views and practices from those of other girls in the neighborhood. She portrayed herself as being the vigilant and responsible partner in her sexual relationship, emphasizing that she used condoms regularly during intercourse.[33] Her boyfriend, Patrick (who was also interviewed in this study), commented that he and Annie usually had unprotected sex without withdrawal, however. At this point in his interview, Patrick smiled guiltily and remarked, "I must be sterile or something…or, I guess we're just lucky." While she never articulated this aspect of her dilemma, it appears that Annie could not reconcile Patrick's preferences and pressure for "natural sex" with her future goals and remain sexually active.[34] Annie claimed that she does not even like sex, and does not mind giving it up. However, her decision reflects a conscious avoidance of sexual desire that has caused tensions in her intimate relationship with Patrick.[35]

Annie nevertheless imagines that she and Patrick will still be together in the future. While they each characterized their relationship as fraught with conflict, both teens expressed deep love for one another. Referring to their shared future, Patrick mentioned in his interview that the couple has talked about buying a house together; Annie disclosed the expectation that Patrick is going to "wait for her" while she goes to college. Patrick confesses that Annie's goals jostle his image of manliness. Clearly, this is a central source of their fighting. However, his traditional views may resonate with Annie's deeper conceptions of femininity and motherhood. Annie considers herself to be Catholic, and these more Catholic notions are evident in her description of "a good wife":

She has to be trustworthy, caring loving…is able to meet expectations, do what she's supposed to do without falling behind. Like, if she has kids, make sure that she can take care of them…The woman is supposed to take care of kids.

Annie believes that the Catholic Church has no right to tell teens not to have sex before marriage. In fact, she declared that there is little about Catholic doctrine she embraces. However, the one aspect of religion Annie consciously and tenaciously holds on to is the promise of forgiveness. In a poignant moment in her interview, Annie revealed the solace she takes in her conflicting experience of sexuality: "I don't need confessions for having sex before I'm married. Only when I ask for forgiveness do I get forgiveness from God."

Ironically, Annie's traditional conceptions of sexuality as sin and motherhood as sacrifice have helped her put off having a baby and strive for academic and occupational achievement. In order not to become pregnant, however, she has also put off experimenting with her own sexual pleasure in her intimate relationship with Patrick. For many girls in Milton, responses to sexual relations are shaped in crucial ways by similar notions of femininity provided by Catholic culture. Yet, this study reveals that the social organization of teen sexuality with its peculiar adaptations of traditional norms in this white ethnic neighborhood is being challenged by more liberal possibilities for redefinition of love, family, and work for young women of this generation.[36]

Teen Sexuality and the Future

Teen sexuality and pregnancy are central means for exploring and establishing adult identities for youth in Milton. For teens in this neighborhood, sexuality is a compelling arena in which boys and girls struggle for control, power, and respect. Socialization of peer culture norms around sexuality and the construction of acceptable body and self-images occur through public and private interactions and complex gender role performances. Peer culture attitudes about and practices of teen sexuality are largely shaped by traditional patriarchal gender relations between parents and other adults in this predominantly Catholic white ethnic community. A double standard operating in the teen peer group puts additional pressures on young women in Milton to conform to traditional and repressive patterns that dominate gender relations in the neighborhood. Requirements for girls to be desirous yet "trustworthy" in intimate relationships reinforce practices of unprotected sex.

Male sexuality is conceived and represented in this peer culture as unbounded and dangerous. Female sexual pleasure and gratification is linked to promiscuity. It is sanctioned by the female peer group in Milton and both encouraged and repressed by the male peer group which reserves the right to both sexual adventure and purity. Many girls with low self-esteem who pledge their intimacy to boyfriends through "natural sex" face pregnancy as a likely outcome of sexual relations. For some young women in this neighborhood, pregnancy and motherhood offer fulfillment and promise independence from the abuse and unhappiness in their own families.

Consequences of the social organization of teen sexuality in this white ethnic neighborhood deeply affect the lives and sense of future of its youth. For many boys and girls in Milton, early pregnancies limit educational and employment opportunities. In this teen peer group, abortion is an unacceptable and stigmatized response to pregnancy. Teen mothers and fathers frequently drop out of high school to take care of and support their babies. Young women in this study who have aspirations for higher education and skilled employment feel that they have no alternative to abstinence to protect their futures from unwanted pregnancy.

The prevalence of sexual activity and the pressures to exchange unprotected sex for intimacy in this peer group make abstinence a difficult response to teen sexuality. Ambitious young women in Milton who have internalized traditional working-class and Catholic notions of femininity and fear their own sexuality get caught in contradictory and often self-defeating sexual patterns.[37] Nevertheless, youth in this study revealed that these traditional perceptions are now competing with more contemporary notions of equality and partnership in sexual and marital relationships that offer alternative life options for teen men and women.

Epilogue

This chapter is based on an original text from an interview study with teens ages 14 to 19 from the broader Milton area published in 1994. Subsequent to this initial study, I have changed my sampling frame and my research questions to focus on experiences of rootedness and dislocation and persistence of community in postindustrial American urban life. My ethnographic research includes extensive participant observation, 60 interviews with local adult residents and community leaders, and historical context on a particular white neighborhood in Milton. In light of my current findings and my experience doing field research, I include in this epilogue some additional reflections on my original study of teen sexuality among inner-city, white youth.

In my subsequent research, I have gained a better understanding of the backgrounds and circumstances of families in Milton. Youth in the initial study vividly and poignantly described often disruptive conditions in their homes as part of the strains of their adolescent experience. Contextual knowledge of their worlds or contact with adults in the neighborhood, however, would have helped me further to corroborate, question, and interpret their stories. During the past three years in the field, I have observed the precarious position of white, working-class residents amidst current economic, social, and political change. Many adults in this neighborhood regularly move between employment, unemployment, and welfare. Multiple generations reside together in row houses, and the household composition often fluctuates with changes in individual marital or employment situations. Adults are also assisted by local social networks of families and neighbors that provide child care and other kinds of financial and material support. This information about challenges parents face in making ends meet and their difficulties and frustrations in raising children helps us to better understand interactions between parents and children in Milton. It also tells us more about adult role models available to teens in this community.

It is also important to note that data from my recent study of a particular neighborhood in Milton do not completely overlap with my original study on teen sexuality in the broader Milton area. In my initial research, I made contact with the teens through organized youth groups and a school dropout prevention program in the local comprehensive high school. Thus, the youth did not reside in the smaller neighborhood or the families I have gotten to know in my extended fieldwork. I believe this is relevant, because Milton is a place where people strongly identify with their particular neighborhood or street corner, and the families who live there. Furthermore, the majority of youth in the original study were residing in neighborhoods that are racially and ethnically mixed (most often white and Puerto Rican). Their daily experiences and interactions with a variety of non-white youth shape their perceptions, attitudes, and identities as "white" teens in ways that are likely to differ from youth in the nearby white section I studied in following years. I did not focus on questions of race/ethnic relations and sexuality in my subsequent research. However, my current data lead me to raise further questions about similarities and differences among the white youth in my first study and those of other racial or ethnic groups from comparable socioeconomic backgrounds. Future research might examine variations in perceptions and experiences of sexuality, pregnancy, and opportunity among white teens in different urban environments.

Another limit to the original study is that I did not combine interviewing with other observational methods. Due to the scope of the initial project, I was not able to engage in participant observations, or to shadow the teenagers in school or other peer group settings. Between focus groups and personal interviews, I had only one conversation with each of the participants. Therefore, I was not able to follow-up with their experiences and development over time. In addition, the teens were not able to establish a rapport with me that might have deepened our exchange. Close and trusting relationships with participants in a study often evolve through extended time and shared activity in the field.

This point is particularly salient with regards to one of the participants in the initial study, whom I called Annie. Of all the teens involved in the study, I had the most contact with Annie. She participated in one of the focus groups as well as a one-to-one interview. In addition, I had several opportunities to talk with her informally in the youth group office where she worked and driving her home after the personal interview. Several months after this research had been published, I learned that Annie had just given birth to a child she intended to raise. She had been pregnant throughout the entire study. Annie did not indicate that she was expecting to have a child; I did not detect her condition. My initial reaction to this information was shock, given her lengthy discussions about her future college education and her moves to break off sexual relations with her boyfriend in order to avoid pregnancy. Yet, I have come to view Annie's omission as revealing important information about herself and about the interview process. She was presenting, to me, a young, white, female graduate student, one particular narrative about her life. In these conversations, she described her dreams of a fulfilling career and marriage in the future while concealing an obviously difficult present reality. The interview data in my study must be seen in light of this information about Annie's pregnancy. However, I believe that my interpretation in the original text captured the contradictions in her attitudes and pressures in her situation that, perhaps, contributed to this outcome.

This chapter is my attempt to represent these teenagers' stories as they illuminate aspects of the social organization of teen sexuality and opportunity for white youth in a working-class and poor urban area. The focus groups allowed me to observe teens interacting, and to record from their discussions and arguments norms and shared complaints of a group of white teenagers. In the personal interviews, I also learned about individual experiences that, taken together, reveal patterns about cultural resources and constraints shaping these teenagers' sexual behavior and perceptions of opportunity. Given my limited contact with these youth, however, I cannot comment on any individual's deeper, internal motivations for becoming sexuality active or for becoming a young parent. This kind of information would be best gathered through long-term relationships and documented in more extended case histories.

In conclusion, I believe that this study offers an excellent opportunity for us to listen to youth talk about their peer culture, their perceptions of sexuality and family life, and their dreams about the future. I asked them, "What would you want adults and policymakers to know about your experiences and your community?" To recapitulate my finding, teen sexuality can be understood as an arena for exploring and establishing adult identities in Milton. Sexual activity, pregnancy, and young parenthood take the place of, or sometimes compete with, educational or career opportunities pursued by youth in other communities. My discussions with these young people illuminated the central role of teen sexuality in their search for adulthood.

- First, youth described sexual relations as a game of control and exercise of power in the face of a sensed lack of control over their lives and futures.

- Second, the form of this game is shaped by traditional gender relations in this working-class and largely Catholic neighborhood.

- Third, the study reveals that it is common for teenagers in Milton to use pregnancy and babies as a means of finding love and becoming independent from their own families.

- Fourth, youth expressed disappointment with, and confusion about, relationships with their parents and some teachers and counselors at school.

- Finally, young women with aspirations for future educational and career opportunities revealed particular difficulties with the role of sexuality in the peer culture and the consequences of these pressures for their self-discovery.

References

Anderson, E. (1990). *Streetwise: Race, class, and change in an urban community*. Chicago: The University of Chicago Press.

Binzen, P. (1970). *Whitetown, U.S.A.* New York: Random House.

Fine, M. (1992). *Disruptive voices: The possibilities of feminist research*. Ann Arbor: The University of Michigan Press.

Gitlin, T. (1970). *Uptown: Poor Whites in Chicago*. New York: Harper & Row Publishers, Inc.

Goffman, E. (1974). *Frame analysis: An essay on the organization of experience*. Cambridge, MA: Harvard University Press.

Goffman, E. (1959). *The presentation of self in everyday life*. New York: Doubleday.

Horowitz, R. (1983). *Honor and the American dream: Culture and identity in a Chicano community* (1992 reprint). New Brunswick, NJ: Rutgers University Press.

Kornblum, W. (1974). *Blue collar community*. Chicago: University of Chicago Press.

Loeb, V. (1992, November 8). In a poor neighborhood, new houses offer hope. *Philadelphia Inquirer*, Local, B1.

Loewenstein, G., & Furstenberg, F. (1991). Is teenage sexual behavior rational? *Journal of Applied Social Psychology, 21*, 957-986.

Luker, K. (1975). *Taking chances: Abortion and the decision not to contracept*. Berkeley: University of California Press.

MacLeod, J. (1987). *Ain't no makin' it: Leveled aspirations in a low-income neighborhood*. Boulder, CO: Westview Press.

Nathanson, C. A. (1991). *Dangerous passage: The social control of sexuality in women's adolescence*. Philadelphia: Temple University Press.

Newman, K. S. (1988). *Falling from grace: The experience of downward mobility in the American middle class*. New York: Vintage Books.

Rieder, J. (1985). *Canarsie: The Jews and Italians of Brooklyn against liberalism*. Cambridge, MA: Harvard University Press.

Rubin, L. B. (1976). *Worlds of pain: Life in the working-class family*. New York: Basic Books.

Swidler, A. (1986). Culture in action: Symbols and strategies. *American Sociological Review*, *51*, 273-86.

U.S. Bureau of the Census. (1990). *1990 Census of Population and Housing, Summary Tape File 3A*. Washington, DC: Author.

Weedon, C. (1987). *Feminist practice and poststructuralist theory* (1993 reprint). Cambridge, MA: Blackwell.

Zelnik, M., Kantner, J. F., & Ford, K. (1981). *Sex and pregnancy in adolescence*. Beverly Hills, CA: Sage Publications.

Notes

1   For the purposes of my study, this white working-class neighborhood is referred to as "Milton." All names of people, places, and local institutions are also pseudonyms.

2   These figures are reported from the 1990 Census on Philadelphia. The figures are an average of the report on educational attainment for Census tracts 160 and 159. These tracts contain most of the families whose children attend the public and Catholic elementary schools discussed here.

3   My contact with children and parents has been as a participant observer in a variety of roles, including community organizer, counselor at a local day camp, and as a resident in the community.

4   Further education does not only mean post-high school education, but also completing high school in some cases. The 1990 Census reports that 46% of the adults in the broader Milton area finished high school; 5% of the adults in the neighborhood had a bachelor's degree or other advanced training. In the smaller area of Milton where I have focused my ethnographic research, on average, 60% had finished high school and 6.7% obtained a B.A. or advanced training.

5   Based on findings in their survey research of patterns of sexual behavior and contraception use among Philadelphia teens, Furstenberg and Loewenstein recommended increasing the availability of contraception to youth. Interventions designed to enhance alternative life options to teen pregnancy have not been

favored due to indeterminate evidence of direct effects of socio-economic variables on teenage sexual behavior. See conclusions in Loewenstein and Furstenberg [1991, pp. 983-4] and in Zelnik et al. [1981, pp. 54-61].

6   This profile is based on the 1990 Census of Population and Housing, Summary Tape File 3A. These data come from the Long Form Sample Data sent to one in six households on average (one in eight households in urban areas). Percentage figures are rounded off to the nearest whole number.

7   Aggregate neighborhood figures represent an average of six census tracts in Philadelphia. It is important to note there was a low response rate to census collection in this lower income area of Philadelphia. The census figures for these tracts were completed by the Census Bureau with methods of imputation and substitution.

8   There has been continued racial and ethnic succession in the Milton area and white flight from the neighborhood in the four years since the 1990 Census. The white teens in this study refer to these ongoing social and economic changes in their assessments of the decay of Milton's infrastructure and economy, as well as the rise in violence between whites and Puerto Ricans in the neighborhood.

9   According to Binzen, the biggest firm in Milton was the Stetson Hat Company, which employed almost five thousand men and women and provided a hospital for the workers during World War II.

10   By the 1950s, residents were already moving out of Milton to new developments in Philadelphia's Northeast or nearby suburbs like Levittown in search of better housing, jobs, and schools. Factories and businesses in Milton were already relocating or shutting down in the 1960s and 1970s. More recently, outmigration of white residents has been spurred by fears of racial and ethnic succession. However, continual job loss in the area and increasing poverty among whites in the neighborhood also contribute to a sense of decline that motivates some old-timers and many of their adult children to move elsewhere.

11   Information on live births by age and race in Milton is based on City of Philadelphia Department of Public Health 1990 Statistics by health district, census tract, sex, age, and race.

According to reports from the American Enterprise Institute for Public Policy Research, the national birth rate to unmarried white mothers in 1990 was 31.8 out of 1,000 women; births to white teens was 29.5 births per 1,000 women. For more information on national teen pregnancy rates, see American Enterprise Institute Sexuality and American Social Policy Seminars, "Rise in Out-of-Wedlock Births Complicates Welfare Reform" News Release, 15 November.

12   The Philadelphia Department of Public Health did not have data on teen births sorted by age and race at the time of this study. A comparison of teen pregnancy among white youth in Milton with the national birthrate of unmarried white mothers is not within the scope of this research.

13   There is little information available on teen pregnancy among Asian youth in the Milton neighborhood. Presumably, rates of pregnancy are lower among daughters of Vietnamese, Korean, Chinese, and Filipino immigrants due to cultural norms against illegitimacy. More research in this area is necessary to substantiate this observation.

14   For a symbolic interactionist discussion of "impression management," see Fine, G. A. (1981). Friends, impression management, and preadolescent behavior. In J. Gottman and S. Asher, (Eds.) *The development of children's friendship* (pp. 257-272). New York: Cambridge University Press.

15   For a discourse analysis of femininity, see Weedon, who cites dress as a potential area for contesting gendered power relations, as "dress...necessarily signifies and is open to different meanings... The effect intended by the wearer is never guaranteed, but this does not negate the potential of dress as a site of conscious sexual-political struggle" [1987, p. 87].

16   For a definitive discussion of symbolic interactionism and role performance theory, see Goffman [1959].

17   See Rubin [1976], who offers a sensitive portrayal of the dilemma of the working-class wife during and after the sexual revolution of the early seventies. She observes that working-class husbands in her interviews embraced open sexuality with greater ease than their wives, whose inhibitions had been deeply ingrained by rigid

female sexual socialization of earlier decades [1976, pp. 134-154].

Also, see Luker's argument about "sex-role confusion" resulting from the women's liberation movement. She observes, "Although it sometimes hard for feminists to realize, the traditional female role, with all its limitations, is nonetheless a comfortable one for many women...many women find the loss of traditional female prerogatives (such as passivity and the right to be protected) frightening" [1973, p. 66].

18 Fine [1992] argues that the discourse of "sexuality as victimization" has gained support among educators in the Philadelphia Public School system who teach girls to "defend" themselves against disease, pregnancy, and "being used." She demonstrates the shortcomings in this approach to female teen sexuality, noting that "the language, as well as the questions asked and not asked, represents female as the actual and potential victims of male desire" [1992, p. 34].

19 Their notions of choice and variability in relationships seem to reflect liberal feminist conceptions of autonomy and equality. For a summary of liberal feminist theory, see Weedon [1987].

20 See Horowitz [1983]. In her study of Chicana girls in Chicago and their management of virginity, passion and motherhood, Horowitz argues, "Becoming an unwed mother can be explained only in terms of the legitimizing values associated with femininity and womanhood, not in terms of ignorance or lack of birth control" [1983, p. 135].

Luker also critiques explanations for unwanted pregnancies which do not consider social structures and cultural meanings surrounding sexuality and pregnancy in her study of contraception decisionmaking [1975].

21 The explanations white teens in Milton give for contraceptive failure or neglect often appear to serve as "techniques of neutralization" for young sexual activity without proper usage of birth control. Such justifications suggest that youth engaging in sexual activity nevertheless are partially committed to dominant social norms restricting teenage sex or they are at least aware of these norms.

For a theoretical account of deviant juvenile subculture and demands of conformity, see Sykes, G. M., & Matza, D. [1957]. Techniques of neutralization: A theory of delinquency. *American Socio-logical Review, 22,* 664-670.

22   In her interview study, Rubin documents similar motivations for teen pregnancy and early marriage reported by working-class men and women who were teenagers in the fifties and sixties. However, it is important to note that there is a crucial difference in the consequences of teen sexuality for working-class youth today from previous generations. Unlike the contemporary situation in Milton, the institution of marriage and norms against illegitimacy were relatively stronger in working-class neighborhoods even during the sexual revolution of the early seventies [Rubin 1976].

23   My subsequent research does not offer further support for this finding about peer pressure for white boys to take care of their children or stay with the mother of those children. However, I have anecdotal testimony suggesting that men who do live in households still want to be seen as the breadwinner. This is the case even if their money comes from informal work, illegal activities, or disability checks. More research in these areas of family life and gender relations in this white working-class and poor neighborhood would be useful to illuminate this dynamic.

24   In my ethnographic research over the past three years, I have discovered that welfare is a complicated and important part of many residents' lives in this community. A number of people I have known and worked with talked with pride about earning their own way. Yet, they eventually revealed that they are currently receiving welfare benefits for themselves and their children in some capacity. If they were not receiving welfare, it was likely that someone in their family was getting some kind of benefits from the state. Interestingly, their presentation of themselves and their attitudes often contradicted their actual practices. People frequently expressed mixed feelings about being recipients themselves through severe judgments of other "undeserving" recipients.

25   Teens in the study noted that interracial coupling tends to occur between Puerto Rican boys and white girls in Milton rather than white boys with Puerto Rican girls. Some youth attributed this pattern to a myth that "white girls are easy" and thus, more desirable to Puerto Rican young men than their Puerto Rican female counterparts. Others said that Puerto Rican guys "went after"

white girls because they are not easy. Maggie felt that it was difficult for white girls to find "nice" white boys in Milton because there are so few in the neighborhood in her age group (late teens).

It is important to note that this portrayal of interracial dating is based on limited discussions of the topic with these teens. It should be taken as a presentation of their views. More research in this area of interracial/ethnic dating is necessary to understand this aspect of social life in a demographically changing urban area.

26   My subsequent research confirms these teens' portrayal of absent fathers and mothers with low self-esteem in Milton. This presentation, however, does not show the complexity of how these problems might be part of particular gender relations in this culture. From talking with local women and observing families in the area, I could detect a strong and persistent value attached to having a man "around" in this white working-class and poor neighborhood. It is common for a woman to stay involved with a man regardless of emotional or financial drain, or even damaging influences he or their relationship may be having on her children. To analyze this further would require more participant observation and long-term case studies of individuals and families in this area.

I would highlight, however, that it is primarily women in Milton who take care of the home and the children. Many of these mothers are working or on welfare to support their families on their own. They also rely tremendously on family networks, particularly female relatives.

27   These "Catholic vestiges" resemble other religious influences, such as Evangelical Protestantism, that contribute to urban working-class cultural norms shaping teen sexuality. Similar characteristics and behaviors also can be seen among the American "Religious Right" in suburban and rural communities. However, Catholic culture seems to have constituted dominant institutional and moral structures in Milton that continue to contour the social organization of teen sexuality today.

28   For a discussion of Catholicism and female sexuality, see Weedon [1987, pp. 96-8].

29   See MacLeod [1987]. In his portrayal of "leveled aspirations" of white boys in a low-income neighborhood, MacLeod captures

the resignation and disaffection of "Whitetown" boys who cannot blame their difficulties on social class status or racial discrimination. MacLeod observes:

Once on the job market, the Hallway Hangers' [white male peer group] inability to secure even mediocre jobs further dampens their occupational hopes...the Hallway Hangers, if the ideology [achievement ideology] stands, are afforded no explanation outside of laziness and stupidity for their parents' failures [MacLeod 1987, p. 141].

30 For an account of culture as "tool kit," see Swidler [1986]. Her conception of culture as a style or set of skills and habits, rather than a set of preferences or wants is helpful in understanding the complex attitudes and experiences of teen sexuality among white youth in Milton. In her discussion of the workings of culture, Swidler refers to a cultural repertoire or "tool kit" consisting of available symbols, stories, rituals, and world views which "people use in varying configurations to solve different kinds of problems" [1986, p. 273].

The impact of local culture on the "tool kits" available to young women in Milton is evident in their experiences and management of femininity, sexuality, and motherhood. It is strikingly apparent in the more subtle yet profound case of girls in this study with future educational and occupational aspirations. Even these young women with a vision of upward mobility rely on the same basic "tool kit" available to "Whitetown" women to manage sexual pressures and expectations of teenage life in Milton.

31 Both Horowitz [1976] and Luker [1975] illustrate the consequences of this "double sin" on female contraceptive behavior in their discussions about Catholicism. Luker explains:

There is a noticeable tendency in this population for Catholic respondents to conform to and reject the Church's teachings at the same time, in a "zero sum" game fashion: to engage in deviant intercourse, but not to compound that "sin" by using contraception, which is both a deviant act by Church standards and an acknowledgment that premeditation precedes the sin [Luker 1975, p. 45].

Based on my subsequent interviews with adult Catholic white women in Milton, I would modify this analysis. The women I spoke with, including those in their 20s and 30s, reported being much more aware and mindful of the messages of the Catholic Church when they were teenagers growing up in this general neighborhood than did the girls in this study. The incidence of teen pregnancy at younger ages (13-16 years old) and/or teen pregnancy without subsequent marriage has skyrocketed among Catholic girls in this area in the past two decades. This trend is also apparent among female students even in the most prestigious citywide Catholic high schools for girls in Philadelphia. Thus, orientations and norms rooted in traditional working-class and Catholic culture in Milton appear to operate on some level. However, they are in a process of transformation with the increasing complexity and confusion in the social organization of the neighborhood, and a decline in exposure to and influence of Catholic doctrine and practice.

32   Fine identifies this conception of female sexuality as "sexually autonomous, responsible, and pleasurable," and the social phenomenon of its absence among teen women as the "missing discourse of desire" [1992, p. 41].

33   Annie's mother is a social worker dealing with AIDS education and prevention efforts. In her individual interview, Annie emphasized her close relationship with her mother. She elaborated on the point that her mother lavishly provides free condoms for Annie and her friends.

34   Given Patrick's frankness about sharing conventional neighborhood male attitudes toward sex and sexuality and Annie's conflict over identifying as a sexually active woman, the interviewer speculates that the couple has had unprotected sex during at least part of their sexual relationship. It is likely that Patrick told Annie that he preferred not wearing a condom; Annie (for a variety of reasons) probably stopped arguing with him about it and eventually ceased sexual activity with him as a result of her discomfort and fears about pregnancy.

See the section, "Epilogue," for subsequent findings on the outcome of this relationship. Also see Harold Garfinkle's appendix on the case of Agnes in his book: Garfinkle, H. (1967). *Studies in Ethnomethodology*, Englewood Cliffs, NJ: Prentice Hall Inc.

35   Fine dramatizes what she terms the "missing discourse of desire" among teen women and the consequences of repressive constructions of female sexuality for young pregnancies and alternative life options [1992].

36   In the original text, I used of the terms "liberal possibilities" and "contemporary notions" in contrast with the traditional conceptions of gender roles in love, family, and work in this working-class neighborhood. In reflecting on my subsequent fieldwork, I do not intend this distinction to be a value judgment against all traditional modes or to exclude potential combinations of these different styles found among families in Milton. The point here is that individual teens in this study themselves held out egalitarian relationships between men and women and working in a fulfilling careers as preferable life options. They also did not openly criticize the common situation in their world of having and supporting children as a teenager. As one young women remarked, "I love my child. I don't regret this…"

37   Fine observes in her study in the Philadelphia Public Schools that the more passive and quiet African American and Latina young women are the ones who get pregnant. Emphasizing the consequences of repressive constructions of female sexuality, Fine remarks, "it may also be the case that young women who do internalize such notions of 'femininity' are disproportionately at risk for pregnancy and dropping out" [Fine 1992, pp. 56-57].

3. Prevalence, Patterns, and Outcomes

Brett V. Brown & Carol Emig

For most American teenagers and young adults, the late teens and early twenties are a time of transition from youth to independent adulthood. The vast majority follow a fairly predictable life course.[1] They complete high school, enter college or pursue some other form of career training, and enter the labor force. Some marry and start a family at this time.

This transition can be a rocky one, even for the most advantaged young people. Some will have a misstep along the way—school failure, unemployment, an unintended pregnancy—but, even within this group, most will not be seriously derailed from the path to independent adulthood.

But what of those who find the passage particularly difficult? What of those young people who find themselves well off the course to independence and self-sufficiency for extended periods in their late teens and early twenties? These are America's disconnected youth. For a substantial time between the ages of 16 and 23, they are not in school, not in a job, and not in the military, nor are they married to anyone who is "connected" in any of these ways. Increasingly, policymakers, scholars, and even casual observers view these young people with concern, because disconnection carries both personal and societal costs. Welfare dependency, criminal activity, and a failure to meet various societal expectations related to family life and citizenship have all, at various times, been attributed to extended periods of youthful aimlessness, drifting, or "disconnection." This chapter provides a brief overview of the reasons for studying disconnected youth, patterns of disconnectedness, and the prevalence of, and characteristics shared by, disconnected youth.

There are many reasons for studying disconnected youth. There is ample research indicating that serious missteps in the transition to adulthood are costly in both personal and social terms. For young women, such missteps include never finishing high school, giving birth outside of marriage, and becoming dependent on welfare. Male youth who are out of school and not at work for long periods are more likely to engage in delinquent behavior and to engage in illegal activities to earn a living. When the transition to adulthood is eventually made, those who experienced these problems often continue to pay long-term penalties in the form of lower earnings and fewer weeks employed. Social costs include higher crime rates, more young children in poverty, and lower economic productivity. Costs to the government include higher transfer payments and social support expenses and lost tax revenues.

The transition to adulthood is in many respects a single process, although one in which many different paths can be taken to make a successful transition. Disconnectedness is an appropriate and useful global measure of failure in this complex social process. By looking at it this way, we can identify those youth who are at highest risk of experiencing difficulties and target them for early interventions that may help keep them connected.

Basic Findings

For our analysis, we use the National Longitudinal Survey of Youth (NLSY), a longitudinal survey designed to document the transition of youth into the labor force.[2] It has been conducted annually since 1979. The sample includes young men and women who were between the ages of 14 and 21 at the time of the initial survey. From this data set, we examined that cohort of youth who were ages 16 through 23 in the 1980s and in their mid- to late-twenties in 1991.

Characteristics

What characteristics were shared by youth not involved in school, work, or marriage for substantial periods of time? Youth who were disconnected commonly experienced poverty and dependency, either on family members or public assistance. Among young persons who were disconnected for three or more years, 77% of the men and 89% of the women had been poor at some point during these years. The vast majority (85% of women and 98% of men) lived with their parents at some point while disconnected. Among the young women, 57% had received Aid to Families with Dependent Children (AFDC), and 64% had received food stamps. Sixty-five percent were living with (and presumably caring for) their own children. The young men spent about half of their nonworking time unemployed and about half out of the labor force (that is, not seeking work). The young women spent about three-quarters of their time out of the labor force.[3]

Gender, Race, and Disconnection

More than one in 10 (11%) of America's youth in the 1980s were disconnected for at least an entire year (52 consecutive weeks) between the ages of 16 and 23. Despite the stereotype of idle young men on the streets, this disconnection was more common among young women. More than 13% of young women were disconnected continuously for at least a year, compared with 9% of young men. As we discuss later, a significant proportion of disconnected young women are unmarried mothers.

Disconnection was particularly pronounced among African American young women. About one in three young African American women were disconnected for an entire year, compared with about one in five young Hispanic women and one in ten young white women (see Figure 3-1). Comparable rates for young men are 23% for African Americans, 13% for Hispanics, and 7% for whites.

When the cumulative experience of disconnection over the entire period of youth is considered, the plight of African American women appears even more troubling. More than one in 10 young African American women were disconnected for four or more entire years between the ages of 16 and 23. This is more than four times the rate for any other group regardless of race or gender.

Figure 3-1. Percentage of Youth Disconnected for Entire Calendar Year Between Ages 16 and 23, by Gender and Race

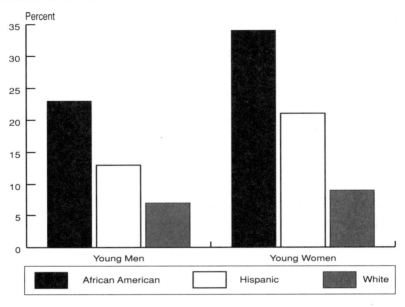

Using a broader definition of disconnection—not connected for at least 26 of 52 weeks—we find that substantial percentages of young minority men and women struggle for many years to make a successful transition to adulthood. More than a quarter (27%) of young African American women and 14% of young Hispanic women were disconnected for four or more years under this less restrictive definition, compared with 5% of young white women. Comparable rates among young men are 18% for African American males, 11% for Hispanic males, and 7% for white males.

Adult Outcomes

Not surprisingly, youths who were long-term disconnected (i.e. for a total of three or more years) between the ages 16 to 23 had much higher rates of poverty and welfare receipt at ages 25 to 27 than did their peers who were never disconnected.[4] Their attachment to the labor force as adults was also more tenuous. Long-term disconnected youth were 13 times more likely than their never-disconnected peers to be poor as young adults. (See Figure 3-2.)

Poverty rates were 44% for men and 56% for women, compared with 3 and 4% among never-disconnected men and women in the same age group. Welfare and food stamp receipt in adulthood was higher among women who had been disconnected for long periods as youth compared with women who had never been disconnected (34% compared with 1% for AFDC and 48% compared with 3% for food stamps).

As young adults (ages 25–27), long-term disconnected youth had family incomes that were less than half the family incomes of their peers who had never been disconnected ($18,200 versus $40,100 for men; $15,400 versus $42,500 for women). Individual earnings followed a similar pattern.

Long-term disconnected youth are also likely to continue into adulthood their difficulty in establishing strong and sustained ties to the labor force. Only 41% of young adult men who were disconnected for long periods during their youth, for example, were employed for a full year[5] in 1990 (at ages between 25 and 27) compared with 75% of young men who were never disconnected as youth. (See Figure 3-3.) Comparable figures for young adult women are 21% and 62%. These employment problems contribute to low rates of health insurance coverage among young adult men who were disconnected for long periods of their youth, since most Americans obtain health insurance through employment.[6] Just over half (51%) of long-term disconnected male youth had health insurance as young adults, compared with 86% of young adult men who were never disconnected as youth. The difference is considerably smaller among young women (73% compared with 91%) primarily because of the availability of Medicaid to low-income pregnant women and to families receiving AFDC.

Youth who were disconnected for long periods were less likely to marry as young adults, possibly because their low earnings potential

Figure 3-2. Percentage of Long-term Disconnected and Connected Youth Who Were Poor as Young Adults (Ages 25-27)

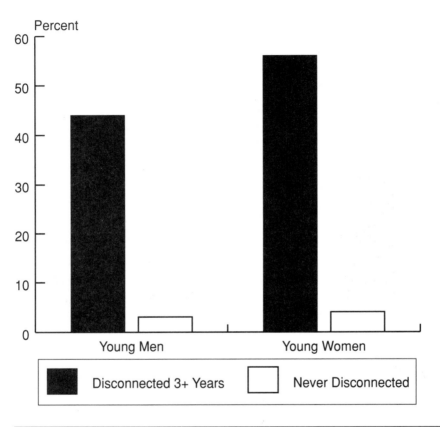

lessened their attractiveness as marriage partners. Fifty-eight percent of young men who were disconnected as youth for three or more years were not married (and had never been married) by ages 26 to 28, compared with 37% of never-disconnected men. Among women, comparable figures are 48% and 24%.

Individuals who are disconnected for long periods in their youth are thus at heightened risk of some continued level of disconnection at least through their late twenties. They are more likely to be poor. Their

Figure 3-3. Percentage of Long-term Disconnected and Connected Youth Employed Full-year as Young Adults (Ages 25-27)

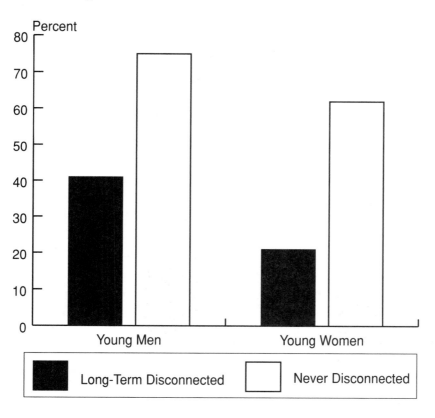

ties to the work force are weaker, and they earn less. They are less likely to marry. Women who were disconnected for long periods in their youth are more likely in their late twenties to receive welfare and food stamps. Separate analyses for white, African American, and His-panic groups (not shown) revealed that the relationships between dis-connection and adult well-being described above hold for each of these groups. For both its personal and its societal consequences, youthful disconnection is therefore cause for concern.

Family and Personal Characteristics

Not surprisingly, disconnected youth are much more likely than connected youth to have grown up in poor families, families receiving welfare, and families headed by single mothers, and they are less likely to have a parent with a high school degree. Comparing young men who were disconnected for 26 of 52 weeks over three or more years to young men who were never disconnected, we find the following:

- 35% of these disconnected young men were from poor families, compared to 10% of connected men;
- 26% of disconnected young men were from families receiving welfare, compared with 6% of connected men;
- 28% of disconnected young men were from single-parent families, compared with 13% of connected men; and
- 45% of disconnected young men lacked a parent with a high school degree, compared with 16% of connected men.

Similar family differences appear in comparisons of disconnected and connected young women.

Long-term disconnected youth were also more likely than connected youth to have dropped out of school and to have had low aspirations, characteristics that make their transition to independent adulthood harder and less certain. Half of disconnected young men and 37% of disconnected young women were high school dropouts. Comparable dropout rates for connected young men and women are 6% and 4%. Only a quarter of disconnected young men aspired as teenagers to a professional or technical occupation, compared with more than half (56%) of connected young men. A quarter of disconnected young women had given birth before age 18. Almost two-thirds (64%) of disconnected young women had received AFDC by age 23.

The experience of disconnection almost always begins early. Nearly 90% of those who are disconnected at ages 20 to 23 were first disconnected as teenagers, and roughly half were first disconnected before age 18—strong arguments for prevention programs that begin in the midteens, if not earlier.

Of those who were disconnected for three or more years, only 19% of the men and 11% of the women had ever participated in a government job training program by age 23. This may reflect a lack of awareness or interest among potential program participants, a failure by the programs to target or reach those most in need adequately, or combinations of these factors.

Youth at Risk of Long-Term Disconnection

Another way to look at the relation between background characteristics and disconnection is in terms of the risks for long-term disconnection associated with certain personal and family background factors. This approach is particularly useful when considering potential early intervention strategies to reduce the incidence of disconnection. Our analyses show many such factors are associated with substantially higher risks of long-term disconnection (for three or more years). (See Table 3-1.) Chief among these are

- **Family poverty.** About one-third of young people who lived in poor families in 1978 (when the youth in this survey were ages 13 to 15) became disconnected for three or more years later in their youth. This is about three times the rate of disconnection among young people from nonpoor families.
- **Family welfare receipt.** Youth who grew up in families that received welfare in 1978 (when they were between the ages of 13 and 15) were at great risk of long-term disconnection. Thirty-four percent of the young men and 40% of young women from such families experienced long-term disconnection, compared with about 10% of youth from nonwelfare families.
- **Low parental education.** The risk of long-term disconnection was substantially greater when there was no parent in the household with a high school degree (26% compared with 9% when at least one parent held a high school degree). The risk was identical for both young men and young women.
- **Single/no parent family.** Youth who lived in households where only one or no parent was present were at substantially higher

Table 3-1. Risk Factors Related to Long-term Disconnectedness* by Family and Personal Background Characteristics

	Young Men	Young Women
Family Background at Ages 13-15		
Poverty		
Poor	30%	36%
Not poor	10%	10%
Welfare receipt**		
Yes	34%	40%
No	10%	11%
Parent(s) lack high school degree		
Yes	26%	26%
No	9%	9%
Family structure		
1 or no parents	22%	26%
2 biological parents	10%	9%
Personal Background		
Becoming a parent before age 18		
Yes	35%	37%
No	12%	11%
High school completion		
Dropout	39%	37%
GED	29%	27%
Graduate	5%	8%
Race		
African American	26%	37%
Hispanic	19%	21%
White	10%	9%

*   Long-term disconnected youth are those who were disconnected for 26 or more weeks per year for a total of three or more years between ages 16 and 23.

**   AFDC or Food Stamps.

risk of long-term disconnection than youth who lived with both biological parents (22% compared with 10% for young men and 27% compared with 9% for young women).

- **Bearing or fathering a child before age 18.** The risk of long-term disconnection associated with bearing or fathering a child before age 18 was surprisingly similar for men and women (35% for young men and 37% for young women).
- **Dropping out of high school.** Youth who dropped out of high school were at much higher risk of long-term disconnection than those who graduated. The risks were about four in ten for high school dropouts, compared with fewer than one in ten for those who graduated. (See Figure 3-4.)
- **More than one risk factor.** For young people who had some combination of two high-risk characteristics, the risk of long-term disconnection often exceeded 50%. Among youth who were from families receiving welfare and who dropped out of high school, for example, 57% of young men and 68% of young women became disconnected for three or more years.

These risk analyses were also carried out separately for white, African American, and Hispanic youth. By and large, the risk factors identified above operate as risk factors for all three groups, with one important exception. For several key family background factors, the risk of long-term disconnection was substantially weaker for African American males than for any of the other groups including black females.

Among young men, for example, whites from poor families were more than three times as likely as those from nonpoor families to become disconnected long-term, and Hispanics were nearly twice as likely. (See Table 3.2.) For black males, however, the increased risk associated with poverty was only one-quarter (from 24 to 30%), and that difference was only marginally significant statistically. For white and Hispanic females, the risks associated with poverty were similar to their male counterparts, and black females from poor families were much more likely than those from nonpoor families to become disconnected (51% compared with 27%). Similarly, risks associated with family struc-

Figure 3-4. Educational Attainment as a Predictor of Long-term Disconnectedness

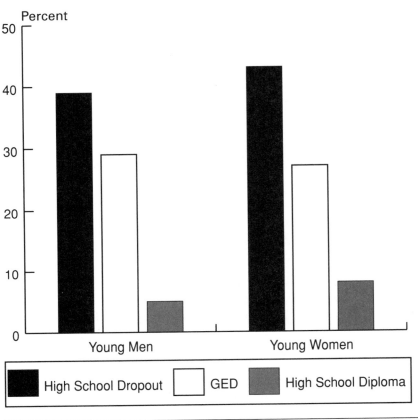

ture, family welfare receipt, and parental education were less predictive for black males than for other groups. In contrast, risks associated with personal characteristics such as high school completion, academic ability, and suspension or expulsion from school were strong and highly predictive for all groups including black males.

Conclusion

From the basic descriptive data presented here, we draw several important conclusions. First, youthful disconnection, particularly when

Table 3-2. Family Poverty and the Risk of Long-term Disconnectedness,* with Differences by Gender and Race

	Poverty Status at Ages 13-15	
	Poor	Not Poor
Young Men		
White	31	9
African American	30	24
Hispanic	29	15
Young Women		
White	23	7
African American	51	27
Hispanic	28	15

* Long-term disconnected youth are those who were disconnected for 26 or more weeks per year for a total of three or more years between ages 16 and 23.

it lasts for several years, is often associated with serious long-term consequences for a young person. Long-term disconnected youth are much more likely to be poor and dependent on public assistance as adults and to have trouble establishing or maintaining stable ties to the labor force or to a spouse.

Second, certain personal and family background characteristics appear to place young people at higher risk of long-term disconnection. These include family poverty, family welfare receipt, low parental educational attainment, dropping out of high school, and minority status. Young people with more than one risk factor are at even higher risk. In a continuing era of tight budgets, these findings could help target limited prevention funds to populations at highest risk.

Third, the degree of risk associated with particular background factors can differ by population subgroup. In particular, family background measures that predicted well to long-term disconnection for most groups were not strong for black male youth. It is unclear why this should be, but, importantly, it suggests that solutions to long-term disconnection will need to be somewhat different for this group of youth.

The data presented in this essay also challenge the common stereotype that it is young males who most often fail to make a successful transition from youth to adulthood. Among young women, African Americans are at highest risk of long-term disconnection.

In the litany of immediate woes and long-term threats that face disconnected youth, it is important to remember that youthful disconnection is not a life sentence. Among disconnected youth, many appear to overcome early setbacks to become independent adults. But many do not, and for this group, the personal and social costs can be quite high. The data described above help us identify those young people most at risk of long-term disconnection, critical information for designing and implementing effective strategies to prevent or correct long-term disconnection.

Notes

1   For a review of life course research and research on the transition to adulthood, see Hogan, D., & Astone, N. (1986). The transition to adulthood. *Annual Review of Sociology, 12*, 109-130.

2   Dr. Peter Tiemeyer of the RAND Corporation used these data to construct weekly activity variables that we used to create most measures of disconnection used in the analyses presented. We are grateful to Dr. Tiemeyer for his generosity in providing these data for use in this research effort. The authors also wish to acknowledge the work of Charles Halla, who performed the statistical programming for the project.

3   The preceding estimates are based on a definition that classifies youth as disconnected for any year in which they were not working, not in school, not in the military, and not married to anyone connected in these ways for a total of 26 or more weeks.

4   The estimates that follow are based on the temporally less restrictive definition that classifies youths as disconnected for any year in which they were not working, not in school, not in the

military, and not married to anyone connected in those ways for a total of 26 or more weeks.

5   Full-year employment is here defined as having been employed for 50 or more weeks during the year.

6   This may also be a result of the types of jobs that such youth have as young adults, jobs that may be less likely to offer health insurance as a benefit.

4. Family Background, Church Attendance, and School Achievement

Linda Datcher Loury*

Many policymakers across the political spectrum emphasize the role of external or structural impediments to economic progress. Many of those on the Right, for example, blame governmental transfer programs for disincentives to work or explain poor performance as the result of lower innate cognitive ability. Many on the Left, in contrast, blame the lack of jobs and discrimination in the labor market for the failure of some individuals and groups to advance.

While structural barriers such as these can certainly inhibit socio-economic success, they are not the only factors that affect outcomes. Clearly, for instance, there are substantial variations in children's educational outcomes across families that are identical in parents' education, work history, income, and other standard measures of social and economic well-being. In particular, many low-income families produce children who perform at or above grade level in primary and secondary school and who attend and graduate from college, even though they grow up in the same neighborhoods as families whose children perform poorly in school and become dropouts.

* The author is thankful for the support of Joan Aratz-Snowden, J. Brooks-Gunn, and Virginia Shipman and for the assistance provided by others at the Educational Testing Service who were essential for the completion of this study. Some of the data and tabulations used in this report were made available by the Inter-University Consortium for Political and Social Research. The data were originally collected for the National Center for Education Statistics. Neither the original sources of the data nor the consortium bears any responsibility for the analyses or interpretations presented here.

According to Loury [1977, 1987], much of this variation may be explained by differences in social capital; that is, the set of resources that inhere in family relations and in the social organization of the community and that are useful for the cognitive or social development of individuals. Within families, social capital that increases children's educational performance may include a wide variety of behaviors and attitudes that promote success. Outside of families, many formal and informal associations (such as churches) provide social support for educational achievement and sanctions against behaviors that compete with schooling. This paper explores the hypothesis that variation in the academic performance of children is due, in large part, to differences in behavior and attitudes within families and to differences in neighborhood and community associations. In the case of the associations, the paper focuses on the effects of church attendance.

The remainder of the paper is divided into three sections. The first summarizes previous theoretical and empirical work useful in analyzing this topic. The second describes the data and presents the empirical results. The last summarizes the conclusions.

Previous Work

Many different family attitudes and behaviors cause children in some families to achieve more in school than others with a similar income. First, families spend different amounts on toys, puzzles, books, or other items that directly or indirectly raise children's performance. Second, there may be even wider differences in ways that families use their time (for example, helping with homework as opposed to watching cartoons). Third, there may be substantial differences across families in the effect that the purchases or the time use has on children's performance.

Some parents' help with homework may improve their children's knowledge and skills more than others. Merely buying a computer for children would not necessary improve their educational performance.

A considerable amount of evidence suggests that such differences in family behaviors affect educational outcomes independent of the family's economic resources. Leibowitz [1974] found that higher reports of time spent in instructional activities raised sons' (but not daughters') IQ scores. Tizard, Schofield, and Hewison [1982] found that inner-city students chosen to read to their parents regularly at home over a two-year period had significantly higher reading test scores by ages 7 to 8 than those of an otherwise identical control group. Amota and Ochiltree [1986] found that more family activities such as outings, playing games together, and talking about television programs increased reading test scores for a representative sample of primary school children. Hess et al. [1984] found that a variety of maternal behaviors were important for predicting children's school readiness at ages 5 and 6 and academic performance at age 12. These included the mother's teaching behavior, communication efficiency, disciplinary strategy, and expectations for achievement. Other evidence comes from Leibowitz [1974], Portes [1984], and Portes et al. [1984].

Additional evidence shows that, besides families, various neighborhood and community associations such as churches and synagogues may affect schooling outcomes. Sander [1992] found that, for both men and women, Jewish family background had a large, positive effect on years of schooling, holding parents, socioeconomic status, ethnicity, and other demographic variables constant. This was followed by the effects of Episcopalian and Catholic backgrounds respectively. Stryker [1981] and Featherman [1971] recorded similar results showing that denomination affected years of schooling.

The usefulness of much of that previous work is limited by three shortcomings. First, it is difficult to separate out the different sources of family and church effects. Studies of the impact of the ways families use their time, for example, capture the effects of both the amount and the quality of time spent in child care. Similarly, past work has shown that the different measures of religious commitment such as church attendance, denomination, and reports of the importance of the individual's religious life tend to be positively related (see, for example, Petersen and Roy [1985]). Thus, the estimated effects of denomination from previous work may also imperfectly capture the effects of other dimensions of religiousness. As such, these effects would overstate the impact of denomination but understate the total effect of religiousness.

The second problem is that the direction of causality is unclear from past studies. While it is certainly plausible that parental behaviors affect children's school achievement, it is also possible that parents are more willing to work with children who respond more quickly to help and suggestions. Similarly, while religiousness may raise educational attainment, it is equally plausible that educational attainment may itself affect religious commitment. Taylor [1988], for example, found that education was positively associated with attendance at religious services and church membership for adult blacks.

The third shortcoming of previous work is that the included measures of family attitudes and behaviors, as well as religiousness, may be correlated with unobserved attitudes, behaviors, and abilities that also affect schooling. Consider, for example, the correlation between education and adolescent church attendance. Parents who encourage or require their children to attend church may systematically differ from other parents in the degree of supervision of their children's activities, in the amount of time they spend with their children [Chiswick 1986], or in a wide variety of other nonreligious attitudes and behaviors that are the true determinants of children's schooling. In addition, children who typically attend church may also differ from other children in their aspirations, in their aversion to criminality and destructive behavior, and in other ways independent of their religious commitment. Similarly, parents who are more likely to purchase educational toys for their children may have higher levels of permanent economic resources, possibly in the form of assistance from relatives or higher expected future income.

Results

This paper builds on the earlier work just outlined. After summarizing the results in Loury [1989] with particular focus on the scholastic achievement of low-income black children, this paper explores whether the types of attitudes and behaviors already identified here continue to exert an important influence on children's academic success even when parents face extreme socioeconomic disadvantages. The second part of the paper focuses on the effect of church attendance in the senior year of high school on total years of schooling. While this work does not capture the full effects of religiousness, it examines the effects of a particular type of religious expression during a relatively crucial period in the schooling process.

The data for the first part of this paper come from the ETS-Head Start Longitudinal Study, a study designed to assess the effects of early education on the cognitive, personal, and social development of young children. Data on children approximately 3.5 to 4.5 years of age were obtained in the initial mother's interview and child tests during the spring and summer of 1969. Subsequent interviews and tests were performed annually until the children were ages 8.5 to 9.5. This study focuses on a subsample of black children who were either enrolled in Head Start as of 1969 or eligible but not enrolled.

The paper analyzes variations in these children's achievement as of September 1971 to August 1972 when they were ages 6.5 to 7.5 and as of September 1973 to August 1974 when they were ages 8.5 and 9.5. Achievement was measured by scores on the first-grade and third-grade reading and math subtests of the nationally standardized Cooperative Primary Tests battery developed by the Educational Testing Service. (See Educational Testing Service [1967] for further details concerning the test.)

In this paper, family background was represented, in part, by the standard indicators of socioeconomic status, such as parents' years of schooling, parents' occupation and employment, and the presence of the father in the household. These variables were supplemented with relatively rare indicators of maternal aspirations for their children and the quality of interaction between mother and child. Mothers, for example, were asked how much schooling they expected their child to complete, how regularly they attended PTA-type meetings, how often they read stories to the child, what kinds of toys they purchased for the child, and whether encyclopedias were available in the home. These variables were measured as of the initial 1969 interviews, as well as in subsequent reinterviews. It is, therefore, possible not only to measure the contemporaneous relationship between children's achievement and parental characteristics, but also to determine whether indicators of maternal attitudes and behaviors early in the child's development (at ages 3.5 to 4.5) have long-lasting effects on academic performance (at ages 6.5 to 7.5 and ages 8.5 to 9.5).

In addition, more direct indicators of mother-child interaction were derived from the Eight-Block Sorting Task [Hess et al. 1984], which was administered in 1969. In this task, researchers asked mothers to teach their children to sort blocks by height (tall or short) and by mark (an X or 0). This type of task is considered to be especially helpful for examining many different aspects of mother-child interaction that may affect learning.[2]

The ETS-Head Start sample used in this paper is clearly a population disadvantaged relative to the general population (see Loury [1989]). Mothers and fathers averaged fewer than 10 years of schooling and more than half the fathers were absent from the household. The distribution of reading and math results shows that mean scores for sample children were less than 50% of total possible scores of 50 and 60, respectively. Achievement varied substantially, however, with standard deviations ranging from 25% to 40% of the sample means.

Family Background

To uncover the determinants of this variation, Loury [1989] analyzes the effects of the background characteristics described earlier on each of the four tests. Some of the results for the 1969 parental socioeconomic status and demographic variables are the same for all four tests. Except for the 1973-1974 math test, boys averaged more than 2 fewer points than girls, holding all other factors constant. In addition, each year of mother's schooling added at least 0.3 points to all test scores.

Some of the other results for the 1969 parental socioeconomic status and demographic variables were largest for the reading tests. Each year of father's education raised scores by over 0.3 points, and the children of full-time working mothers scored almost 2 fewer points on the 1971-1972 reading test. The absence of a father lowered 1973-1974 reading scores by more than 3.5 points.

In the literature, these types of results point to the role of external or structural impediments to economic mobility. Note, however, that test scores vary considerably among children who are the same along these dimensions. This variation stems in part from the differences in parental behavior measured in 1969. Children whose mothers read to them several times a week scored 2.5 points higher on the 1971-1972 reading test and almost 5 more points on both 1973-1974 tests. Each additional year of mother's educational expectations for children raised 1973-1974 reading scores by 1 point. Children living in households with an encyclopedia averaged about 3 more points on both 1973-1974 tests. Children whose mothers participated in groups mainly concerned with education at least once every two weeks (such as PTA or Head Start) enjoyed a similar advantage on the 1971-1972 math test.

Other indicators of specific maternal behaviors and attitudes were obtained by observing mother-child interaction during the Eight-Block Sorting procedure in 1969. All the significant effects were limited to the 1971-1972 tests. The hostility rating, for example, had a large and significant negative effect on the math scores, and each point of the praise index raised both reading and math scores by at least .3 points. If mothers used a lot of positive verbal feedback with task-specific information during the sorting procedure, math scores averaged more than 8 points higher. Finally, children of mothers who used bribes or pleading to influence the child during the sorting task scored about 1.5 points lower on the reading and math tests. In general, an affectionate and directed style of conveying information to children is significantly correlated with higher achievement.

These results support the contention that differences in family behavior and attitudes have large and important long-term effects on children's academic performance. Family characteristics measured in 1969 when children were ages 3.5 to 4.5 continue to exert a significant influence on the extent of success (especially in the case of reading achievement) up to five years later.

The pattern of results suggests that parental behavior has a much larger impact on reading than on math scores. As we have seen, many parental characteristics affect one or both reading scores but do not influence either math score. One explanation is that early math performance depends more on innate ability and is, therefore, less amenable to parental intervention. The pattern of results also indicates that different types of behavior may have a greater impact on different periods in the child's development. While reading to the child in 1969 significantly raised 1971-1972 reading scores, the largest effects were observed in the 1973-1974 reading and math test results. Similarly, educational aspirations and encyclopedia ownership did not affect children's performance until the later scores. In contrast, the style of maternal interaction with children seems most important for the younger group. Only the 1971-1972 test outcomes were affected by the nature of the interaction as indicated by the Eight-Block Sorting Task. These results are consistent with a variety of theories of cognitive development [Rotter 1966; Wachs & Gruen 1982], which see a considerable age specificity in the relation between environment and development.

Not only are 1969 parental characteristics and behaviors correlated with children's achievement in 1971-1972 and 1973-1974, but, as might be expected, parental attributes measured in 1973 affect children's outcomes in 1973-1974. The impact of the contemporaneous variables on reading scores is especially noteworthy. Reading scores increased by 1 point for each additional year of schooling mothers expect their children to achieve, by more than 3 points if there was an encyclopedia in the household, by more than 4 points if the child owned more than 12 books, and by about 1.5 points each if the child owned the following items: paints, records, musical instruments, a children's dictionary or encyclopedia, and puzzles. The significant effects for the math score were limited to educational expectations and toys owned.

Maternal employment in 1973 in white collar, craft, or machine operator occupations (but not as laborers or service workers) raised children's reading and math performance. This change from the negative effects of full-time work on children's achievement as of ages 6.5 to 7.5 indicates that the mother's absence from the household does not inhibit performance of older children as it appears to do for the younger group. Instead, either the higher financial resources or the other positive benefits associated with employment in jobs other than laborer or service worker overwhelm any possible negative influences due to less time available for child care activities.

It is difficult to determine precisely the source of all the estimated effects described here. Higher parental schooling may reflect greater financial resources, more time spent in child care (see, for example, Hill and Stafford [1980]), or greater productivity in using goods and time to raise the quality of the child's achievements. The two latter explanations seem most likely, since some measures of family economic status, such as father's employment and occupation and number and type of family possessions, had little effect on outcomes.[3] For similar reasons, it seems likely that the negative impact of full-time work may capture reduced time spent in child-care activities. Full-time workers are likely to have greater rather than fewer financial resources *ceteris paribus*, and part-time work does not have a similar negative impact on children's performance.

Even the interpretation of proxies for specific behaviors and attitudes is unclear. Simply purchasing an encyclopedia for all low-income black children, for example, is not likely to raise third-grade reading test scores by 3 points. Similarly, providing paints, records, musical instruments, a children's dictionary or encyclopedia, and puzzles is not likely to increase reading and math scores by 8 and 5 points, respectively. A more plausible interpretation is that the included measures are proxies for a constellation of attitudes and behaviors that jointly alter children's performance. Parents who have the measured attitudes and engage in the indicated behaviors may also differ from other parents in many unobserved ways that also contribute to children's scholastic success.

It is noteworthy that almost half the variation in children's reading performance is accounted for by the measured family characteristics. This finding suggests that a large fraction of the variation in children's reading performance may result from systematic differences in family attitudes and behaviors. Thus, even though all these families were severely constrained in the number of quality-enhancing goods that could be purchased, these limitations do not preclude activities that promote high achievement.

An alternative explanation assumes that the causality runs in the opposite direction. That is, parents' behavior depends on children's performance rather than vice versa. Parents with children who perform well in school are motivated to have higher expectations and allocate their income and time differently from parents of children who perform poorly. The results in this paper, which point to long-term effects of differences in parental behavior and attitudes, provide evidence against this contention. They suggest that efficacious parental behavior precedes knowledge about scholastic performance. In addition, comparing children with similar 1971-1972 reading scores shows that poor early performance does not prevent parents from having an important and positive impact on their children's later achievement.

This portion of the paper does not analyze the effect of nonfamily associations since the ETS-Head Start data have little consistent information on such items. Many previous studies, however, have looked at the effect of community socioeconomic characteristics on children's educational achievement. They have found a strong positive correlation as in the case of parents, education, and occupation noted here.

Church Attendance

As indicated earlier, variations in community socioeconomic status are not the only source of community effects. Individuals affected by the same socioeconomic constraints may vary considerably in their choice of association. One potentially positive source of academic performance is church attendance. This paper reports the results of Loury [1996], which used data from the high school and beyond sophomore and senior cohorts to analyze the effects of church attendance on schooling. A nationally representative sample of 1980 high school sophomores and seniors was interviewed to determine a variety of characteristics of young adults.[4] The original 1980 interviews, as well as follow-up studies in 1982 and 1986, included questions about participation in church activities and schooling. Because of data limitations, the analysis was restricted to those who attended the twelfth grade.[5]

One way to determine the effects of church attendance on schooling in a given year is to measure difference in schooling between individuals who are otherwise identical except for church attendance. This approach is subject to the some of the problems mentioned earlier. Any effects of church attendance, for example, may simply reflect unobserved nonreligious attitudes, behaviors, and abilities that affect both schooling and religiousness.

These problems can be minimized by comparing the effects of church attendance during the senior year of high school with the effects of church attendance at other times. The latter would reflect factors other than religion that affect both schooling and religiousness. Thus, any gain in schooling due to church attendance during the senior year relative to earlier or later church attendance would capture the effects of this type of religious commitment at a crucial time in the school decision-making process over and above that due to these nonreligious factors.

The analysis for 1980 seniors shows that, holding constant a variety of background characteristics, the difference between church attendance in 1980 (during the senior year of high school) and church attendance six years later in 1986 equals 0.341—that is, 0.250-(0.091)—for white women and 0.213—that is, 0.333-0.120—for blacks.[6] Similarly, the difference between church attendance in 1982 (during the senior year of high school) and church attendance in 1980 (during the sophomore year) equals 0.190 for sophomore white women—0.199-0.009—and 0.430 for sophomore blacks—0.405-(0.025).[7]

The differences between white men and white women may reflect a declining importance of religion for men compared with women. Sander [1992] compared the effects of denomination on years of schooling for cohorts born before 1930, between 1930 and 1944, and between 1945 and 1959. He showed that all of the large and significant effects for men declined from older to younger cohorts. The direction of the changes for women was the same, but the sizes were much smaller. The differences between white men and blacks may occur because black churches are more likely to be a source of subcultural differences "due to distinctive doctrines, religious experiences, social solidarity, organizational environment, or lifestyles."[8]

Several observations can be made about the minimum estimate of the additional 0.2 years of schooling attributable to church attendance for blacks and for white women. First, these are differences in senior year church attendance relative to church attendance at other times. Second, these estimates are for individuals with the same religious denomination who report themselves equally religious. Third, the effects of sophomore year attendance are small and insignificant. These observations suggest that the social act of church attendance during the senior year of high school accounts for the estimated effect rather than the general level of religious faith that the individual holds or has been exposed to while growing up.

Loury [1996] also suggests that other indicators of religious commitment are likely to be important determinants of schooling. For both white sophomores and seniors, those who reported that they were not religious attained significantly less schooling than the group who reported they were somewhat religious, and those who reported that they were very religious acquired significantly more. The results imply a difference of 0.27 years of schooling between seniors who were very religious and those who were not religious at all and a difference of 0.48 years of schooling between sophomores who were very religious and those who were not religious at all. These same variables had a much smaller effect on blacks.[9]

Summary

The results of the first part of this paper imply that, while socioeconomic barriers constrain the possibilities of low-income children, they do not preclude many such children from being successful in school. The evidence presented here is consistent with the view that much of the variation in performance between children is systematic and not simply the result of random luck or external factors beyond the control of low-income parents. Thus, the attitudes and behaviors necessary to overcome handicaps of limited financial resources are within the realm of possibility for some of these parents. It is also consistent with the contention that differences in family behavior and attitudes have large and important long-term effects on children's academic performance. Although these findings are clearly tentative, they suggest that programs aimed at altering parental behavior may be useful in helping to overcome the effects of economic disadvantage on children's scholastic achievement.

The second part of this paper examined the effect of a particular type of social capital, namely, that associated with church attendance during the senior year of high school, on total years of schooling. The main problem with estimating the effect of church attendance on schooling is that individuals who attend may have greater ability or may have attitudes more consistent with higher schooling than a random sample of the population. This paper relies largely on differences in the effects of church attendance before, during, and after the senior year of high school to control for spurious correlation between church attendance during the senior year and total years of schooling. It shows that church attendance adds about 0.2 additional years to total schooling for white women and at least as much for blacks. Church attendance has no significant effect on the years of schooling of white men.

References

Amota, P., & Ochiltree, G. (1986). Family resources and the development of child competence. *Journal of Marriage and Family, 48,* 47-56.

Chiswick, B. (1986). Labor supply and investment in child quality: Study of Jewish and non-Jewish women. *Review of Economics and Statistics, 68,* 700-703.

Educational Testing Service. Cooperative Test Division. (1967). *Handbook: Cooperative primary tests.* Princeton, NJ: Educational Testing Service.

Ellison, C., & Gay, D. (1990). Region, religious commitment, and life satisfaction among black Americans. *Sociological Quarterly, 31,* 123-147.

Featherman, D. (1971). The socioeconomic achievement of white relio-ethnic subgroups: Social and psychological explanations. *American Sociological Review, 36,* 207-222.

Hess, R., Holloway, S., Dickson, W., & Price, G. (1984). Maternal variables as predictors of children's school readiness and later achievement in sixth grade. *Child Development, 55,* 1902-1912.

Hill, C., & Stafford, F. (1980). Parental care of children: Time diary estimates of quantity, predictability, and variety. *Journal of Human Resources, 15,* 219-239.

Leibowitz, A. (1974). Home investments in children. *Journal of Political Economy, 82,* Slll-S131.

Loury, L. (1996). High school church attendance and schooling. Unpublished paper.

Loury, L. D. (1989). Family background and school achievement among low income blacks. *Journal of Human Resources, 24,* 528-544.

Loury, G. (1987). Why should we care about group inequality? *Social Philosophy and Policy, 5,* 249-271.

Loury, G. (1977). A dynamic theory of racial income differences. In P. A. Wallace & A. LeMund, (Eds.). *Women, minorities, and employment discrimination* (pp. 153-176). Lexington, MA: Lexington Books.

Petersen, L., & Roy, A. (1985). Religiousness, anxiety, and meaning and purpose: Religions' consequences for psychological well-being. *Review of Religious Research,* 49-62.

Portes, P. (1984). Longitudinal effects of early-age intervention on family behavior. Paper presented at the Annual Meeting of the American Educational Research Association, April.

Portes, P., Franke, S., & Alsup, R. (1984). Parent-child interaction processes related to scholastic achievement in urban elementary children. Unpublished manuscript. University of Louisville, Department of Educational Psychology and Counseling.

Rotter, J. B. (1966). Generalized expectancies for internal versus external control of reinforcement. *Psychological Monographs* 80.

Sander, W. (1992). The effects of ethnicity and religion on educational attainment. *Economics of Education Review*, 11, 119135.

Sebring, P., Campbell, B., Glusberg, M., Spencer, B., & Singleton, M. (1987a). *High school and beyond 1980 senior cohort: Third follow-up (1986) data file user's manual*. Washington, DC: Center for Education Statistics.

Sebring, P., Campbell, B., Glusberg, M., Spencer, B., & Singleton, M. (1987b). *High school and beyond 1980 sophomore cohort third follow-up (1986) data file user's manual*. Washington, DC: Center for Education Statistics.

Shipman, V. C. (1971). *Disadvantaged children and their first school experiences: Structure and development of cognitive competencies and styles prior to school entry*. PR-71-19. Prepared under Grant H-8256, Department of Health, Education, and Welfare. Princeton, NJ: Educational Testing Service.

Stryker, R. (1981). Relio-ethnic effects on attainment in the early career. *American Sociological Review*, 46, 212-231.

Taylor, R. (1988). Structural determinants of religious participation among black Americans. *Review of Religious Research*, 30, 114-125.

Tizard, J., Schofield, W., & Hewison, J. (1982). Collaboration between teachers and parents in assisting children's reading. *British Journal of Educational Psychology*, 52, 115.

Wachs, T., & Gruen, G. (1982). *Early experience and human development*. New York: Plenum Press.

Notes

1. For more information about the sample, see Shipman [1971].
2. Specifically, the tester observed (1) the level of affection toward the child, (2) the number of responses to the child's inattentiveness, (3) the amount of positive and negative verbal feedback, (4)

the amount of praise and criticism, (5) the extent to which the child is encouraged to reflect before responding, and (6) the mother's control system or influence technique (that is, bribe, encouragement, pleading, reasoning, firm command, threat, physical restraint, or physical punishment).

3. The survey measured the number of televisions, radios, stereos, and automobiles that each family owned.

4. See Sebring et al. [1987a, 1987b] for further information about the sample.

5. Questions about church attendance were not asked for sophomores who dropped out of school before the senior year.

6. The black figures were constrained to be the same since they were virtually identical at 0.210 for women and 0.204 for men.

7. As in the case of the seniors, the numbers for black males and black females were almost identical at 0.44 for women and 0.40 for men.

8. See Ellison and Gay [1990].

9. Ellison and Gay [1990] obtained similar results for blacks in their analysis of life satisfaction.

5. Listening to Young, Inner-City African American Males

Kathryn Taaffe McLearn & Shawn V. LaFrance*

Adolescence is a time of great opportunity. It is also a time of vulnerability and risk. The literature abounds with reports that identify the risk factors such as poverty, single-parent homes, poor schools, and unsafe homes and neighborhoods that contribute to adolescents engaging in risk-taking behaviors such as experimenting with drugs, unprotected sex, dropping out of high school, and delinquency [Lerner 1995; Goddard 1991]. While risk-taking behaviors may seem prevalent in the inner city, an important insight to emerge from scientific inquiry is that the problem behaviors tend to "cluster" in some individuals. A young person who abuses alcohol and drugs, for instance, is also at high risk of teenage parenthood, engaging in crime, and dropping out of school [Hamburg 1992]. Troubled young people are also more likely to report low interest in school or education and low expectations on the part of parents and teachers. Environmental and family risk factors also tend to cluster and thus increase the likelihood of risk behaviors for youth living amid certain economic and social conditions.

Unfortunately, low-income young African American males who reside in disadvantaged urban neighborhoods grow up with many conditions likely to increase risks. They often live in poverty, are poor for a longer time, and are more likely to live in single-parent households than other adolescents [Chalk & Phillips 1996]. These risk factors tend to result in a large share of young African American males who drop

* The authors wish to acknowledge Linda Greenberg for her contributions in preparing this manuscript and Karen Davis and Cathy Schoen for their helpful comments in reviewing the manuscript.

out of high school, are unemployed, are incarcerated, or are drug addicted [Mincy 1994; Wilson 1996]. In addition, adolescents from poor families, and often minority backgrounds, are more likely than their middle- or upper-income peers to reach adulthood ill prepared for work and family responsibilities.

Not all disadvantaged young African American males, however, are troubled. Many overcome difficult circumstances. Recently investigators have been interested in understanding the protective factors that allow adolescents, and especially disadvantaged adolescents, to beat the odds and increase their chances to lead successful adult lives [Spencer et al. 1993; Connell et al. 1995; Zimmerman et al. 1995; Taylor & Roberts 1995].

A 30-year longitudinal study by Werner and Smith identified three clusters of protective factors that distinguished resilient high-risk adolescents from other individuals who develop problems in adolescence:

- personal characteristics of the youth, such as average intelligence, at least, and engaging temperament and social skills that involve family members;
- growing up in a family with parents or other dependable adults, such as grandparents, whose child-rearing practices are positive and appropriate; and
- a broad community support system such as school, church, youth group, or work that offers stable support and consistent guidance [Carnegie Corporation 1995].

In particular, family and community supports are key in helping to shape the life course trajectory of many at-risk adolescents. Having parents and other caring adults, such as a teacher, coach, employer, or mentor, can foster interpersonal and decision-making skills that help young people be resilient in the face of adversity or difficult challenges.

High school graduation is seen as a pathway to becoming a productive adult. Completing high school is perhaps the most important action that adolescents can take to improve their economic prospects. In 1992, a high school graduate earned almost $6,000 a year more than a high school dropout [Feldman & Elliot 1990]. Here again, studies indicate that obstacles can make this basic hurdle a challenge for many disadvantaged African American young men, but many are resilient and stay in high school and graduate despite enormous odds. Research by Connell and his colleagues suggests that family support, young peoples' sense of control or failure in school, and their own sense of self-worth or emotional security with others regulate their actions in school over and above the economic conditions of their family or neighborhood [Connell et al. 1994].

To learn more about the obstacles and factors helping young people become productive adults, the Commonwealth Fund, a New York City-based national foundation that undertakes independent research on health and social issues, funded in 1993 a study of young African American males in four cities to identify factors associated with school success of young men and the characteristics faced by those who dropped out of high school.

The Survey

For this study, Lou Harris and Associates conducted 30-minute face-to-face interviews with 360 African American males ages 17 to 22. The young males resided in inner-city census tracts in New York, Los Angeles, Chicago, and Atlanta that were at least 70% African American. This created a sample universe, according to the survey firm, that was representative of 54% of the African American population in each city.

To select the sample, Lou Harris and Associates created maps of city blocks. Interviewers recorded the addresses of 100 housing units in the neighborhoods. Nearly 5,000 housing units were screened. About half of the units were deemed ineligible because of vacancy, language barriers, unavailability of an adult, no males, or no African Americans. From the remaining lists of units, Lou Harris randomly selected 360 participants; 79% of households with a young African American agreed to participate.

There were 90 respondents from each city. For this survey, it was believed that respondents would participate more willingly if the interviewer was not perceived as a threat. For that reason, the majority of interviewers were female, middle-aged, and African American. By design, one-half of the young men interviewed had dropped out of high school; the other half were still attending high school, had graduated, had received a GED, or had gone on to college.[1] The interviews were conducted between October 1993 and March 1994.

Results

Generally, the survey found that African American males who succeeded were more likely to report that the presence of caring adults—parents, teachers, employers, and mentors—in their lives was important to their success in high school. The opportunity for part-time work experience while in high school and participation in youth programs were also reported to be key factors in their success. Looking more closely at the family characteristics of these young men revealed that certain parental characteristics and behaviors appeared to be associated with these young men remaining in school and that young men who stayed in school were less likely to engage in risk-taking behaviors.

Educational Support from Parents and Teachers

Young African American men who succeeded in school reported parental support (80%) and teacher support (64%) as the most important factors that helped them stay in school. Those who dropped out of school said that more parental support (39%) and better teachers (36%) would have helped them to stay in school.

Young men who succeeded in high school were more likely to report that their parents were involved in supervising homework (p<. 01) and in visiting their school and teachers (p<. 01) than reports of those who dropped out of school. (See Figure 5-1.) More than half (57%) of young African American men who graduated reported that having a place to study was important. For those students who dropped out of school, more than a quarter (27%) said having a place to study would have helped them to stay in school.

Young African American men who completed school were more likely than those who dropped out of school to perceive their teachers as

Figure 5-1. Parent Involvement in Education

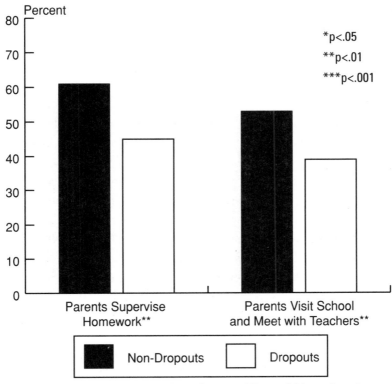

Percent

*p<.05
**p<.01
***p<.001

Parents Supervise
Homework**

Parents Visit School
and Meet with Teachers**

■ Non-Dropouts   □ Dropouts

Source: The Commonwealth Fund Pilot Survey of Young African American Males in Four Cities, Louis Harris and Associates, Inc., 1994.

more competent at teaching (p<.01) (see Figure 5-2). Three out of four students who stayed in school reported that their teachers were interested in how well they were doing in class, perceived their teachers as encouraging further education, and said that their teachers instilled hope in their future. In contrast, only half of the dropouts had such positive teacher experiences (p<.001).

Enrollment in academic programs (39% v. 14%, p<.01) or vocational programs (35% v. 23%, p<.01) was significantly more prevalent among those who graduated than those who dropped out of school. In con-

Figure 5-2. Educational Experiences

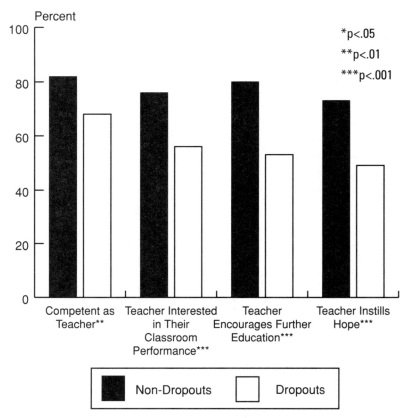

Source: The Commonwealth Fund Pilot Survey of Young African American Males in Four Cities, Louis Harris and Associates, Inc., 1994.

trast, students who dropped out of school were more likely than those who stayed in school to have been enrolled in general education programs (52% v. 38%, p<.01).

Work Experience

Half of young African American males who succeeded in school, as compared with only a third of those who dropped out of high school, had a job while in school (p<.001) or participated in a summer job

Figure 5-3. Participation in Work and Youth Programs

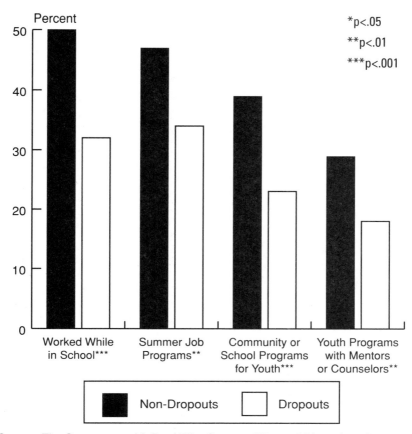

Source: The Commonwealth Fund Pilot Survey of Young African American Males in Four Cities, Louis Harris and Associates, Inc., 1994.

program (p<.01) (see Figure 5-3). Sixty percent of students who stayed in school said that participating in a summer job program helped them succeed, and 78% of these same students reported that a job training program helped them stay in school.

A high proportion of young African American males residing in low-income urban areas are unemployed. Young males who were in school, however, were significantly more likely to be employed full- or part-time than those who dropped out of school (49% v. 35%, p<.01). More than two-thirds of those who dropped out of school and were seeking employment believed that they lacked sufficient education (78%) and job skills (76%) to compete in the labor market.

Youth Programs

More young African American men who succeeded in high school than those who dropped out of high school participated in a community, school, or church program that had activities for young people (p<.001) (see Figure 5-3). Young men who stayed in high school were also more likely to have participated in programs that had mentors or counselors compared with those who dropped out (p<.01). Two-thirds of those who stayed in school reported that participating in programs with a mentor or counselor helped them stay in high school.

For the young men in this study, those growing up in self-rated poor families were the least likely to participate in summer job programs and youth programs. Only one-fourth of young African American men from very poor families in these four urban communities, compared with near half of those with good or steady incomes (25% v. 44%, p<.01) participated in youth programs.[2] Those from very poor families were less likely to participate in job training programs, compared with those from families with steady to good incomes (17% v. 29%, p<.05). Fewer young men from very poor families participated in community, school, or church youth programs, compared with those from families with steady to good incomes (20% v. 33%, p<.05).

Protective Family Characteristics

The mothers of the young African American men who succeeded in high school were almost twice as likely as those who dropped out of school to have been married while their sons were growing up (p<.001) (see Figure 5-4). More than half of the young men who stayed in school, compared with those who dropped out of school, reported that their father had lived with them while they were growing up (51% v. 41%). More young men who succeeded in school than those who dropped

Figure 5-4. Mother's Marital Status and Relationships with Parents

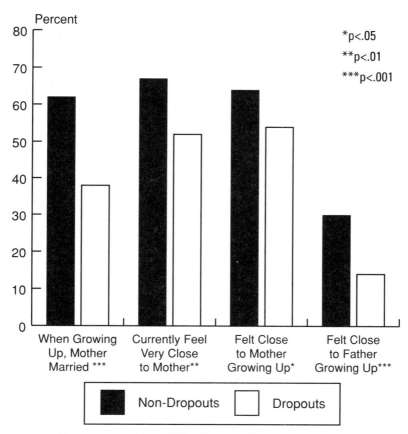

Source: The Commonwealth Fund Pilot Survey of Young African American Males in Four Cities, Louis Harris and Associates, Inc., 1994.

out reported feeling close to their mothers at the time of the survey (p<.01) and close to their fathers or male guardian when they were growing up (p<.001). Those who succeeded in high school were more likely than those who dropped out to report that their mother had graduated from high school (91% v. 81%, p<.01).

The young African American men who succeeded in high school were less likely than those who dropped out to have grown up in many different locations (p<.05) or in unstable families where parents had substance abuse or mental health problems (p<.05) (see Figure 5-5). Adequate family finances also seemed to be associated with school success. More than a third of those who stayed in school reported that their families received public cash assistance through Aid to Families with Dependent Children (AFDC) or Medicaid, compared with nearly two-thirds of those who dropped out of school (p<.001). The majority of those who succeeded in school, compared with those who dropped out of high school, reported that their family usually had enough money or had a steady or good income (p<.001). Similarly, those who stayed in school were much less likely than those who did not report that their families were poor and had a hard time getting enough money (8% v. 28%, p<.001).

Health

A majority of those who succeeded in school reported that their health was excellent, compared with those who dropped out (54% v. 43%, p<.05). The young African American men who stayed in high school were more likely than those who dropped out to take a positive attitude toward themselves (92% v. 71%, p<.001). They were less likely to report being depressed, with one-third (34%) of those who stayed in school having depressive symptoms, compared with nearly half (48%) of those who dropped out of school. One in 20 (5%) of those who stayed in school as compared with the more than one in ten (11%) of those who dropped out of school reported thoughts of suicide in the previous year (p<.05). Finally, those who graduated and stayed in school reported that they were more likely to have better skills in managing conflict with others than those who dropped out of school. Specifically, students who graduated were less likely to threaten others, act out in anger, break or hit something, or do something reckless when trying to resolve an argument than those young men who dropped out of school (see Figure 5-6).

Figure 5-5. Family Stability and Income

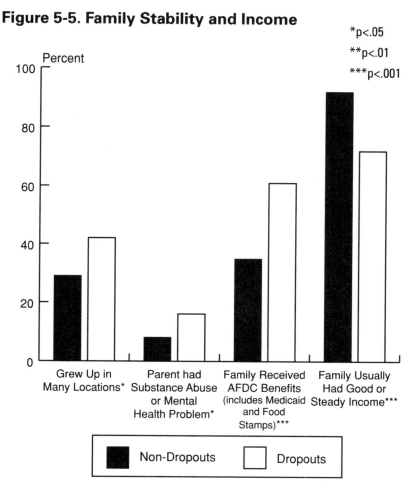

*p<.05
**p<.01
***p<.001

Source: The Commonwealth Fund Pilot Survey of Young African American Males in Four Cities, Louis Harris and Associates, Inc., 1994.

Young African American males who stayed in school were three times less likely to report having an inhibiting disability, handicap, or chronic disease (3% v. 9%, p<.01). While there was no significant difference between those who succeeded in school and those who dropped out on being hospitalized (38% v. 34%), the reasons for their hospitalization differed. Only 13% of those who stayed in school and had been hospi-

Figure 5-6. Conflict Management and Risk-taking Behaviors

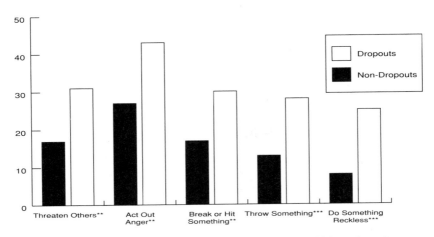

Source: The Commonwealth Fund Pilot Survey of Young African American Males in Four Cities, Louis Harris and Associates, Inc., 1994.

talized were admitted with stab or bullet wounds, as compared with 44% of those who dropped out of school.

In this study the young men who succeeded in high school were significantly less likely to report being engaged in risk-taking behaviors. Those young men who graduated from high school were less likely to be in gangs (p<.001), experiment with drugs (p<.001), or be involved in the juvenile justice system (p<.001) than those young men who dropped out of school (see Figure 5-7). In addition, more than one in four (29%) of those who stayed in school, compared with about two out of five (41%) of those who dropped out of school, had children.

Although there are some significant differences between the young African American men who graduated and those who dropped out of high school, both groups demonstrated positive attributes. The majority of all men in the study had strong self-respect (see box on p. 146). A majority helped out family members or friends who had problems taking care of themselves or needed help in taking care of children, and

Figure 5-7. Family Stability and Income

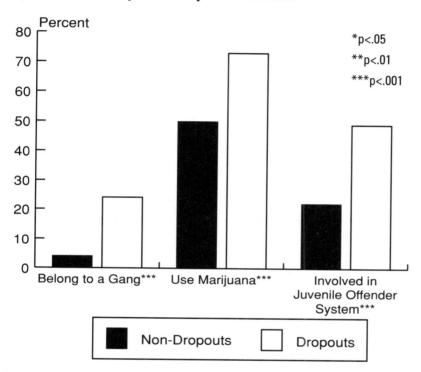

Source: The Commonwealth Fund Pilot Survey of Young African American Males in Four Cities, Louis Harris and Associates, Inc., 1994.

nearly one-fifth of these young African American men performed volunteer work in their communities. Contrary to some perceptions, most of these young men from the inner city were not involved in gangs. Many did not drink alcohol or use marijuana, and more than 8 in 10 did not use hard drugs, such as cocaine or heroin, nor had they spent time in prison.

Discussion

No single policy can guarantee that adolescents will grow up into healthy productive adults. Yet, the findings from this survey suggest that a num-

---

Portrait of a Young African American Male

- 85% have strong self-respect
- 63% are caregivers to family members or friends
- 19% volunteer in their communities
- 86% are not involved in gangs
- 39% do not drink alcohol
- 38% do not use marijuana
- 86% do not use hard drugs
- 82% never spent time in prison

Source: The Commonwealth Fund Pilot Survey of Young African American Males in Four Cities, Louis Harris and Associates, Inc., 1994.

---

ber of protective factors seem to be associated with school success and fewer risk-taking behaviors among inner-city young African American men. The findings suggest that young men view the presence of caring adults (such as parents, teachers, mentors, and employers), as well as working and participating in youth programs, as helpful to staying in and completing high school.

This study indicates that parental involvement is important to adolescents. Although the young African American men in this study are at an age when they are moving toward independence, the findings reveal that they are still connected to their families. They reported that what their parents said and did made a critical difference in helping them complete high school. The vast majority of those who stayed in school reported that their parents had high expectations for them and expected them to finish high school. These parents supported their sons by supervising homework, providing a place to study, and visiting their sons' schools or teachers.

It is not surprising—but important to emphasize—that young men in this study who succeeded in school were more likely to be growing up in two-parent homes with steady family incomes. These young men also reported that they were growing up in stable circumstances in which they felt close to their parents, their parents did not abuse substances or experience mental health problems, and the family did not change residences often. But the critical role of parents in the lives of adolescents is often neglected in community programs, youth development initiatives, and public policies.

Other research finds that a good educational experience is another key ingredient in a young person's success in the first two decades of life [Hahn 1999]. Teacher interest, competence, and support were all reported in this survey to be associated with helping disadvantaged young African American men stay in school. The young men who stayed in school reported that their teachers instilled a sense of hope and belief in the student's ability to affect their academic outcomes. The findings also suggest that an academic or vocational curriculum, rather than a general education program, may help young African American men stay in school longer. A more challenging academic or vocational curriculum would likely make school more interesting for these young men, and it may also provide more opportunities for teachers to instill hope and to encourage further education.

A surprising finding in this study was that having a job while in school may be associated with remaining in school. Again, the young men reported that the relationship with a caring adult—their employer—was an important factor in their staying in school. Specifically, the results suggests that in addition to "having a job," the nature of the relationship in which the employer respects them, gives them hope for the future, and self-confidence could also help young African American men living in inner cities.

In this study young people report that mentors were important in their lives, a finding echoed in other studies [Sipe 1996; Galbo & Demetrulias 1996]. Those young men who stayed in school were more likely to report that youth programs helped them stay in school. Others have found that youth programs can connect adolescents with caring and reliable adults who provide social support and guidance while offering the youth opportunities to be of service to their community

[Loury 1999]. Unfortunately, many men in this study did not have access to youth programs in their communities.

The findings also suggest that staying in or finishing high school can serve as a protective factor against engaging in risk-taking behaviors. As other studies indicate, being in school enhances the opportunities for these inner-city young African American men to develop interpersonal relationships with caring reliable adults in their schools, homes, workplace, and communities [Connell et al. 1994; Walker 1996].

This study of young African American males points to the importance of program and policy initiatives that keeps them in school, including opportunities to form positive relationships with parents and other adults that will enhance the young person's sense of self-worth and hope in the future. The essential ingredients are attainable—supportive parents and teachers, investments in schools, mentors, summer jobs, and youth programs at critical stages in the lives of young African American men can help them develop into healthy productive adults. The return on the investment is significant for the young men themselves as well as the communities in which they live. We need to and can do a better job.

References

Carnegie Corporation of New York. (1995). *Great transitions: Preparing adolescents for a new century.* New York: Carnegie.

Chalk, R., & Phillips. D. A. (Eds.). (1996). *Youth development and neighborhood influences: Challenges and opportunities.* Washington, DC: National Academy Press.

Connell, J. P., Halpern-Felsher, B. L., Clifford, E., Crichlow, W., & Usinger, P. (1995). Hanging in there: Behavioral, psychological, and contextual factors affecting whether African American adolescents stay in high school. *Journal of Adolescent Research, 10,* 41–63.

Connell, J. P., Spencer, M., & Aber, L. J. (1994). Educational risk and resiliences in African American youth: Context, self, action, and outcomes in school. *Child Development 65,* 493–506.

Feldman, S. S., & Elliott, G. R. (Eds.). (1994). *At the threshold: The developing adolescent. Cambridge*: Harvard University Press.

Galbo, J. J., & Demetrulias, D. (1996). Recollections of nonparental significant adults during childhood and adolescence. *Youth & Society, 27*(4), 403–20.

Goddard, L. L. (1991). You can teach wisdom. In B. P. Bowser (Ed.), *Black male adolescents: Parenting and education in community context* (pp. 202-207). Lanham, MD: University Press of America.

Hahn, A. (1999). Extending the time of learning. In D. Besharov (Ed.), *America's disconnected youth*. Washington, DC: CWLA Press.

Hamburg. (1992). *Today's children: Creating a future for a generation in crisis*. New York: Times Books.

Lerner, R. (1995). *America's youth in crisis: challenges and options for programs and policies*. Thousand Oaks, CA: Sage Publications.

Loury, L. D. (1999). Family background, church attendance, and school achievement. In D. Besharov (Ed.), *America's disconnected youth*. Washington, DC: CWLA Press.

Mincy, R. (1994). Introduction. In R. Mincy (Ed.), *Nurturing young black males* (p. 12). Washington, DC: The Urban Institute Press.

Sipe, C. L. (1996). *Mentoring: A synthesis of P/PV's research: 1988–1995*. Philadelphia: Public/Private Ventures.

Spencer, M., Cole, S., DuPree, D., Glymph, A., & Pierre, P. (1993). Self-efficacy among urban African American early adolescents: Exploring issues of risk, vulnerability, and resilience. *Development and Psychopathology, 5*, 719–39.

Taylor, R. D., & Roberts, D. (1995). Kinship support and maternal and adolescent well-being in economically disadvantaged African American families. *Child Development, 66*, 1585–1597.

Walker, G. (1996). *Back to the basics*. Conference paper. American Enterprise Institute, Washington, DC, May 16.

Wilson, W. J. (1996). *When work disappears: The world of the new urban poor*. New York: Alfred A. Knopf.

Zimmerman, M. A., Salem, D. A., & Maton, K. I. (1995). Family structure and psychological correlates among urban African American adolescent males. *Child Development, 66*, 1598–1613.

Notes

1   Among those who succeeded in high school, 71% had graduated and 29% were still in high school.

2   Respondents defined their families' income in the following terms: (1) *being very poor*: "had a hard time getting enough money"; (2) *being poor*: "poor, but usually had enough money"; (3) *having a steady income*: "had a pretty steady income"; and (4) *having a pretty good income*: "had a pretty good income and were able to buy special things."

6. The "Hallwalkers"

Hillard Pouncy

On Philadelphia's West Side, 10 blocks from the Schuylkill River that runs through the city, University City High School (UCHS) sprawls over a large city block. Although it is similar in many respects to the inner-city comprehensive schools that ethnographers discuss in their work on urban general education youth [MacLeod 1987; Kozol 1995; Kozol & Fine 1991; Devine 1996], it differs from them in that it is surrounded by universities and hospitals that offer the types of jobs that could help poor youth pull themselves out of poverty. UCHS's neighbors include four higher educational institutions (the University of Pennsylvania, Drexel University, the Philadelphia College of Pharmacy and Science, and a branch of the Community College of Pennsylvania), a high-technology urban research park (the University City Science Center, including the Ben Franklin Technology Center), and a three-hospital cluster operated by the University of Pennsylvania. In addition, a vocational education center is nearby, as are many restaurants and small employers that typically service universities and hospitals.

As originally conceived, UCHS was meant to serve as a science magnet school that would seek the city's best students for programs that local university faculty would help design. The plan fell through, and the school became a comprehensive neighborhood school. In 1994, the school's students were below the city average on statewide competency tests in math, reading, and science. Only 19% were at their grade norm for math, 29% for reading, and 11% for science. Philadelphia schools themselves fall below the state average: only 27% of the city's students are at their grade norm in math, 36% in reading, and 21% in science, compared with about 80% of students in the city's neighboring suburbs.

William Yancey, Senior Research Associate of Temple University Center for Research in Human Development and Education, pooled data from Census Bureau, health, and police department files for each Philadelphia student's neighborhood and generated a weighted average of demographic and "trouble" variables for each school [Yancey et al. 1995]. Compared with average Philadelphia students, UCHS students were both more likely to be poor and from "troubled" neighborhoods. In 1997, for example, 54% of UCHS students were from families on welfare, and 86% qualified for federal reduced-price lunches. By comparison, 42% of all Philadelphia students were from families on welfare, and 74% qualified for the federal reduced-price lunch program. In 1994, UCHS was ranked among the top 15% of schools on Yancey's "trouble" index. The students came from neighborhoods with high arrest rates for drugs and violent crimes, high rates of syphilis, high rates of teenage births, high rates of babies with low birth weights, high rates of tuberculosis, and high rates of lead poisoning [Yancey et al. 1995].

Of the approximately 2,500 students who attend UCHS, 97% are black, 1% are Asian, 1% are Latino, and 0.6% are white. In 1994, the school had a larger Asian population, but city officials relocated many Asian students after serious violence broke out between blacks and Asians in the 1993-94 school year.

Five years ago, a community group, the West Philadelphia Improvement Corps (WEPIC), and the Center for Community Partnerships at the University of Pennsylvania began sponsoring courses that brought college students to the school to engage in community service projects and to write research papers. More recently, a team comprising two undergraduate students of University of Pennsylvania anthropologist Peggy Sanday, along with two UCHS students, conducted research at the school.[1] Their documentation of the school's disorder was much in keeping with other ethnographic studies of inner-city schools. They noted that many youngsters were so bored, and school discipline was so lax, that some students spent their days in the halls avoiding classes. This chapter is largely based on their research [Strange & Phillips 1996], as well as on surveys conducted at the school by its staff, and the observations of others, including Peggy Sanday; the principal, James Lytle; and staff at the Center for Community Partnerships.

"Losing That Future Feeling"

Even school administrators describe UCHS's appearance as a modern prison. The three-story yellow-brick building has narrow windows covered by metal security bars. Two years ago, the school was organized so that administrative offices occupied the first floor. The second floor housed the general education students and was covered in graffiti and littered with trash and burned-out lights. The third floor, where the college-bound students met, had little graffiti and "beautiful academic murals depicting gene replication, how tadpoles become frogs" [Brooke & Strange 1996, p. 3]. Recently, the school has been reorganized so that college-bound and noncollege youth are not so segregated.

Hallwalkers congregated on the second floor. "Hallwalking is defined by the school administration as the intentional act of an individual or group of students who leave class without permission (via a note from a teacher), or do not come to class but are on school grounds while school is in session. These students are usually found walking around the school, always without a note (there are also students who obtain notes but never return to class)" [Brooke & Strange 1996, p. 15]. Because the school cafeteria is also on the second floor, hallwalkers easily mingle with lunch crowds, making it even harder for overwhelmed security people to spot them.

The University of Pennsylvania students distinguished between two types of hallwalkers: subject hallwalkers and chronic hallwalkers. (They did not identify how many in either group were frustrated third-floor college-bound students who came down to join the hallwalkers, and how many were refugees from second-floor general education classes.) Subject hallwalkers were bored by a specific class or subject. According to the researchers, they felt unchallenged in class or turned off because the class was "slow." They never reported that they were avoiding a class because it was too hard. Chronic hallwalkers, on the other hand, avoided all their classes—hard or not—to spend as much of the day as possible in the halls. This group told the Penn students that they were generally dissatisfied with their education and saw little connection between school and their future.

The presence of chronic hallwalkers validated research by other scholars, including Mercer Sullivan, author of *Getting Paid* [1997]. He details the reaction of disadvantaged youth to declining economic opportunity, discrimination, poverty, fatherlessness, poor schools, and indifferent teachers, painting stark pictures of what life is like once these youth become disconnected. Many general education youth see little connection between school—a nuisance at best—and getting paid—what they care most about. At a time when the labor market increasingly links skills and good jobs, chronic hallwalkers are less likely to see such a connection. How does this play out in their lives? Do they eventually drop out to chase money and other gratifications, or do they struggle on and graduate? Similarly, do subject hallwalkers eventually grow even more bored and turn into chronic hallwalkers?

In-Crowds, Out-Crowds, and Changing Crowds

As ethnographers in training, the Penn students cataloged the school's various cliques and captured their language, dress, thoughts, and views. Their work fits in with other classic studies of urban schools that identify in-crowds and out-crowds and label them with colorful names: hallway hangers, brothers, jocks, those who act white or do not, burnouts, brains, the popular set, earls, lads, etc. [Gelabert 1997; MacLeod 1987; Kozol 1995; Kozol & Fine 1991; Devine 1996; Willis 1977; Fordham & Ogbu 1986]. [The latter two terms are British working-class terms for bright, committed students (earls) versus soccer fans and turned-off blokes (lads).] They found that the hallwalkers were the "in-crowd."

One problem with ethnographic research on urban schools is that researchers are often so focused on the difficulties of collecting evidence that they leave the impression that change is unlikely. For example, Philippe Bourgois, author of *In Search of Respect: Selling Crack in El Barrio* [1995], suggests that disadvantaged urban youth consciously develop a culture of opposition. They reason that they should not strive to excel in school or on the job, because any initial success will inevitably be followed by rejection and discrimination. Pedro Gelabert has challenged the idea that disadvantaged youth were deeply embedded in an oppositional culture [Gelabert 1997]. The Penn students, like Gelabert, found little evidence that hallwalkers at UCHS were so attached to an oppositional culture that it precluded the possibility of change. Instead they found that

> students ... make (conscious or unconscious) decisions about which classes they feel are necessary to attend and which classes they will attend just enough to pass. These decisions made by the students vary on what they feel school should teach them. Thus, the school curriculum becomes a patchwork quilt where the student picks and chooses which classes he/she will attend because they are about real life, or which classes they cut because they are 'boring' and not about real life. [Strange & Phillips 1996, p. 15].

Such an orientation makes it possible that if the school's patchwork of courses and other arrangements were changed, the boredom and hallwalking might decline. This supposition is consistent with school reform ideas developed by Phillip Cusick [1991, 1973]. As one of Cusick's interpreters put it:

> High school is designed so as to reward scholarship. But since most students will not be rewarded as scholars, the school must provide an alternative reward system which will attract the loyalty of a larger second group of students in order to obtain the loyalty of at least a large minority of the school: the second reward structure is inter-school athletics and the fraternity

/sorority-like social whirl of service clubs and student
government. But this is a system which leaves out most
students, who are neither "brains" nor "popular." It
leaves many students feeling unwanted or unattached.
[Crain 1997, p. 151]

Viewed from this perspective, the subject hallwalkers are students
who sought scholarly rewards but did not find them. The chronic
hallwalkers are students left out of a school's implied contract, and thus
they present a bigger challenge to educators, for these hallwalkers must
first be connected to school before they can be attached to the workplace.

University City High School's Response

In the 1993-94 school year, the level of disorder at UCHS, particularly
that involving Asian and black students, was particularly high. In that
school year, there were 67 serious incidents, a 150% increase from the
previous year. Twelve of these were assaults involving fellow students,
eight were attacks on school employees, and nine were assaults on teachers. One student was stabbed.

In 1994-95, the school's disorder finally attracted public attention.
A Philadelphia newspaper called the school a sea of chaos: "Right now
…that common area where all the kids are, is like hanging out on a
street corner in Philadelphia" [Bello 1995].

During spring vacation, late in the 1994-95 academic year, the school
system replaced the principal at UCHS with Dr. James "Torch" Lytle,
a Stanford Graduate School of Education alumnus. Lytle, like the majority of staff and faculty at UCHS, is white, and he acknowledges the
need to recruit faculty with backgrounds similar to those of his students.

In his first full academic year on the job, 1995-96, Lytle began a
series of changes that reduced the school's violence and eventually put
an end to much of the hallwalking. The main change, which affected
how decisions were made at the school, grew out of his belief that chaos
theory, derived from physics, can be applied to educational administration.[2] As he described it:

Within two weeks of my arrival we were required to cut the school's $11,000,000 budget by almost 10%, so a demoralized community was now being confronted with new leadership and a significant reduction in its resources. I decided to use the budget cut as an opportunity to help the school generate about $500,000 we could reallocate to support new programs and priorities. The whole process was conducted publicly—no deals, no secrets. We also agreed to subdivide the school into six (now ten) small learning communities, or schools-within-a-school, in which students take all but their physical education classes. In the process we shifted the school's core organizing construct from subject/department to caring/support/personalization.

In Lytle's first year (the same year the Penn students began their study), the disorder had subsided to the point that researchers observed that vandals and troublemakers represented only a small minority of students at the school. The new security problem was the hallwalkers. A year later (1996-97), the hallwalkers were gone. At the same time, the school reduced the size of its security force. Lytle's "chaos" plan

- Shifted departmental organization to self-contained small learning communities, each with its own faculty and section of the building. Eventually, there were ten such communities,[3] and each had a different character, so that some provided stronger classes for subject hallwalkers (e.g., Academic and Community Empowerment, Business Academy, Excel—Performing Arts, Health, Law and Government, Magnet, Marathon 2000, Motivation and Technology, and Journalism). For chronic hallwalkers, the school created a special small learning center called the Opportunity Center, which provided additional attention, nurturing, and individual instruction.
- Reorganized the photocopying center into an activity center run by special needs students, who had also been hallwalkers and unable to sit still in class.

- Gave each small learning community its own counseling, special education, and security staff.
- Reduced the number of assistant principal and department head positions.
- Replaced the cafeteria that hosted hallwalkers with a bright, shiny food court.
- Introduced student-run, nonprofit businesses—rebuilding and selling computers, selling web-page design and computer graphics services—that became the focus of two of the small learning centers.
- Arranged for 18 graduate students from the University of Pennsylvania's Graduate School of Education to be teacher interns.
- Created a twilight, or after-school program, for dropouts.

As a result of the school's success within the eight areas listed above, it was able to establish a school management consulting business providing budget, scheduling, and planning services to other troubled high schools. The consultancy business charges a $175,000 retainer, which the central school office allocates to any additional school expenditures it chooses. Its clients include several New Jersey school districts and a Kansas City school.

By the academic year 1996-97, the school's disciplinary problems had declined so significantly that, among 23 schools with a high level of disciplinary problems (of the 43 in the Philadelphia system), UCHS went from the top of the list to the bottom. Even though the school accepted 111 youth back from probation, incarceration, or other disciplinary assignments, only 14 of the 2,000 students at the school left for disciplinary reasons. UCHS proved more capable of intervening successfully on disciplinary issues than most schools. Its number of graduates rose above 300 for the first time in 10 years. Between 1996 and 1997 alone, the number of graduates increased from 250 to 328.

Lytle's efforts to address the hallwalker problem involved several public education innovations at the center of current reforms: career-focused education, dropout retention, development of pathways to college, and small learning communities tailored to student needs, with a leadership style built on decentralization and staff empowerment. These efforts seemed to end hallwalking. But a larger question remains: Can such reforms increase academic achievement, decrease the number of dropouts, and, by extension, decrease the chance that high school graduates will become disconnected? So far, the evidence on the effectiveness of three such efforts—career-focused education, dropout prevention, and the development of pathways to college—is mixed. Researchers speculate that implementation matters: If done incorrectly, these otherwise promising educational innovations may exacerbate existing problems and increase disorder, while another style of implementation may reduce disconnection and launch youth toward productive careers. The UCHS experience can help separate what works from what does not.

The Two Faces of Career-Focused Education

The UCHS principal and many other educators argue that career-focused education can reach hallwalkers and other youth untouched by a regular curriculum, interest them in school, and prepare them for a job or college [Pouncy & Hollister 1997]. Lytle, for example, attributes his school's improved graduation rate to the career-focused education some of the school's small learning communities have begun to provide.

Other school districts have had success with school-to-career programs and note that the programs work well for youth from disadvantaged backgrounds. This year, for example, at Oakland (CA) Technical High School's Health and Bioscience Academy, 91 of the 93 seniors are going to college. It is also true, however, that only 60 out of 240 African-American freshman males made it to their senior year. Very few of those 60 were enrolled in the Health Academy. Thus, school-to-career programs seem to have two faces. One promises outreach to hallwalkers—like the UCHS effort. The other rejects such youth, as the initial outcomes for graduates of school-to-career programs like Oakland's Health Academy attest.

New York City's Career Magnets

New York City tried to operate its school-to-career programs, or "magnet schools" in ways that would both reach out to hallwalkers and maintain high standards. Officials sought to maintain high skill levels, while increasing access by introducing a lottery. The New York City system includes 59 programs at 31 high schools.

The city's eighth graders take reading and math exams, and the exam results are ranked on a six-part scale. Students on the bottom rung are labeled below average in reading and math skills. Students on the top rung are labeled above average, and the two-thirds in the middle are labeled average. As originally intended, the city's career magnet was to be selective—or elitist, as one educator put it. For political reasons, however, the city added a lottery, so that about half of the students are admitted to the program randomly. In the eighth grade, each youngster fills out an application for high school that makes it as easy as possible to apply to a career magnet. (Students in the top 2% are exempt from the lottery and are given their first choice whenever possible.) At each level—below average, average, and above average—the city runs separate lotteries that give even very low-skilled youth access to otherwise very selective programs.

> Each academic career magnet program could only admit one-sixth of its students from those with above grade level reading scores…and another one-sixth from students from those reading below grade level (the other two-thirds coming from those within one standard deviation of the area mean). And finally, they required that half of the students in each of those reading groups be admitted by lottery. [Crain 1997, p. 11]

As a result, about one-third of the city's students now attend career magnet programs.

The lottery is important to policymakers, because it is one method for resolving tensions between quality and access. It has the effect of guiding low-achieving students into rigorous, selective programs. Thus, the system suggests what might happen if such youth were to receive an education focused on a career that could yield a middle-class income. If it works, perhaps school-to-work programs can address the disconnection problem.

Crain conducted an assessment of the effectiveness of all the career magnet programs, hoping that the randomly assigned admissions element would permit a scientific experiment. They analyzed the records of 9,176 lotteried students, then conducted focus interviews with 110 graduates and four-hour life history interviews with 30 of those students. The experiment, however, did not incorporate a perfectly random assignment, because only youth who applied for career magnet programs were involved. In a perfect random assignment experiment, youth would be picked independently of their preferences to eliminate the effects of selection, so that even those did not want to attend a career magnet would be assigned to one. Nonetheless, because the number of applicants was greater than the available slots, those who were rejected were randomly rejected—a variation on being randomly selected to attend. This arrangement allowed researchers to determine whether general education youth could take advantage of school-to-career programs if these were offered. The experiment is analogous to what would happen if all youth who might conceivably want to attend Harvard were entered in a lottery, and its findings tell us what might result if the UCHS hallwalkers who wanted to enter selective career magnet programs were actually able to do so.

In their interviews with the New York graduates, Crain and his colleagues found large differences between graduates of the two programs, sufficiently large that the research team could not explain them away by citing a higher dropout rate among career magnet attendees (see below).

In the life history interviews, Crain refined this finding, identifying nine major positive outcomes of the programs for youth who graduated:

- **Reduced risky behaviors.** Forty-one percent of career magnet graduates reported no risk behaviors—they never smoked, did not regularly drink alcohol, never used drugs, and never became pregnant or made someone else pregnant. Only 19% of youth in the control group—those who attended regular comprehensive schools—said the same.

- **Increased the amount of career-related course work.** Career magnet graduates averaged 13.4 hours/credits of career-related course work, compared with 5.2 such hours/credits among comprehensive students.

- **Augmented students' feelings of safety.** Crain found this was true even when the magnet program was located in a comprehensive school building that the comprehensive school youth found unsafe.

- **Increased student earnings.** After graduation, career magnet students who worked earned about $1 more per hour than their comprehensive peers. They also earned $1 an hour more a year or two later (a starting hourly wage of $7.27, as compared with $6.28).

- **Changed students' friendship networks.** Career magnet graduates were more likely to develop new friends at school who were likely to express an interest in a future career (17% more likely than the friends of comprehensive peers, as reported by the graduates themselves).

- **Affected student expectations.** Career magnet graduates were more likely to perceive their parents as willing to sacrifice financially for college. This was a particularly strong finding, because it meant that a young person who was the first in the family to go to college might inspire his or her parents to offer financial support. It might also mean that the youngster misperceived reality, but the "misperception" signaled that the career magnet had helped bond youth to their families so strongly that they gave their families credit for something that the families might, in fact, not do. Zellman and Quigley [1997] could explain 21.3% of the variation in youth who perceived a parent as willing to spend money on college by citing attributes associated with career magnet schools.

- **Improved students' language skills.** Career magnet graduates were usually more confident in English class, independent of their immigrant status.
- **Promoted multiple improvements.** In a pool of 110 interviewees, youngsters with all the above attributes were 32.3% more likely to have graduated from a career magnet program.
- **Encouraged further education.** After graduation, career magnet students earned more college credits than their comprehensive peers. They averaged 37.7 credits within two years of graduation, as compared to 30.9 credits for the comprehensive high school graduates.

Other studies reinforce the findings of Crain and his colleagues. Larry Rosentock, former head of Rindge Latin in Cambridge, Massachusetts wrote:

> As a former high school teacher and principal, I visited 23 cities last year with the New Urban High School Project, looking at school-to-work programs. What we consistently found was that those who complete such programs are entering postsecondary institutions at significantly higher rates than their counterparts who are not in such programs. [New York Times 1998]

The Other Side of the Question

A career magnet lottery winner with an average reading level is, however, also more likely to drop out of high school. Fourteen percent of the lottery winners in career magnet programs dropped out in the four years following the eighth grade, as compared with 11% of their peers in comprehensive schools. Among career magnet "ultra seniors" (those who stay in high school beyond four years), the dropout rate was 29% five years after the eighth grade, versus 16% for their peers in comprehensive schools. The career magnet graduation rate was also lower. Twenty-six percent of the career magnet lottery winners graduated four years after the eighth grade, as compared to 31% of lottery losers. Five years after the eighth grade, the graduation rate of average-reading-level career magnet lottery winners was 9% lower than that of average-reading-level students in comprehensive schools (see Figure 6-1).

A UCHS hallwalker who attended a New York career magnet school might graduate after trading in old friends, reducing risky behaviors, and training more intensely for a job. That student would earn more at work and would be more likely to attend college, where he or she would take more courses than his or her general education peers at comprehensive schools. The chances that the hallwalker might drop out of school, however, would also be higher.

Crain commented, "There is a major problem with these schools: they have a low graduation rate that cannot be justified by the quality of the students they admit. We think this is a fixable problem: If we are right, then we have uncovered a workable strategy for high school reform which should have wide applicability to low and moderate income areas, and especially to minority students. If it is not fixable, and these good schools can only do what they do by driving graduation rates down, we will have identified one of the ugliest Hobson's choices in education" [Crain 1997, p. 1].

As implemented in New York City, the career-focused effort seemed to exacerbate a problem. By their nature, selective school-to-career programs operate more aggressively than college-preparation courses to prepare students for demanding clients. Thus, rather than produce graduates who will fail employment standards, the programs flunk out even more hallwalker-type students than traditional college-bound programs. The idea that reforms might increase dropouts is discouraging, because UCHS already has a high dropout rate.

Dropouts, or Just Ultra Seniors?

Urban schools like University City High School have dropout prevention strategies—the paradox is that the more successful the strategy, the more controversial it is likely to become. In a typical year, UCHS accepts about 700 hundred freshmen, approximately 100 of whom never

Figure 6-1. Graduation Rates by Lottery Outcomes

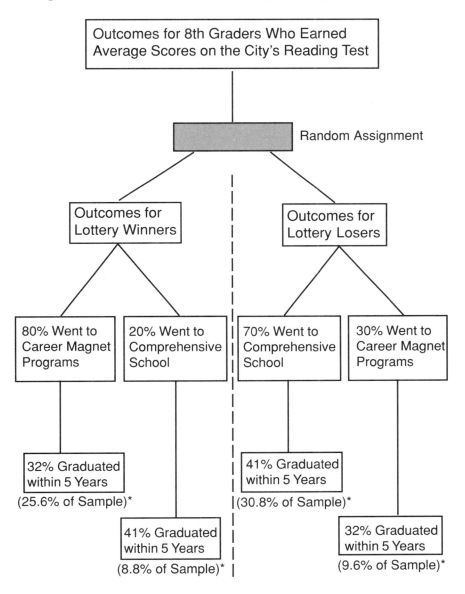

* 25.2% transferred to another another school system.

Source: New York City's Career Magnet High School Lottery, 1992.

arrive. "They are phantom students and probably dropped out of middle school, but the school system still carries paperwork on them" [Lytle 1998]. About 300 graduate four years later, leaving the school with an average dropout level of between 50% and 60% of its students.[4] To recover students from that pool of dropouts, UCHS operates a twilight or after-school retention program, as mentioned earlier. The school captures 80 to 100 students from that dropout pool and expects to graduate them. When UCHS factors such students into its calculations, it believes that 50% of its current students will graduate on time, about a third will drop out, and another 17% will become ultra seniors (students who take longer than four years to graduate).

However, solving one problem—drawing dropouts back to school to become ultra seniors—creates new problems, as recent events in New York City illustrate.

The New York City Board of Education Division of Assessment and Accountability's cohort study of New York City students who started high school in 1988 found that 21% had dropped out by 1992—the year they would have been expected to graduate. By 1995, an even larger segment of 1988 freshman (24%) had dropped out [New York City Board of Education 1997]. Thus, of 82,935 students who began high school in 1988, only 40% graduated from high school on time. Of the others, 14% were discharged, meaning they left the city school system and could be verified as belonging to another school system. Another 21% dropped out, as just noted, but 25% were ultra seniors. Three years later, enough of those ultra seniors dropped out to push the dropout rate up to 24%. Many ultra seniors graduated, however, so that the graduation rate for the incoming class of 1988 was 57%.

Table 6-1 shows that New York City's dropout levels have declined marginally (from 26.2% to 22.6% over five years), while its student retention rates have increased, indicating that more youth are struggling to graduate. These findings are consistent with the theory that even as the significance of a high school degree declines, youth in fact struggle harder to attain it, so that they can at least begin an effort to secure stronger skills and credentials.

Table 6-1. New York City Graduating Cohort, 1986 to 1992

Class of 1986	4 yrs > 8th Grade	7 yrs > 8th Grade
Dropouts	21.8%	26.2%
Graduates	41.0%	57.3%
Discharged	12.3%	14.4%
Still enrolled	24.9%	2.1%
Class of 1987	**4 yrs > 8th Grade**	**7 yrs > 8th Grade**
Dropouts	22.4%	27.0%
Graduates	39.2%	56.9%
Discharged	11.6%	13.7%
Still enrolled	26.8%	2.4%
Class of 1988	**4 yrs > 8th Grade**	**7 yrs > 8th Grade**
Dropouts	20.8%	24.4%
Graduates	40.1%	57.3%
Discharged	13.8%	15.2%
Still enrolled	25.3%	3.1%
Class of 1989	**4 yrs > 8th Grade**	**6 yrs > 8th Grade**
Dropouts	20.9%	24.8%
Graduates	38.0%	53.1%
Discharged	15.7%	16.4%
Still enrolled	25.4%	5.7%
Class of 1990	**4 yrs > 8th Grade**	**5 yrs > 8th Grade**
Dropouts	19.2%	22.6%
Graduates	37.6%	49.5%
Discharged	15.3%	15.9%
Still enrolled	27.8%	12.0%
Class of 1992		
Dropouts	17.2%	
Graduates	38.9%	
Discharged	16%	
Still enrolled	27%	
Class of 1992		
Dropouts	16.0%	
Graduates	48.3%	
Discharged	16.5%	
Still enrolled	35.3%	

Source: Eileen Foley, "Half the Battle," Office of the Comptroller, Office of Policy Management. New York City, February 1993. (Class of 1992 from Crain, unpublished report). Used with permission.

The ultra senior phenomenon in some respects mirrors the dropout phenomenon, since the reasons ultra seniors give for staying longer or not graduating on time are similar to the ones youth used to give for dropping out. "Their academic slide often begins well before their late teens—around the end of junior high and sometimes earlier—when it seems impossible to be cool and a good student at the same time. All have been kept back a grade at least once and in most cases twice" [Archibold 1998, pp. B1-B3].

One such ultra senior, describing his friends, told a journalist: "They didn't like school, so I didn't like school." This was George Osorio, who, after repeating the ninth and eleventh grades, finally came around a couple of years after realizing that "I was getting old and I didn't want to stay another term. I finally figured out what classes I needed to take and saw what I needed for my diploma." After five-and-a-half years in high school, he is on track to graduate in June and plans to go on to Bronx Community College to study television technology, an idea that came to him from watching MTV [Archibold 1998, pp. B1-B3].

Even at best, allowing youth to continue past four years reduces a UCHS dropout rate of 40–50% to approximately 24%. Yet, compared to a national cohort, UCHS and New York City have higher dropout rates, even when ultra seniors are factored in. In 1988, the National Center for Education Statistics (NCES) sponsored a cohort study of sophomores who were to become the high school graduating class of 1992. According to the NCES report, 11% of the youngsters who were in the eighth grade in 1988 had dropped out by 1992 (their senior year). Two years later, however, about 3% of the class had dropped back in and graduated, making the final dropout rate 7%.[5] UCHS's corresponding dropout rate, taking into account "dropins," was 33%, and New York City's corresponding rate was 25%.

By another national yardstick—"event" dropouts—UCHS and New York City public schools compare favorably, however. Event dropouts are the proportion of youth between the ages of 15 and 24 who have dropped out of school during any 12-month period. The national event dropout rate is 5.7%. In his 1998 annual report on the nation's educational system, U. S. Secretary of Education Richard Riley referred to this event dropout measure when he said, "The [national] dropout rate is holding at around five percent. This means that some 500,000 young people are still short-changing their lives and dropping out." New York City's event dropout rate compares favorably at 5.4%, and the UCHS rate is about 8%.[6]

Increasing Access to College or More College Dropouts?

A less well-known attribute of some urban high schools is that, once their students graduate, almost all of them attend college—even if that means that they only take a few courses. This also means, however, that postsecondary institutions have become the new major location of disconnection for urban youth. Over the past 20 years, the financial advantage of a college education has increased. The earnings of male high school graduates declined sharply, from $27,000 in 1979 (in 1993 dollars) to $20,000 in 1993 (the median earnings of 25- to 34-year-olds), while the earnings of male college graduates fell only slightly (from $30,000 to $29,000). The earnings of female high school graduates also declined slightly (from $15,000 to $14,000), while the earnings of female college graduates climbed from $17,000 to $23,000 [Murnane & Levy 1996; Murnane 1995; Hamilton 1990; U. S. Department of Labor 1995]. In the past—in the factory-driven labor market of the 1960s [Licht 1992]—general education youth could earn more than $32,000 per year (in 1993 dollars) doing production work in a Ford Motor Company plant.

Given this increased earnings gap, UCHS administrators have sought to increase the number of its graduates who go to college. Currently, administrators estimate that about 66% of the school's 200 to 300 graduates go to college or junior college, and another 25% to 30% take jobs or enter the military. Although this college access rate is in keeping with current national college attendance rates, it is actually low for an urban system. In large cities like Philadelphia and New York, college access rates are higher than national averages, because graduates can enroll in community colleges at relatively affordable rates. In New York City, one study estimates the college attendance rate among city high school graduates is as high as 85% [Crain 1997].

Nationally, NCES found that 71% of youth who graduated high school in 1992 took courses at a four-year or two-year college within two years of graduation.[7] This figure rises to 75% when trade school youth are included.[8]

Although the college access data suggest that more youth are embarking on college courses, youth who start a college education do not necessarily finish. For urban youth, disconnection may result even from dropping out of college. In regards to nonurban youth, particularly rural youth, the MDC research group in Chapel Hill, North Carolina, has concluded that some rural college dropouts are skill dropouts, meaning people who secured the job-relevant skill they sought and had no need for a credential.

Nationally, college dropouts may not be a problem. Fifty to sixty percent earn a degree, and many pick up credits.[9] For these students, disconnection is an unlikely outcome. For example, 66% of the 1972 high school cohort completed college, a level that barely changed among the class of 1982—65%. Early evidence for the class of 1992 suggests that the flat trend continues—66% will complete college within six years of high school graduation.[10] New York City, however, manifests a different pattern, one that may also prove characteristic of Philadelphia: Fewer than 17% of those enrolled in 1992 graduated from a two-year college within four years [Levy 1998, p. B1].

Although New York City's graduates attend college in record numbers, they also take remedial courses in record numbers. Of the six CUNY community colleges that enroll about 37% of all undergraduates in the city system and about 45% of first-time freshmen, an average of 87% of enrolling students failed one or more of the college placement tests in reading, writing, and mathematics. These subjects must be made up in remedial courses. About 21% of the instruction at the community colleges involves remedial coursework [Arenson 1998, p. B7].

The Quantity/Quality Conundrum

These outcomes for high school students confront urban policymakers with a conundrum. Permitting or even encouraging higher rates of ultra seniors may lower dropout rates, but it increases the number of interactions between adult and adolescent students. For this reason, New York City Mayor Rudolph Giuliani has challenged the city's policy that permits high school attendance beyond four years—the ultra seniors—and instead proposes separate evening and weekend facilities for adult high schoolers. "Mr. Giuliani wants to phase in a policy that would require students who stay beyond five years to complete their education at night or weekend schools. This, the mayor reasoned, would also give such students better preparation psychologically and emotionally for the job market. But critics suggest that Giuliani's plan would destroy hope and place a barrier to ultra seniors" [Archibold 1998, p. B1]. Critics believe that the proposal may increase dropout rates.

The city's college access rates have likewise become a political problem. In a State of the City address, Mayor Giuliani also expressed dismay at the policy's effect on community colleges, threatening to pull city funds from CUNY's community colleges unless they toughened standards. Specifically, he proposed to continue the city's current level of funding, but to divide the money between CUNY and other educational institutions that would teach the remedial courses, a move that would cut CUNY's enrollments by 75% [Levy 1998].

To fix quantity-based programs that they believe sacrifice quality, the mayor proposes quality-based policies that may sacrifice quantity. There is no evidence that ratcheting up the quality of graduates, separating ultra seniors from regular students, and moving weak graduates out of the postsecondary system will decrease disconnection. In fact, some believe such efforts will increase disconnection. These choices give the mayor and New York City schooling officials a quality/quantity conundrum.

Implementation Matters

New York City's attempt to improve access to its selective career magnet system may have increased student competence while making weaker students more likely to drop out. This suggests that the "how" of school system reform—how school systems implement promising programs—matters more than the "what" of specific programs.

Lessons from the Crain report, the UCHS experience, and other field studies yield four ideas that may help urban school systems capture the benefits of advanced career-focused programs like the New York City career magnet schools while avoiding higher dropout rates.

Early Work-based Learning

Crain and his colleagues argue that the career magnet dropout problem may be linked to the lack of career-oriented classes in the early high school years: "We can only speculate, because we have no direct data from a large enough sample of tenth grade classrooms, but it is possible that by the tenth grade students are both bored and frustrated by the relatively small amount of career content in their classes and frustrated by the high level of difficulty of those classes. Such difficult courses are likely to be used by school staff to identify those students who are most likely to be suitably qualified for internships, career-related jobs, and the advanced classes to prepare them for employment"[11] [Crain 1997, p. 248]. That is, because schools do not provide internship opportunities until the eleventh or twelfth grade, and because teachers assign students to those internship programs based on prior classroom performance, many students who would benefit from work-based learning never experience it. By the time they are old enough to qualify for current programs, they already view school as irrelevant, and their interest in learning has waned.

In contrast, if middle-school students, who are idealistic and energetic and who have little knowledge of proper office behavior, were allowed to participate in internship programs, the positive experiences they acquire during such programs might spark enthusiasm for learning as they begin to understand the importance of school. Ideally, such programs would occur in settings in which the students would be treated as responsible adults-in-the-making, thus engaging young people with the world before boredom and disillusionment set in.

Flexible Pathways

In some career magnet high schools, faculty currently teach tenth-grade classes as if all students were headed for prestigious programs in securities and finance. This approach favors students who are interested in selective colleges. But the New York City system includes six other programs: accounting, business, computer science, business law, marketing, and secretarial science and information systems. Crain suggests that moving students among the various programs when boredom or frustration sets in should reduce the dropout rate. Similarly, health career magnet programs include small theoretical medical programs for students headed for four-year colleges, but there are also eight other programs, including practical nursing, nursing assistance, dental assistance, dental laboratory work, medical laboratory work, medical accounting, medical office, and medical secretarial work. Again, academically strong nursing students might increase their level of rigor and go into the medical science program, while laboratory majors who did not like blood work or found the academics too rigorous might move over to medical office work.

Multiple Exits

Currently, most career-focused programs begin with an "all aspects of the industry" introductory sequence, as mandated by the School to Work Opportunities Act of 1992. Crain and others now suggest that highly selective career magnet programs should apply an "all aspects of the industry" framework to students exiting the program as well. With continuing career counseling and continuing work experiences, general education youth can fight frustration and boredom and may remain attached to a program in which they keep their final career options open.

Counseling and Feedback

The small learning centers of UCHS, with their emphasis on counseling and support and on resolving Cusick's "maintaining the contract" element, are good examples of how this idea works in practice. A good career-focused program must combine elements of the selective New York City career magnet academic programs with UCHS' focus on counseling and nurturing less-skilled youth. That combination was what Cusick had in mind for reaching hallwalkers.

Such a combination of more intensive counseling and monitoring, à la UCHS small learning communities, and an advanced career-focused education, including early internships and multiple exit points, may reduce the dropout rate while securing the qualitative gains of a career focus. Furthermore, such a program could accommodate ultra seniors and, at the same time, restrict interactions among adolescents and young adults. Implementing such a program might improve the lives, and lessen the disconnection, of many inner-city youth. But while the chapter has so far focused only on the problems of young people in the inner city, the effects of disconnection are not limited to urban areas. The society as a whole pays a price for its failure to involve youth in preparing for their own futures.

All general education youth face the same challenge of earning a middle-class income. Some speculate that the skinhead phenomenon in the suburbs and among urban middle-class white youth is also a manifestation of the frustrations and despair expressed by urban gangs. In Denver, for example, after a "good kid" went bad, *The New York Times* blamed the young man's descent on the changing economy. In profiling Mattheus Reinhart Jaehnig, a disconnected Denver skinhead who killed a police officer late in 1997, the *Times* reporter claimed that Jaehnig's life was a window into how "neo-Nazi" groups nationwide tap into the frustrations of disconnected young people, "offering them solace with a scapegoating view of the world" [Brooke 1997, p. A8]. The report said that Jaehnig's main problem was that he was an "unskilled worker in a high-tech world." The article did not blame his parents, German immigrants who had done well in Denver. (Jaehnig's father was an intellectual, a peace advocate, a pastor, and a school principal.) The paper also did not blame the Denver educational system. Mattheus was dyslexic and a slow learner, but he had gone to good schools. His family sent him to the school his father founded. There Mattheus was given special tutoring until the tenth grade, when he transferred to a regular Denver high school and was so far behind his peers that he was put in a special class for slow learners. He withdrew after only one semester, and that is when he joined a group of white "punk" youngsters, who in turn joined the Denver Skins, a skinhead hate group. He was also an unwed teenage parent who withdrew from his teenage girlfriend and their child.

Ultimately, however, Jaehnig was presented as an isolated, nonsystemic case. Most other general education students in his school were not dropouts or ultra seniors. Most were not disconnected.

The *Times* conclusion appears somewhat utopian, if we consider the possibility that some types of concentrated family-based problems in middle-class communities may be producing outcomes similar to those in poor communities. This possibility was raised in a *New Yorker* piece on a predominantly white suburban community that was filled with skinheads from good families. In that article, William Finnegan focused on Mindy Turner, a high school dropout, and her friends who live in Antelope Valley, a predominantly white Los Angeles suburb that grew in population from 60,000 in 1980 to 220,000 in 1994 [Finnegan 1997]. It is a story about a murder involving youth who saw few opportunities ahead.

The problem in Antelope Valley was that it concentrated many dual-earner couples who commuted long hours to their jobs in Los Angeles, so that most of their children had become latchkey kids. "Parents can't afford after-school care and often don't return from their epic commutes until long after dark." In such a landscape, "the teen-pregnancy rate is high, so is juvenile crime—particularly burglary." In that environment, the main youth activity is a street war raging between a white-supremacist skinhead gang known as the Nazi Low Riders and a rival gang of antiracist skinheads who call themselves Sharps—Skinheads Against Racial Prejudice. "And at the local high school, Palmdale High School, out of a graduating class of about four hundred, only six students went into the University of California system. Less than ten percent of the class went on to any four-year college at all."[12] Bedford-Stuyvesant or Watts is hardly likely to yield a starker example of disconnection than that.

Everything New Is Old Again

The pairing of disconnection and schools has a history. Three decades ago, the 1967 Task Force Report on Juvenile Delinquency and Youth Crime, sponsored by the President's Commission on Law Enforcement and Administration of Justice [President's Commission 1967], made similar associations and reached similar policy conclusions. Disconnection, they concluded, was at the root of juvenile delinquency, and they too could not decide whether it resulted from other causes or was somehow a cause unto itself. But the Commission was certain of two points: the "opportunity thesis" forward by Richard Cloward and Lloyd Olin was correct in its view that "crime and juvenile crime in particular could be prevented by giving youth a sense of stake in society," and schools, particularly high schools, were key to delivering a credible message of opportunity to America's youth.

> Schools should assume a greater responsibility for preparing students for the future. They should help raise the aspirations and expectations of those students capable of higher education and should prepare them for it. This is the objective of the Upward Bound programs sponsored by the Office of Economic Opportunity. Present programs for students not headed for college should also be reviewed and revised. Vocational training programs removed from industry often provide highly unrealistic training, and often it is for obsolete jobs. Schools should concern themselves with job placement for their graduates; it is already common for col-

leges to have placement offices and for industry to recruit directly from colleges. [President's Commission 1967, p. 53]

The President's Commission, and the scholarship supporting it, anticipated Steven Hamilton's observation that American noncollege youth can no longer afford to flounder for years before settling into a career. The Commission failed to anticipate that preparation for both college and the world of work were about to become equally rigorous. It slid into the presumption that work-bound students were those "not capable of higher education."

In the Commission's mind, the nation needed to build on-ramps leading from high school to good opportunities and good jobs that lifted inner-city youth above discrimination, poverty, and poor schools. The modern school-to-work movement updates the Commission's original view of an on-ramp that must not only lift poor youth over those problems, but also lift them over a skills barrier in which 70% of good jobs require education beyond high school.

In large urban school systems, even youth who graduate from high school and attend college may leave their college experience without securing needed skills. Even a high school degree combined with some college attendance does not end the risk of disconnection.

In West Philadelphia, the staff at University City High School may or may not know about these studies and theories, but they do know that two years ago their hallways were filled with bored and frustrated youth from some of Philadelphia's most violent and troubled neighborhoods. By making their hallways more secure and their classrooms smaller and more nurturing, and by showing more concern about the careers and future of their general education youth, they have begun to show how schools can address the root issues leading to disconnection.

References

Archibold, R. C. (1998, January 19). At Bronx school, 'ultra-seniors' ponder graduation. *New York Times*, B1-B3.

Arenson, K. W. (1998, January 30). Some CUNY officials are cautious about mayor's proposal, but others see disaster. *New York Times*, B7.

Bello, M. (1995, March 20). High school is a sea of chaos. *The Philadelphia Daily News*, p. 5.

Bourgois, P. I. *In search of respect: Selling crack in El Barrio* (New York: Cambridge University Press, 1995).

Brooke, J. (1997, December 13). From close family to world of hate. *New York Times*, A8.

Crain, R. L. (Ed.). (1999). *The effects of academic career magnet education on high schools and their graduates.* Berkeley, CA: National Center for Research in Vocational Education.

Cusick P. A. (1991). *The egalitarian ideal and the American high school: Studies of three schools.* New York : Teachers College Press.

Cusick, P. A. (1973). *Inside high school: The student's world.* New York: Holt, Rinehart and Winston.

Devine, J. (1996). *Maximum security.* Chicago: University of Chicago Press.

Finnegan, W. (1997, December 1). The unwanted. *The New Yorker 73*, 60-79.

Fordham, S., & Ogbu, J. U. (1986). Black students' school success and the burden of 'acting white.' *The Urban Review, 18*, 3.

Gelabert, G. M. (1997). *Street ethos, surviving high school: A qualitative study of immigrant and American-born students in an inner-city high school.* New York: NYU School of Education.

Hamilton, S. F. (1990). *Apprenticeship for adulthood: Preparing youth for the future.* New York: Free Press.

Kozol, J. (1995). *Amazing grace: The lives of children and the conscience of a nation.* New York: Crown.

Jaynes, G., & Williams, R. M., Jr. (Eds.). (1989). *A common destiny: Blacks and American society.* Washington, DC: Committee on the Status of Black Americans, Commission on Behavioral and Social Sciences and Education, National Research Council.

Kozol, J., & Fine, M. (1991). *Framing dropouts.* Albany, NY: SUNY Press.

Levy, C. J. (1998, January 30). Giuliani demands community colleges drop remedial help. *New York Times*, B1.

Licht, W. (1992). *Getting work: Philadelphia, 1840-1950.* Cambridge, MA: Harvard University Press.

Lytle, J. (1998, March). Author interview.

MacLeod, J. (1987). *Ain't no makin' it.* Boulder, CO: Westview Press.

Murnane, R. J. (1995). The growing importance of cognitive skills in wage determination. In R. J. Murnane, J. B. Willett, and F. Levy's contribution to The National Bureau of Economic Research Working Paper Series. Cambridge, MA: National Bureau of Economic Research.

Murnane, R. J., & Levy, F. (1996). *Teaching the new basic skills: Principles for educating children to thrive in a changing economy.* New York: Martin Kessler Books; Free Press.

National Center for Education Statistics [NCES]. (1997). *Access to postsecondary education for the 1992 high school graduates.* Washington, DC: Author.

New York City Board of Education, Division of Assessment and Accountability. (1997). *Assessment/accountability report: The class of 1996, four-year longitudinal report and 1995-1996 event dropout rates.* New York: Author.

New York Times. (February 10, 1998). School to work programs set students back; "The glue that holds." Letter to the Editor. Response to the editoral by Lynne Cheney (February 3, 1998) on the failure of school-to-work reforms.

Pouncy, H., & Hollister, R. G. (1997). Net impact evaluation of school-to-work: Contending expectations. In *Evaluating the net impact of school-to-work: Proceedings of a roundtable.* Washington, DC: U.S. Department of Labor, Employment and Training Administration Employment and Training Administration.

President's Commission On Law Enforcement and Administration of Justice, Task Force on Juvenile Delinquency. (1967). Task force report: Juvenile delinquency and youth crime. Washington, DC: U.S. Government Printing Office.

Strange, A., & Phillips, B. (1996, May). *Hallwalking: An ethnography.* Unpublished paper for Cultural Pluralism, Anthropology 561, Dr. Peggy Sanday, University of Pennsylvania.

Sullivan, M. (1986). *Getting paid*. New York: Cornell University Press.

U. S. Department of Labor. (1995). *Skills, standards and entry-level work: Elements of a strategy for youth employability development*. Washington, DC: Author.

Willis, P. E. (1977). *Learning to labor: How working class kids get working class jobs*. New York: Columbia University Press.

Yancey, W. L., Saporito, S. J., & Thadani, R. (1995). *Neighborhoods, troubles and schooling: The ecology of Philadelphia's public schools*. Philadelphia: National Center on Education in the Inner Cities, Temple University Center for Research in Human Development and Education.

Zellman, G. L., & Quigley, D. D. (1997). Career magnet schools: Effects on student behaviors and perceived parent support. In R. L. Crain (Ed.), unpublished book manuscript.

Notes

1 All material used with permission of the authors. I also acknowledge the work of their University City High School student assistants, Jamil Ryder and Candace Watson.

2 "The potent force that shapes behavior in…fractal organizations …is the combination of simply expressed expectations of acceptable behavior and the freedom available to individuals to assert themselves in non-deterministic ways." Cited by Lytle from M. Wheatley [1993].

3 Much of this part of the citywide effort to encourage small learning environments itself anticipates federal legislation before Congress that would allocate $200 million annually on such learning efforts nationally, in coordination with the Mott Foundation's 21st Century School Initiative.

4 Officially, the school system counts dropouts as youth not in school in October who have not been in school for a year. This "event" dropout rate in 1994 was 8%.

5 The cohort dropout rates for the eighth-grade class of 1988 show that, by the spring of 1992, 10.8% of the 1988 cohort of eighth graders were out of school and had not completed a high school program. Some of these dropouts completed a high school program during the following summer, so that by August 1992, the

size of this group was reduced to 10.1%. By August 1994, only 7.2% of the cohort remained as dropouts who were not working towards completing high school. NCES reports that these dropouts, relative to their peers who completed high school, were less likely to participate in postsecondary education; on average, they earned lower incomes; and they were more likely to be unemployed or out of the labor force. They were also more likely to make early transitions into adult roles—to have children and marry or live in marriage-like arrangements. "A comparison of cohort dropout rates from the 1980 and 1990 sophomore classes shows that 9.9% of the students who were sophomores in 1980 were high school dropouts by August of the 1981-82 school year. For the sophomore class of 1990, the cohort dropout rate was lower, with 5.6% of the students who were counted as sophomores in 1990 counted as dropouts by August of the 1991-92 school year. This amounts to a 43% reduction in the sophomore to senior dropout rate over the decade" [NCES 1997].

6   As calculated by the City Board of Education's Division of Assessment and Accountability on city youth enrolled in high school until the age of twenty-one. The rate is about the same each year, because some dropouts drop back in or find an alternative certification program, and others grow too old to be included. The U.S. Department of Education also monitors cumulative dropouts between the ages of 15 and 24. With roughly 500,000 new dropouts added each year, the nation's cumulative or status dropout rate—the proportion of young adults aged sixteen to twenty-four years who were considered dropouts in October 1995—was 12% of the 32.4 million students in that age group in the United States in 1995; nearly 3.9 million young adults were not enrolled in a high school as of October 1995. New York City's cumulative dropout rate compares unfavorably with these national standards—it is about 25%.

7   The U. S. Census Bureau estimates the college access rate within two years after high school graduation at 66% for youth between 16 and 24. Discrepancies between census estimates and cohort measures are long-standing. Mark Lopez suggests that the discrepancy may largely be the inclusion of dropouts in the Census Bureau's sample. The NCES cohort studies monitor postsecondary

access only among high school graduates. Also cohort studies slightly inflate college access rates by including trade schools and nontraditional colleges. But when trade school attendance was excluded from the NCES data cohort, the result is approximately 71%. The vocational education percentages are as follows: private for-profit vocational institutions, 3.1%%; private nonprofit two-year institutions, 1.0%; and public less than two-year institutions, 0.2%.

8   The way in which data are collected has policy ramifications. Although both the Census Bureau and NCES found increased college access rates in the 1990s among all youth, and among minorities in particular, they disagree about the 1980s. Census estimates suggest that black enrollment declined in absolute and relative terms compared to whites. Cohort studies suggest that black enrollment declined only relative to whites, while increasing in absolute terms. For example, in the book, *A Common Destiny*, a report on the state of race relations in the 1980s, educators puzzled over a serious decline in black access rates to college after 1975 (see Jaynes & Williams [1989]). Again, the discrepancy is likely the result of the Bureau's tendency to include high school dropouts in its tabulations.

9   Assuming, however, that an associate degree or college credential has its own value in the job market and beyond, Clifford Adelman at NCES [1997] made a participation ladder to give a sense of how far youth get before they drop out (this calculation assumes that 3 credits equal a college course, and 160 credits are needed to graduate a college program).

- Incidental students earned no more than 10 credits—13% (60% gone within a year).

- Amorphous students with more than 10 credits but less than two year's worth of credits started in community college attended more than one college and left a curricular trail—24%.

- Peripatetic students have more than 60 credits but no degree; most started in a four-year college, 70% attended more than one school, and a majority wandered from one major to another—8%.

- Credential earners—6% of those enrolled earn a certificate, another 9% earn an associate degree and 40% earn a bachelor's degree. (The number earning a bachelor's degree increased from 22% in 1984.)

10 Some groups have experienced declines. White college completion rates, for example, declined from 68% in 1982 to 62% in 1992. Asian students completed college at a rate of 81% in 1972, but this figure declined in 1982 to 79% in 1982 and 73% in 1992. Among black and Latino youth, the numbers have increased. Black completion rates, 49% in 1972, decreased to 42% in 1982, then rose to 52% in 1992. Latino completion rates were 44% in 1972; they rose to 49% in 1982, and to 52% by 1992.

11 Crain believes that part of the problem may be that career magnet teachers are fighting back against less-skilled general education youth by dropping them out. They may be measuring students against standards that apply to the most demanding jobs in a given field. It would be as though teachers in college-bound programs tried to flunk out students who might do well at an average college because they could not compete for Brown or Berkeley. Instead, Crain and his colleagues suggest that career magnet faculty should prepare less-skilled students for less demanding jobs in their field.

12 See Finnegan [1997, p. 70]. When Cloward and Olin first presented their opportunity thesis, the "Ozzie and Harriet" nuclear family was the American ideal. As Sara McClanahan notes, the two-parent household with a breadwinner-father, a homemaker-wife and two or more children was more ideal than reality even in the 1950s and 1960s. Since then, this family style has become rarer, so that by 1985, only 16% of American households fit its description (another 7% were nuclear, husband-as-breadwinner families with no children). Another 14% of American households were single-parent households (8% were single-employed-parent households, 6% were single-homemaker-parent households). The most dominant household formation is now the dual-earner couple—35% (21% with children, 14% without). The remaining 29% were single people without children—including cohabiting couples.

In its heyday, the "Ozzie and Harriet" family style is credited with providing such support for children that the President's Commission considered it a bulwark against juvenile delinquency.

"Research findings, however, while far from conclusive, point to the principle that whatever lies in the organization of the family, the contacts among its members, or its relationships to the surrounding community diminishes the moral and emotional authority of the family in the life of the young person also increases the likelihood of delinquency" [Finnegan 1997, p. 45].

James Coleman built upon this research when he suggested (in *Equality of Education Opportunity*) that making sure public schools had enough students in them from middle-income, presumably intact families was the most efficient way to deliver educational opportunity—hence his support for bussing inner city youth to middle-class school districts. In this sense, he concluded that good families fix bad schools.

Although dual-earner households averaged $46,629 in 1985 versus $13,012 in average earnings for single-mother households, dual-earner couples may not be the bulwark against disconnected youth that they once were.

7. Improving Links Between High Schools and Careers

Robert I. Lerman

Enhancing the educational and employment success of disadvantaged urban and minority youth is critical if the United States is to reduce its high rates of poverty, social and family disruption, and alienation. Unfortunately, many current patterns are not promising. As of 1992, 60% of disadvantaged 12th grade urban students had math proficiencies below the basic level [Mullis et al. 1993]. Unemployment remains extremely high for minority and disadvantaged youth. As of March 1995, more than one in four 18- to 21-year-old males from low-income families were neither working nor in school. In 1996, when the overall unemployment rate was only 5.4%, unemployment among 16- to 24-year-old black out-of-school high school graduates was 23% [U.S. Bureau of Labor Statistics 1997].

These impersonal job statistics mask much more serious social problems related to the poor career options of disadvantaged and minority youth. Wilson [1987] sees the deteriorating job market for young black men as the underlying cause of the rising rates of mother-headed families and a growing underclass. Between 1960 and 1989, the proportion of black children living with two parents dropped from about 67% to about 38%. To Anderson [1991, 1994], the alienation associated with what he calls "endemic joblessness" has led to an oppositional street culture that can engulf even young people from "decent" homes. Unable to gain self-respect through solid performance at school or on the job, street youth (especially young men) prove their manhood by showing their peers that they can conquer women sexually and become a father and that they can steal something from another and flaunt it. The tragic levels of street crime have made murder the leading cause of death of young black men.

Many suspects are implicated in this increasingly intractable problem. Concentrated poverty weakens the ability of schools to raise educational performance. Low academic achievement for some youth can ultimately bring down others, as peer pressure works against those trying to succeed [Ogbu 1990]. The declining wages of less skilled men and even high school graduates further reduce the attraction of working hard to do well in high school, especially in a peer culture that takes a short-term view of life. Crime arises not only from direct economic incentives but also from the necessity of preserving self-respect through violent behavior. Anderson [1994] notes that prison may enhance a young man's reputation after the toughening experience.

These phenomena are widespread and have become worse among low-income black youth. Bound and Freeman [1992] calculate that 20% of black 18- to 29-year-old male dropouts were incarcerated in 1989, a rise of 12.7 percentage points since 1980. By the mid-1980s, nearly one in three young black women had become an unwed mother by age 21. The effects on schooling and jobs are disastrous. According to Bound and Freeman, the rising share of black dropouts with criminal records may have accounted for 70% of the decline in employment rates between 1979 and 1989. In recent work, Freeman [1996] estimates that 10% of 25- to 34-year-old men were in jail, in prison, or on probation; 12% of dropouts and 34% of black male dropouts were actually incarcerated. Crime and violence have extended to schools and affected the innocent. By 1988, nearly one in five black eighth graders did not feel safe in his own school.

The racial dimension complicates the problem by creating a vicious circle. The history of blatant racial discrimination and salient examples of continuing discrimination add to the bitterness of many inner-city youth against the system and to their expectations that hard work in school will not pay off. Employers, sensing that a lack of basic skills and an unwillingness to work hard are common among lower-class blacks, discriminate by attributing the highly visible traits of blacks to individual black job applicants [Holzer 1992]. Even employers in the neighborhood are unlikely to take a chance on youth who lack a credible reference [Kasinitz 1993]. The evidence of continuing discrimination reinforces the rejection by ghetto black youth of the mainstream system and rationalizes their lack of effort in school.

How can we escape from this vicious circle? How can student motivation increase significantly enough to help school reforms succeed? In what ways can disconnected students be confident that achieving academic success will pay off in the job market?

The Importance of Education

In any consideration of how to improve public policies to deal with these problems, a good place to start is the school system. Since virtually all disconnected youth go through the public schools, it is a place they can be reached. Although schools are not primarily responsible for the weak educational achievement of disconnected students, the structure of the school system and how it interacts with the job market certainly weaken the motivation of young people, especially the economically and socially disadvantaged. Performing well in school does not clearly translate into better jobs. The link between school and careers is largely absent for the vast majority of high school students. Students rarely have a good idea about a wide range of middle-level careers and what skills will be required to succeed in these careers. In short, schools may be failing to provide economically disadvantaged students with what they need and what employers demand for entry-level jobs with career possibilities.

An article in *The Economist* [1996] points out that we cannot count on training programs to overcome the problems of the unemployed. In country after country, publicly funded training schemes are found to have a solid logic but fail in practice. The evidence goes well beyond the absence of earnings gains for young people participating in the Job Training Partnership Act programs. Few countries have been able to document significant positive impacts from youth training programs outside the mainstream structure of education and training.

The purpose of this paper is twofold: first, to examine what employers demand for entry-level workers and, second, to consider the school's role in helping disconnected or disadvantaged youth to meet these demands.

The main argument of the paper is as follows:

- The evidence is strong that employers are increasingly demanding higher skills for many types of jobs potentially available to disconnected young adults.

- The skills of many such youth are often inadequate to meet employer demands associated with good careers.

- While improving academic skills is critical, relying entirely on increasing academic standards within a school-based approach to remedy the skills problem is unlikely to be successful without improving student incentives to learn.

- Only by moving to a career-based approach that emphasizes well-structured work-based learning are we likely to exert a major influence on the life chances of disconnected young people.

The academics-only approach ignores differences in modes of learning and creates a single hierarchy based on one type of intelligence. Under the current system, unless a student excels in schooling and aspires to a selective college, he or she often sees little reason to study hard enough in high school to learn important skills. Most believe they will be able to go on to college in any event, and few see any direct and immediate benefit for their careers [Bishop 1989]. As of 1992, virtually all (96%) high school seniors said they plan on going to college, including nearly 90% of seniors scoring in the lowest 25% of test takers [U.S. Department of Education 1995]. Yet, despite the high expectation of attending college, most young people will not graduate from a four-year college or even a two-year college. As of 1995, only one-third of all 25- to 34-year-olds had graduated with an A.A. or B.A. degree, and less than 25% of black men had done so. Of those in the bottom quartile, success is even rarer.

Despite the reality that only a minority of students complete even an A.A. degree, students, parents, teachers, and educational policymakers today see college as the only pathway to success. Partly as a result of that attitude, the educational and job market systems spend far too little time and resources making high school students aware of the possibilities for good jobs in careers that do not initially require academic degrees. This approach is extremely shortsighted for two important reasons. First, even if we doubled the rate graduating with at least an A.A. degree, we would still have to help the remaining noncollege youth prepare seriously for careers. Second, there is a growing realization that combined school-based and work-based programs often reengage students in the learning process and lead them to pursue postsecondary education.

The inadequate attention to careers in high school is especially problematic for young people whose parents and friends are unemployed or in unskilled jobs. Since these students cannot learn about or gain connections to these careers through informal channels, the absence of good formal channels to these jobs becomes a major disadvantage. The emphasis on academic methods of learning works to the disadvantage of many students who achieve more through hands-on learning in realistic settings. Finally, the current system prolongs adolescence and an adolescent peer culture, thereby slowing the maturation process and weakening constructive interactions with adults.

In my view, the country must simultaneously move toward improved academic standards and diversifying the methods of teaching both academic and technical skills. We must create many more well-structured and demanding career options that students can enter through a combination of high school and community college education together with work-based training. Today, students with only a high school education have few ways to enter skilled careers in their late teens or early 20s. Many suffer from a mismatch between what schools provide and what the job market demands. They ultimately may be able to land a stable job and become productive [Klerman & Karoly 1994] but usually at a lower wage and a lower level of capability than they could have achieved under a better system. For disconnected youth, the weaknesses in our country's links between school and work have a much more devastating impact on the young people themselves (in the form of higher unemployment and poverty) and on the rest of society (in the form of higher crime rates). We now have a chance to make fundamental changes in the relationship between educational and job market institutions. Success in these efforts is vital if we are to reduce significantly the number of disconnected youth.

What Employers Require of Entry-Level Workers

There are many ways to assess what employers demand of entry-level workers. To begin, we must recognize that the employers are heterogeneous, operate in very different markets, and thus may call on a range of different needs. Educators and policymakers often overlook this simple point because schools (especially high schools) use a relatively homogeneous curriculum.

One approach to determining employer demands is to ask them directly what they would like to see in an entry-level employee. Unfortunately, the results can be misleading. Often, an employer will say that he or she simply wants an employee who will show up on time, be honest, listen and respond to supervision, and have a positive attitude toward work. Those who have probed more deeply into this matter find that these statements are usually more indicative of the low expectations of employers than a listing of what employers would actually want from their entry-level workers.

Another common view is that employers want entry workers with only solid basic skills. This view has validity for many types of jobs. But the question is, do these workers actually use such skills on the job?

Several studies of employers have determined that, indeed, the vast majority of even entry-level workers do require more than basic competencies in computation, math reasoning, clear speaking, and writing. Packer and Wirt [1992] reported on a New York State study of 1,400 jobholders in 300 large and small businesses. The jobs represented a cross section of positions not requiring a college degree but involving some career path. They included such jobs as practical nurse, auto body repair, inventory clerk, and salad chef. The results documented that skills well beyond minimum competency levels were necessary in the great majority of these positions. In many cases, the job requirements went beyond the skills expected of those entering college. Packer cites several competencies that are required but not emphasized in schools. The jobs demanded more speaking and listening skills, for example, than the writing skills stressed in schools. Other important skills included having knowledge of a system and its interrelated procedures, reacting constructively to positive or negative criticism, working well as a team member, using information systems, setting priorities, and having good personal work habits. Packer argues that these topics are rarely even taught in schools and are certainly not emphasized.

Another large recent study of employers also found that even entry-level workers use what Packer calls the "extended basics." Holzer [1996] conducted a survey of more than 3,000 employers in four metropolitan areas. Again, the jobs were going to workers with less than a B.A. degree. Employers were asked about how frequently their most recently hired worker undertakes specific tasks: dealing with customers in person, dealing with customers over the phone, reading paragraphs, writing paragraphs, doing arithmetic, and using computers. The vast majority of noncollege jobs required several of these skills every day. More than half the noncollege jobs even required working daily with computers, and more than half involved reading paragraphs daily, and nearly half had to write paragraphs at least once a week. About three-fourths had to do arithmetic at least once a week, with 65% having to do arithmetic daily. Nearly 80% involved working with customers.

The Holzer survey also asked employers about hiring requirements for noncollege jobs, such as requiring a high school diploma, general job experience, specific experience, references, and previous training. For nearly three of four noncollege jobs, a high school diploma, general experience, and references were either "absolutely necessary" or "strongly preferred" by employers. In addition, employers demanded or strongly preferred specific experience as qualifications for two of three of the noncollege jobs in the central city. More than 40% wanted vocational or other training as well. Thus, those without a range of skills and qualifications face great difficulties finding even noncollege jobs.

The recruitment and hiring strategies of employers are also relevant to the ability of disadvantaged youth to begin careers. According to the Holzer survey, employers frequently give tests, check the educational attainment, and consult the criminal record of applicants. Nearly all interview the candidate and expect good English and verbal skills, politeness, and motivation on the part of the job candidate.

Overall, Holzer estimates that only a small proportion of noncollege jobs in cities involves the types of educational levels and other qualification levels currently held by disadvantaged youth. For example, 96% of noncollege, central city jobs require a high school diploma, training, experience, or references. About 90% require both a high school diploma and general experience. As a result, many disadvantaged youth will have difficulty qualifying for positions because of their inability to meet the employers' expectations. Of course, in a tight labor market or when wages are low, employers may be willing to accept a worker who, on the surface, appears less qualified than the employer wishes.

Before the young worker has a chance to get a job, he or she must be able to apply. Yet, given employee recruitment practices, even the more active disadvantaged job seekers may be unable to find out about the job. In the Holzer survey, employers often filled jobs through informal channels. About 26% of hires came through as referrals from current employees and another 12% from acquaintances or others. Private employment services referred about 10% of the successful hires. Thus, nearly half the hires obtained jobs through mechanisms frequently inaccessible to disadvantaged young people. Employers are sometimes unwilling to take a chance even on people in the same neighborhood who lack a credible reference. In his study of the Red Hook neighborhood of Brooklyn, Kasinitz [1993] found that employers discriminated against local residents because they associated them with crime and poor work attitudes. The discrimination was not entirely racial, since members of other racial groups in the area were also cast as undesirable and since employers did hire "black" West Indian immigrants. Employers relied on referrals from existing workers to allow them to determine which workers would be reliable and honest.

The job requirements, screening devices, and recruitment strategies clearly place disconnected youth at a serious disadvantage in the job market. Although black males are a heterogeneous group, their average attributes unfortunately weaken their chances to find jobs. Holzer reports that the more jobs require the various types of tasks described above, the less likely it is for a black male to obtain the job. He reports that each task lowers the hiring of black males by one to eight percentage points and each required credential by one to three percentage points. In addition, differences in the job tasks associated with various groups of workers account for a large proportion of the wage differences among labor force groups.

The work of Bishop [1995] strengthens these findings. In a survey of members of the National Federation of Independent Business, employers cited occupational skills as the ability that mattered more than any other single factor in their hiring decisions. Fully 40% rated already having the occupational skills as the most important attribute. Another 14% of employers placed this skill second. Moreover, it is not simply some employers' bias, but rather their actual experience with entry workers that influences their preferences. Of new employees who had been on the jobs for at least a year, employers found that those with occupational skills performed better than those with more academic skills. Moreover, wage gains of the occupationally skilled rose most [Bishop 1995, pp. 79]. Although Bishop finds that verbal and math abilities did not directly affect the productivity of most workers, these general skills contribute indirectly by affecting the individual's ability to attain the necessary occupational and job-specific knowledge that produces good performance [Bishop 1995, pp. 11].

According to Bishop, there is considerable evidence that it is the *effect* of specific skills on the productivity of workers that generates the higher wages for more skilled workers. The evidence comes from studies on the effects of relevant work experience on job performance and wages and on the effects of occupationally relevant job knowledge on productivity and performance on the job. Bishop cites work summarizing hundreds of studies documenting these relationships. He points to evidence that assessments of technical competence and other cognitive abilities do better in predicting job performance in technical, craft, and machine operator positions than personality traits do.

In the early 1990s, the U.S. Department of Labor sponsored the Secretary's Commission on Achieving Necessary Skills (SCANS) to define the skills needed for employment, propose acceptable levels of proficiency, suggest effective ways to assess proficiency, and develop a dissemination strategy for the nation's schools, businesses, and homes [U.S. Department of Labor 1991]. Using a sample of 50 jobs, SCANS studied how proficient workers needed to be in each foundation skill and competency by asking 20 people to rate the skill levels required for job tasks identified by the job analysis. On the basis of their analyses, SCANS called for moving beyond standard school curricula in several ways. The report specified foundation skills that included such capabilities as listening, speaking, decisionmaking, problemsolving, mental visualization, and knowing how to learn, as well as reading, writing, and math skills. In addition, the SCANS report specified a large number of workplace competencies:

- managing time, money, material and human resources
- acquiring, evaluating, organizing, interpreting, and communicating information
- using computers to process information
- participating as a member of a team
- teaching others

- serving clients

- exercising leadership

- possessing negotiation skills

- working with cultural diversity

- understanding systems; monitoring and correcting performance

- selecting, applying, and maintaining technology

The project described a number of innovative methods for teaching these skills in schools and training programs.

Another approach to learning about what employers want is to use focus groups. While focus groups are too small for broad, general applicability, they permit a more in-depth and potentially more revealing set of motivations by employers. Zemsky [1994] summarizes relevant parts of the discussions of focus groups of small and large employers in eight cities. A major purpose was to determine what incentives might best encourage employers to participate in youth apprenticeship programs. Zemsky reports that employers in the focus groups are generally not interested in and often highly averse to hiring young people in high school or immediately out of high school. At the time the interview took place, the nation's unemployment rate was well above the current 5.6%. As a result, most employers did not have to reach into the pool of inexperienced youth, nor were many interested in developing an apprenticeship program. Many of the employers provided examples of their frustration with young people. They were said to lack discipline as well as communication, numeracy, and literacy skills; to be unwilling to do dirty jobs; and to show little respect for authority. A common complaint was that they had to go through hundreds of job applications to find someone who had the appropriate skills and attitudes.

Employers stated their strong preference for workers who had demonstrated their reliability and basic skills in other jobs, including fast food and retail establishments, or with temporary help agencies. Apparently, the temporary help agencies were able to offer credible references for the individuals applying for jobs. Firms did not wish to try out young workers but wanted instead to wait until the aging and sorting processes made clear which workers had the requisite skills, discipline, and motivation. One employer admitted that it was not what the high school did or did not do but the reality that he could be confident only with a worker who had already reached his mid-20s. When asked about possible motivations for participating in a youth apprenticeship activity, the employers generally responded by emphasizing the program's ability to serve as a screening device to find the best of the young workers.

A different picture about whether young workers can meet the demands of employers emerges from a companion study of employers participating in cooperative education programs. Lynn and Wills [1994] surveyed employers who had hired students to discuss their views on the ability of young people to meet job requirements, as well as on their perceptions of how a major traditional school-work program operates. These employers generally reported a favorable attitude toward their young employees. When asked whether the students are productive workers, 60% strongly agreed, and 33% somewhat agreed. About 86% of employers stated they were satisfied with the school's ability to provide students with the necessary skills, and 70% reported no significant problems with students. Nearly half expressed interest in expanding their participation in the cooperative education program; the major reason the other employers had little interest was their lack of available work. As reported by Zemsky, Lynn and Wills found that the screening function of the programs was extremely important for participating employers.

Certain conclusions follow from this discussion about the relationship between employer requirements and the access to jobs among disadvantaged youth. First, there is clear evidence that the vast majority of noncollege jobs require more than the most basic skills. Indeed, most demand specific experience, credible references, certifications, often the ability to pass a test, and no criminal record. General skills must exceed the basics, specific skills are a major advantage, and other job-related attributes are important. Second, many employers have little confidence in young workers or in disadvantaged workers. Without a screening system that allows young people to obtain a credible reference, many disadvantaged youth are unlikely to obtain entry-level jobs. Third, the experience of employers participating in existing and limited cooperative education programs suggests that under the appropriate circumstances, a wide array of firms would hire young workers.

Improving the Match Between What Schools Teach and What Youth Need

Young people who drop out of high school experience the most serious problems in the job market, account for a high proportion of criminal activity, and have the highest rates of nonmarital parenting. Further, those who have low academic achievement, as indicated on the Armed Forces Qualifying Test (AFQT), are most likely to experience long-term disconnectedness. According to Besharov and Gardiner [1999], 30% of the men and 40% of the women scoring in the bottom 25% of the AFQT were disconnected from school, work, and marriage for at least three years.

Certainly, the limited success of these young people results from many factors, including family background, neighborhood devastation, and peer pressure. It is important to ask, however, whether educational policymakers and school officials have adopted the appropriate strategy to improve the chances that these young people can achieve some success in the job market and in other constructive aspects of their lives. In particular, do schools offer these young people the types of education, training, and other support that will help them effectively respond to the demands of the job market?

The general thrust of school reforms has been to raise academic standards for all students. While high standards for all students are a sound goal, too many educators have viewed the means in a narrowly structured, school-based setting. As a result, they have paid too little attention to the specific career needs of disadvantaged youth and others at high risk of dropping out. None of the National Education Goals specify any occupational or career outcomes for students or any systemic changes that improve school-employer links or develop work-based learning. The 1996 education summit did call for employers to give added weight to school transcripts and other measures of school performance, partly as a way of improving incentives for students to perform well in high school.

Most dropouts report that lack of interest is one of their primary reasons for leaving school. Why should the additional requirements increase their interest in school or their incentives to perform well?

There is an increasing recognition that student effort is at least as important as physical facilities, class size, and even the educational level of the teachers. A Department of Education-sponsored monograph, *Education Reforms and Students at Risk: A Review of the Current State of the Art* [Rossi & Montgomery 1994], states the issue this way:

> Researchers increasingly conceptualize poor educational performance as the outcome of a process of disengagement that may begin as early as a child's entry into school. According to this model, students who do not identify, participate, and succeed in school activities become increasingly at risk of academic failure and dropout. In order to improve student achievement and persistence, the model suggests that the school climate must foster "investment" behavior and schools must encourage student involvement in academic and extracurricular activities by stimulating their interest, increasing their personal resources (e.g., remediating skill deficiencies), and rewarding their efforts. [U.S. Department of Education, no date]

Simply adding standards with little relevance to disconnected students is unlikely to create this type of "investment" behavior, especially in light of peer pressure that often turns students away from working hard in school. Peer pressure and its impacts on behavior increase significantly as young people enter adolescence. It becomes critically important in the high school years. For disconnected students to become invested in their learning, the payoff to learning must become clearer and more immediate and, ideally, must reorient an entire peer group.

The primary emphasis of today's education reformers is high and clear standards. A study by investigators at Public Agenda [Immerwahr & Johnson 1996] reports strong public support for standards and for applying them to students in inner cities as well as middle-income and affluent districts. Minority parents and teachers also want schools to raise academic expectations for inner-city children. A majority of parents believe that higher expectations will encourage improved performance. But parents attach an even higher priority to the role of schools in emphasizing good work habits such as being responsible, being on time, and being disciplined, as well as the value of hard work. They see education reformers as out of touch with average people by stressing "creativity" without teaching children the basics, having students use calculators when they cannot yet do basic arithmetic, mainstreaming children with special educational needs, and instituting bilingual education.

While providing high and clear standards is important, they are unlikely to have a major impact on disconnected students. Although teachers generally support the establishment of standards, only a small proportion (17%) views the absence of clear standards as a major problem. Some are skeptical of standards as the latest fad and as failing to deal with the more fundamental problems of resource scarcity. Moreover, most teachers believe their students are already achieving adequate standards.

Another issue is that standards for high school students and the associated courses are driven primarily by college entry requirements. Since schools wish to avoid tracking and students see few options other than college, the courses emphasized by colleges and universities are extended to the entire student body, but often in a form that varies substantially in the level of sophistication and quality. The results have too often been to de-emphasize the practical steps that could improve the motivation and the educational success of disadvantaged youth. Rarely are the standards linked to a concrete, nonacademic objective that students find compelling. (One exception is the standard of the National Collegiate Athletic Association for performance on the Scholastic Assessment Test.)

The SCANS skills are better grounded in the world of work than traditional academic standards are. One hopeful sign is that some schools are beginning to use the concepts and approaches embedded in SCANS, even for young students. A fourth grade class, for instance, puts together all the tasks required to publish a book, including preparing budgets, schedules, and materials. Educational consulting organizations, publishers, and software companies are developing products based on the SCANS skills. At this point, it is still too early to determine whether this effort to improve the match between what schools teach and what employers require will be widely implemented and, if implemented, will succeed.

In general, however, schools still place far too little importance to preparing young people for careers, especially students from disadvantaged areas. Only one in three teachers believes that a high school education is important in providing knowledge and skills that help young people on the job. Despite the large share of young people working part time or moving into the job market immediately after high school, most schools ignore the role of the workplace as possible learning environments.

A large body of research [Stern et al. 1990] documents the earnings gains of young people from having a job during their school years. Recent evidence indicates that disconnected students gain even more from working than do other students. Chaplin and Hannaway [1995] demonstrate that, even though working in high school often reduces or delays the completion of a young person's years of education, the overall impact on earnings is still positive. Among disconnected youth, working between 15 and 29 hours per week as a sophomore in high school resulted in more than 25% higher earnings 8 to 11 years later as compared with those who had not worked while in high school. The impact was only about a 10% earnings gain among all other sophomores. Despite the positive effects of holding a job and despite the high rates of employment among American teenagers, schools have generally ignored the work patterns of their students and paid little attention to those wishing to enter careers immediately after high school.

I am not suggesting that schools become employment agencies. Schools could, however, do more to recognize what employers require of career workers as well as build on the interests of students in jobs and careers to motivate them to learn more effectively: schools could encourage the work-based learning that can ultimately improve the ability of young people to achieve academic goals. Although postsecondary education is certainly desirable, it should not become the enemy of improved career-based programs for those who do not wish to attend college immediately after high school or for those who might otherwise drop out before completing high school. Indeed, initial results from pilot projects suggest that those inner-city students who participate in well-structured school-to-career programs are actually more likely to enter college than they would have had they participated only in the standard classes [Jobs for the Future 1995].

The U.S. Department of Education review of education reforms for disconnected youth cites research on dropouts that stresses the importance of engaging students in a range of school-related activities. By the time students are in high school, many choose to work for pay. Disconnected students are especially eager to earn some money to help support their families and pay for their own activities. In general, schools have nothing at all to do with the job-holding activities of high school students. Some programs, however, such as cooperative education, manage to develop some links between the schools and the employers. Access to and success in these jobs depend on maintaining adequate school performance and thus school-based links with employment are one way of engaging young people.

Although the evidence provides mixed findings on the special efficacy of cooperative education over other types of employment, some studies show that school-linked part-time jobs provide better learning opportunities, reinforce learning in school, and improve work attitudes more than unsupervised work. In a survey of students in jobs that were school-supervised and in jobs not supervised, Stern et al. [1990] reported that 63% of students in school-supervised jobs reported that they "make good use of special skills ... learned in school" in comparison with only 20% in settings not supervised by the schools. Those in school-supervised settings were more than twice as likely (77% to 36%) to say that the jobs taught new skills useful in future work. High proportions of both groups said that their jobs let them get to know people over age 30, but the proportion was still substantially higher (89% to 70%) in school-supervised settings.

Stern found that job characteristics of the type emphasized in school-supervised placements were positively and significantly related to the work attitudes of students. Such attitudes as feeling a responsibility to do a decent job whether or not the supervisor is around and a sense of pride in the work accomplished were closely linked to job quality. Cynical attitudes (like "working is nothing more than making a living" and "people who take work home don't have a very interesting home life") were much less likely among those holding jobs with characteristics promoted in school-supervised programs.

Recently, I spoke with a career counselor at an inner-city high school in Washington, D.C. This counselor teaches students about the job market, helps prepare them for jobs, places them in part-time positions, asks graduating seniors about their postgraduation plans, and attempts to find full-time positions for those not going directly into college. The counselor was overwhelmed by the large numbers of students and faced an acute shortage of the most basic resources. Still, for qualified students, he had plenty of access to part-time and entry-level jobs. Unfortunately, the peer culture within the school and the weak academic preparation of many students limited the numbers of students who would perform adequately on the job. Some of those referred by the counselor had such bad work habits and demeanor that he lost credibility with the employer.

The prevailing culture of the school limited the success of this counselor. The school did not demand modes of dress and behavior important in the workplace. The school did not have any well-developed mechanism for helping young people focus on career streams and relate their studies to subsequent success. The school was oriented only toward higher education for some groups and jobs (rather than careers) for others. Few young people in the school gained a realistic understanding of the earnings and job attributes of various occupations. As a result, when genuine opportunities for entering apprenticeships in high-paid construction occupations arose, few students ever looked into the area.

The School-to-Work Legislation

In recognizing the weak career link in today's high schools, Congress passed the School-to-Work Opportunities Act (STWOA) in the spring of 1994. The primary goal of the law is to stimulate government, education, and employer communities to create systemic changes that alter how students learn in high school and how they connect to careers. The act called on educators to do more to expand career awareness, to integrate academic and occupational learning, to use project-based learning, and to teach generic skills demanded in the new workplace. Schools are expected to increase the extent of project-based and contexualized learning. In addition, the act promoted work-based learning integrated with school-based courses and connecting activities, such as helping schools and employers use skill standards, job matching, job placement, and technical assistance to employers, teachers, mentors, and counselors.

STWOA has offered time-limited investments (akin to venture capital) to state and selected local governments willing to build on these concepts and remodel their systems for preparing young people for the job market. State and local sponsors have wide discretion in how they use the federal funds and in the choice of school-to-career (STC) program components they emphasize. The legislation mentions several career-oriented approaches:

- **Youth apprenticeships** are two- to three-year programs combining intensive work-based learning with related school-based subjects with the aim of helping students reach designated standards and achieving formal certification in a career stream.

- **Career academies** are schools within high schools that have a career focus around which courses, internships, and other student activities are organized. Students in the academy form a cohort and stay together through their high school years.

- **Tech-prep programs** typically involve structured career-focused programs of two years in high school and two years in a community college. A key element is the close cooperation between community colleges and high schools to develop articulation agreements that specify how high school and postsecondary courses fit together coherently.

- **Internships and cooperative education** provide work experience to students over one semester or a full year. Although students are able to relate some of their work experiences to their schoolwork, the links are often weak, and the experiences rarely provide in-depth education and training toward a career.

While efforts to improve the career focus of high schools are only beginning to take hold, they show considerable promise, especially in reducing the number of disconnected youth.

School-to-Career Approaches and Potentially Disconnected Youth

The benefits of school-supervised employment and, even more important, well-structured school-to-work programs, are of special significance for disconnected students [Lerman 1996]. First, the use of learning in context not only helps students see the relevance of what they are studying, but also helps them gain the self-confidence many of these students lack through their capability to accomplish tasks. Early experimental evidence from New York City's Career Magnet Schools [Crain et al. 1992] indicates that programs that give students a career focus improve their achievement in general subjects, including reading and math. Students in well-structured school-to-career programs report that their classes are more interesting, they have gotten more help planning for college, and they have better relationships with their teachers [Jobs for the Future 1995].

Second, by improving the formal system of placement in training and jobs, STC programs can reduce the disadvantage of poor youth with respect to informal channels to jobs. Inner-city youth lack knowledge of the middle range of jobs and lack access through informal channels. Many firms hire by word of mouth or through other informal channels. As noted above, employers increasingly require credible references, especially for inner-city applicants. Those with the fewest connections to jobs—without a working father, or uncle, or aunt—are at a serious disadvantage in learning about jobs and in gaining the experiences that yield positive, credible references. STC programs offer a formal mechanism in which employers can have confidence and can try out marginal workers. A career-based system can also help inner-city high school students learn more about job and career opportunities in suburbs or other parts of a city. Without this orientation, inner-city youth will become increasingly disadvantaged, as the spatial mismatch between the inner city and the suburban labor markets worsens.

Third, school-employer programs can reduce the negative influence of peers by exposing young people to constructive adult peer groups. The peer pressure to become involved in crime and drugs and to parent children outside marriage can be intense. When the child has only one parent present and he or she is poor, overcoming these influences is extremely difficult. School-to-career programs lead to a natural mentoring process in which the mentor-trainer has a stake in the success of the apprentice not only at the work site but in academic studies as well. Apparently, school-linked employment experiences are more likely to involve these constructive relationships than other jobs and certainly more than relating exclusively to other students.

Fourth, by starting early, STC programs help inner-city youth before they experience serious trouble. Given their poverty, few disadvantaged young people are willing to accept long delays for uncertain returns that might come several years into the future. Moreover, the wait could prove disastrous for those that might otherwise become involved in crime or unwed teenage parenthood.

Fifth, intensive STC programs give employers the chance to watch young people as they learn critical skills. The young disconnected or minority worker has a chance to demonstrate his or her individual strengths during a probationary period after which employers can make their long-term hiring decision. In the absence of this tryout period, minorities and disadvantaged youth generally suffer most from stereotypes held by employers who expect a lack of motivation and basic skills. Unlike other programs for disconnected youth, STC programs are broad based and intended to encompass a wide segment of students.

Finally, improved outcomes for the broader group, including average students, are important. Unless the job and career prospects improve for the typical students who complete high school and do not go on to college, it will be exceedingly difficult to improve the careers of potential dropouts or persuade them that it is worthwhile to study hard and resist temptations to complete high school.

Early indications are that school-to-work programs motivate students and reduce the mismatch between what schools do and what employers demand. They are helping young people gain recognized work experience, specific as well as general skills, and access to supervisors who could provide credible references. In addition, such programs are teaching the informal skills required to succeed on the job, including the discipline and demeanor employers demand. They are providing informal mentors at the work sites. They are exposing young people to the technologies in actual operation, as opposed to the often obsolete equipment found in schools. They are broadening the interests of young people and making them more aware of a wide range of careers. Moreover, they seem to be stimulating students to do better in school and to increase their chances of entering a postsecondary education program.

A number of high school academy programs provide compelling stories of reorienting young people, even in difficult communities. Oakland Technical High School in California, for example, which serves a largely disconnected population, developed a Health Academy Program and has apparently been able to increase the motivation and career success of many young people entering the program. The Finance Academy Program in Baltimore, operating in an inner-city school with mostly low-income students, has managed to develop standards and a high status program. The program has entry requirements, a dress code one day a week, four days of job shadowing, and a summer internship with an insurance company, bank, or other financial institution. Despite their modest supplements to the standard high school education, these programs have already created such an appeal that more students apply than can be served, and many students increase their efforts while in the 9th and 10th grades to have a chance to enter the programs. One unfortunate aspect of the Baltimore program is that relatively rigid high school graduation requirements set by the state of Maryland appear to limit the ability of students to take advantage of work-based learning opportunities employers would offer during the school year. Here is a case in which standards set from above may be undermining student success.

Even more elaborate and extensive programs have begun to operate in Wisconsin through its youth apprenticeship programs. The state has established well-developed curricula for school-based and employer-based education in occupations ranging from finance to printing, from biotechnology to auto technology. Already, more than 1,500 students have begun their apprenticeship sequence. The programs are all oversubscribed.

Other leading school-to-career systems are operating in several cities, especially in Austin, TX; Boston, MA; Louisville, KY; Milwaukee, WI; and Philadelphia, PA. Many offer work-site learning integrated with a strong academic curriculum in several industries. In Louisville, more than 7,000 students are currently pursuing integrated academic and technical studies in the 14 magnet career academies. Each academy is structured to provide students with the breadth and depth of knowledge required for both postsecondary learning and employment. In Milwaukee, students are engaged in community- or work-based learning experiences. Students are expected to spend at least 25% percent of their time engaged in projects that are multidisciplinary, directly connect academic skills and work, and lead to complex learning and problem solving. Philadelphia's small learning communities (SLCs) generally operate as part of the Philadelphia High School Academies system. This school-within-a-school approach to education reform enrolls students beginning in the ninth and tenth grade and provides them with an integrated curriculum and a range of career exploration opportunities, including paid work experience during school and possibly a job upon graduation.

In emphasizing STC programs as an important element in helping disconnected as well as mainstream youth, I do not mean to say that the education and skill development are not essential in the early grades. But even the other approaches recommended by the U.S. Department of Education monograph for disconnected students seem to build on the same concepts present in the STC approach. Among them are curriculum changes that emphasize

- "real-world experiences to attract student interest" and "integration of academic and vocational skills so that students are well-prepared for both college and the job market"

- assessments based on the recognition of student accomplishments and demonstrated mastery of various tasks; use of smaller academic units within large schools, or "schools-within-schools"

- team teaching

- nonstigmatizing youth programs involving mentoring and skill development

- again, connections to work and college through school-to-work apprenticeship programs and university outreach

A final set of gaps between schools and employers is in the use of technology and materials. Since disconnected students are much less likely to have personal computers at home, they may need more school-based or work-based outlets to become adept at using the computer. Even more basic is the use of textbooks. Unfortunately, in some inner-city schools, students are not allowed to take their textbooks home. Fear of theft is understandable, but the result is to deprive students of the chance to learn and to demonstrate their foundation skills in such areas as honesty and managing materials.

Making the New Models a Reality

The underlying goals embedded in the School-to-Work Opportunities Act are to expand beyond existing school-employer links, to move beyond traditional vocational education and cooperative education toward a school-to-career concept. At this point, we have a long way to go.

A large number of purely school-based improvements could prove effective. The expanding private and public sector efforts to move the skills identified in the SCANS report into the mainstream of teaching practice is a hopeful development. Such an effort could prove particularly beneficial to at-risk youth and should be promoted. Other approaches to improving basic skills are critical and, according to the modest but real gains in National Assessment for Educational Progress scores, are beginning to pay off.

Yet, without a fundamental change in the underlying incentives and peer influences students face, the improvement in basic skills is likely to be inadequate to the task of expanding job options for at-risk youth. The high school years are a critical time in which at-risk youth can either succumb to negative peer pressure or move constructively into adulthood. Expanding education about and experience with careers, linking schools with career options, and developing serious work-based learning programs are all vital components of an concerted effort to give hope to at-risk students. Such experiences will help them see directly how working hard in school, developing good work habits and personal skills, mastering fundamental competencies and at least some specific skill, and resisting negative peer pressure will pay off.

The modest demonstration efforts in these directions are promising. But leadership at all levels is required to ensure that the school-to-career movement induces substantial employer participation and does not simply become another ineffective school reform.

References

Anderson, E. (1991). Neighborhood effects on teenage pregnancy. In C. Jencks and P. E. Peterson (Eds.), *The urban underclass* (pp. 375-398). Washington, DC: Brookings Institution.

Anderson, E. (1994, May). The code of the streets. *Atlantic Monthly*, 80-94.

Besharov, D. (Ed.). (1999). *America's disconnected youth: Toward a preventative strategy.* Washington, DC: CWLA Press and The American Enterprise Institute on Public Policy Research.

Bishop, J. (1995). *Expertise and excellence.* Working Paper 95-13. New York: Center for Advanced Human Resource Studies. New York State School of Industrial and Labor Relations, Cornell University.

Bishop. John. (1989, January-February). Why the apathy in American high schools? *Educational Researcher, 18,* 6-10

Bound, J., & Freeman, R. (1992, February). What went wrong? The erosion of relative earnings and employment among young Black men in the 1980s. *Quarterly Journal of Economics, 107,* 201-232.

Chaplin, D., & Hannaway, J. (1995). *High school employment: Meaningful connections for at-risk youth.* Presented at the annual meeting of the Association for Public Policy Analysis and Management, November 1995.

Crain, R., Heebner, A., & Si, Y.-P. (1992, April). *The effectiveness of New York City's career magnet schools: An evaluation of ninth grade performance using an experimental design.* Berkeley, CA: National Center for Research in Vocational Education.

The Economist. (1996, April 6). What works?

Freeman, R. (1996, Winter). Why do so many young American men commit crimes and what might we do about it? *Journal of Economic Perspectives,* 25-42.

Holzer, H. (1992). *Youth and the labor market of the nineties, in dilemmas in youth employment programming: Findings from the Youth Research and Technical Assistance Project.* Washington, DC: Employment and Training Administration, U.S. Department of Labor, 1992.

Holzer, H. (1996). *What employers want: Job prospects for less educated workers.* New York: The Russell Sage Foundation.

Immerwahr, J., & Johnson, J. (1996). Americans views on standards. Public agenda. Background materials for the National Education Summit, Palisades, New York.

Jobs for the Future. (1995). *Promising practices. A study of ten school-to-career programs.* Cambridge, MA: Author.

Kasinitz, P. (1993, November 26). The real jobs problem. *The Wall Street Journal,* A8.

Klerman, J., & Karoly, L. (1994, August). Young men and the transition to stable employment. *Monthly Labor Review,* 31-48.

Lerman, R. (1996). Building hope, skills, and careers: Making a US youth apprenticeship system. In I. Garfinkel, J. Hochschild, & S. McLanahan (Eds.), *Social policies for children* (pp. 136-172). Washington, DC: The Brookings Institution.

Lynn, I., & Wills, J. (1994). *School lessons, work lessons: Recruiting and sustaining employer involvement in school-to-work programs.* Philadelphia: National Center on the Educational Quality of the Workforce, University of Pennsylvania.

Mullis, I., Dossey, J., Owen, E., & Phillips, G. (1993, April). NAEP 1992: *Mathematics report card for the nation and the states.* Washington, DC: Office of Educational Research and Improvement, U.S. Department of Education.

Ogbu, J. (1990, Spring). Minority status and literacy. *Daedalus*, 141-168.

Packer, A., & Wirt, J. (1992). Changing skills in the U.S. workforce: Trends of supply and demand. In G. Peterson & W. Vroman (Eds.), *Urban labor markets and job opportunity* (pp. 31-65). Washington, DC: The Urban Institute Press.

Rossi, R., & Montgomery, A. (Eds.) (1994). *Educational reforms and students at risk: A review of the current state of the art.* Washington, DC: U.S. Department of Education.

Stern, D. (1990, December). Quality of students work experience and orientation toward work. *Youth and Society*, 263-282.

Stern, D., & McMillion, M., Hopkins, C., & Stone, J. (1990, March). Work experience for students in high school and college. *Youth and Society*, 355-389.

U.S. Bureau of Labor Statistics. (1997). *Employment and earnings: January 1997.* Washington, DC: U.S. Government Printing Office.

U.S. Department of Education. (no date). Student engagement. Available on-line at http://www.ed.gov/pubs/edreformstudies/edreforms/chap5b.htm.

U.S. Department of Education. (1995). *Digest of educational statistics.* Washington, DC: Author.

U. S. Department of Labor. (1991). *Secretary's commission on achieving necessary skills: What work requires of schools. A SCANS Report for America 2000.* Washington, DC: Author

Wilson, W. J. (1987). *The truly disadvantaged.* Chicago: University of Chicago Press.

Zemsky, R. (1994). *What employers want: Employer perspectives on youth, the youth labor market, and prospects for a national system of youth apprenticeship.* Philadelphia: National Center on the Educational Quality of the Workforce, University of Pennsylvania.

8. Focus High Schools

Paul T. Hill

Today's public high schools can be described in many ways: as shopping malls that try to cater to the diverse tastes of jaded customers, as playgrounds, and as advanced forms of day care that allow adolescents to get older without doing undue harm to themselves and to others. They can also be seen as places where young people get their last chances to learn modern survival skills—literacy, some mathematics, and some understanding of technology—on a full-time basis before becoming parents or working to support themselves. High schools are, for good or ill, all these things, but they must be much more. High schools must be links between young people and the institutions of adult life—the labor market, particular employers, higher education, the military (in some cases), cultural institutions, churches, political parties and representative institutions, and local government.

Though many high schools still perform this critical linking function, others no longer do. Suburban and middle-class high schools still connect students to an even more powerful linking institution, the college or university. Urban high schools serving the poor, however, are much less successful in connecting students to the institutions of adult life. This is attributable to several causes, not least of which is the difficulty of the task. Compared with high schools in which virtually all students will attend four-year colleges, high schools serving non-college-bound students must prepare students for a more diverse set of futures. Typically they also serve many students with poor academic preparation, who are burdened by poverty and turbulent family and neighborhood circumstances.

In the past three decades, the horizons of urban high schools have narrowed. In response to concerns about students' weak preparation in basic skills, they have created remedial reading and arithmetic programs. In response to rights mandates and federal categorical programs, they have created special education programs that treat as many as one-quarter of their students as handicapped. In response to diminishing student interest and increasing chaos in inner-city families and neighborhoods, many have emphasized the therapeutic content of students' experience and made the schools centers for the delivery of social services. The new emphases come at the expense of other goods—in particular, the teaching of more challenging (and interesting) subjects and skills that normally serve as marks of adult competence in our society. Such skills include, for example, the abilities to take in and use new information, to adapt one's work to changing needs, to contribute time and effort to voluntary organizations, to follow public affairs, and to find competent help when necessary.

These changes in the priorities of urban high schools are understandable, especially for the majority of teachers and principals, whose job satisfactions come as much from engagement with children as from scholarship and the teaching of subject matter. And nobody can say that students can do without basic skills or that their needs for food, shelter, safety, and consolation should be ignored. But the new priorities elbow out the essential functions of high school—namely, the creation of adult levels of knowledge and capacity for analysis, judgment, and self-management, and the ability to deal effectively with adult economic, social, and political institutions.

Are the challenges of modern urban life too much for high schools to manage? Or can high schools do a better job of serving as the students' link to the institutions of adult life? This chapter argues the latter—that high schools can be much more effective, especially for the low-income urban youths whom they now serve least well. The argument is based on my own work on effective urban high schools, much of which is reported in *High Schools with Character* [Hill et al.

1990]. That study compared three kinds of inner-city high schools: comprehensive neighborhood schools that serve all comers and offer highly diverse programs to meet a variety of needs, special-purpose public schools (including schools that prepared students to work in specific labor markets or industries), and inner-city parochial high schools. The study identified school features that motivate low-income children to work and learn, and suggested how these features can be made more broadly available to urban public high school students.

The Study

We studied 13 schools, all located in East Coast, inner-city neighborhoods and serving seriously disadvantaged African American and Puerto Rican youths. All the schools, including the ones operated by Catholic parishes, served large numbers of students from one-parent homes, living on welfare or below the official poverty thresholds. The New York City Student-Sponsor Partnership Program, the largest program we studied, pays tuition for New York City students in inner-city Catholic high schools. Partnership students are 60% African American and 40% Puerto Rican. Two-thirds of their families are on welfare, and only 10% live with two parents. Partnership students are poorer and more heavily minority than are New York City high school students on average, and their rates of welfare dependency are about average for students in the public high schools serving the lowest-income students.

The program expressly seeks out students who are struggling in public schools, or who face other serious challenges, such as the lack of a fixed address. Before entering the program, students must be attending public junior high or middle schools. The vast majority of students selected are those achieving at or below the average performance level for the poverty-area junior high schools they attend.

The eight schools studied most intensively were in New York City. Three were Catholic high schools with large numbers of Partnership students, two were regular neighborhood comprehensive public high schools, and two were public schools that provided specially focused vocational or academic programs for a cross section of New York City students. Finally, one was a special school designed for students who had failed in regular high schools and were assigned there for a "last chance" at education.

Results

The study's main finding is that a demanding high school, that is, a school that teaches academic subjects in the context of a curriculum designed to prepare students to work in a particular industry (such as health), can motivate and focus students and faculty alike. The direct result is that students are more likely to attend school consistently, master core subjects, graduate, and be prepared for college work. A school with a definite and well-understood purpose can teach things that standard comprehensive high schools cannot. There are three reasons for this.

- First, because it is focused on the application of knowledge, such a school teaches that subjects such as science, mathematics, and language have uses and must in fact be used together in real life.

- Second, because it intends to give students an understanding of the world in which they will live and work, such a school remains engaged in a broader community, not isolated as an ivory tower institution.

- Third, because it requires teamwork and mutual support among teachers of different subjects, such a school shows how members of effective adult organizations must cooperate and be accountable to one another.

Table 8-1 compares outcomes for 1989-1990 seniors in the three groups of schools that we studied.

As the table shows, students in the Catholic and special purpose public schools graduate at a much higher rate than do students in the neighborhood comprehensive schools. The vast majority of graduating seniors in the first two groups of schools take the Scholastic Aptitude

Table 8-1. Comparative SAT Scores of Graduating Seniors in New York City Neighborhood Comprehensive, Special Purpose, and Catholic Schools (1990)

Schools	Percentage Graduating	Percentage Taking SAT	Average Combined SAT Score	Percentage Above Mean for Blacks
Neighborhood Comprehensive	55	33	642	<30
Special-Public	66	>50	715	>40
Catholic - Partnership program students	82	85	803	>60
- All students	95	85	815	>60

Note: The data do not include seniors in special-purpose public schools for students who had failed in neighborhood comprehensive schools. The excluded students tend to be older and more troubled than the average neighborhood comprehensive-school students and to come from lower income environments. They graduate at near the average rate for neighborhood comprehensive school students, but are unlikely to aspire to four-year college.

Source: *High Schools with Character* [Hill et al. 1990].

Test (SAT), which is required for entry into selective colleges or universities. Though some of the special purpose public schools prepared students for jobs, most graduates were qualified and motivated to go on to four-year colleges. In contrast, fewer than one-third of the graduating seniors in neighborhood comprehensive schools take the SAT. The SAT scores differ profoundly. The scores of the neighborhood comprehensive school students fall far below national and focus school averages. Based on the mean scores and distributions provided by the New York City Board of Education, we calculated that only 4% of SAT takers in the neighborhood comprehensive schools had scores above the national average.

Test scores of students from special-purpose public schools approached the national mean for African American students, and Catholic school Partnership students comfortably exceeded it. Partnership program students in the Catholic schools, many of whom entered below grade level, scored nearly as well as their tuition-paying Catholic school classmates. Differences in family characteristics and student motivation may explain some of these performance differences. But the conclusion is inescapable: Outcomes for disadvantaged students in focus schools exceeded those for the same students in neighborhood comprehensive schools.

Consistent with the student achievement results, we found more important similarities than differences among Catholic and special-purpose public schools, and we saw dramatic differences between these schools and the neighborhood comprehensive schools. For the purposes of analysis we combined Catholic and special-purpose public schools into a single category, which we called *focus* schools, and compared them with neighborhood comprehensive public schools.

The essential feature of a focus school is a positive commitment on the part of everyone concerned to influence and change students so they can be prepared for responsible adult roles. Focus schools have clear and explicit missions, defined in terms both of the kinds of values and abilities graduates are expected to possess, and of the ways in which the school intends to help students gain those attributes. Nonfocus schools, including most of the neighborhood comprehensive schools that serve urban youth, have diffuse missions, defined in terms of processes rather than student outcomes.[1]

As organizations created to deliver programs and fulfill mandates, nonfocus schools are vague and diffident about their goals for graduates. Because they are preoccupied with the process of instruction, most see themselves as specialized institutions that neither depend on nor contribute to the missions of churches, businesses, the broader local government, or political interest groups. If such organizations will contribute money, the school is glad to take it. But the school resists any form of contact that might be construed as taking direction from these other institutions.

Focus schools, however, regard formal academic instruction as one of a variety of methods by which they prepare students for adult life. Compared with regular public comprehensive schools, focus schools are more likely to require students to perform public service, attend city council or other government meetings, study local businesses and the structure of the local economy, and debate controversial issues. Focus schools intend to help students understand key institutions and to be able to cope with them successfully. Focus schools' orientations differ from one another: some have ideological or political biases— mostly concerning the role of business in society and public responsibility for the poor—that they try to pass on to students. Though they embody different assumptions about society and students' eventual place in it, they are also committed to making students competent and effective adults in the broadest sense.

Many factors can give focus to a school: a specific theory of education, as exemplified by Montessori, Sizer, Paidea, or various Catholic religious orders; a broader theory of society, as exemplified by the Afrocentric curriculum and some forms of progressive education; or a commitment to prepare students to work in well-defined professions or industries. An effective school can be built around any of these focuses, because all of them set clear goals for graduates, establish the need for serious collaboration among staff and students, establish a mission for the school, and mold students as well as instruct them.

Though some forms of focus schooling are hard to build in the public sector, others are not. Secular theories like that of Sizer [1984, 1992] do not establish religion, and as long as they are not the only model offered, they do not unduly constrain students' or parents' options. Industry-focused schools are workable and highly desirable in public school systems, because they can promote economic growth while motivating and leading students.

Focus schools resemble one another, and differ from neighborhood comprehensive public schools, in two basic ways. First, a focus school has a clear, uncomplicated mission centered on the attributes it hopes to instill in students to prepare them to function in adult society. The Catholic schools have missions derived from their vision of the responsibilities and accomplishments of an intelligent Christian adult. The special-purpose public schools have similarly compelling visions of the graduates they hope to turn out. Some strive to produce artists, scientists, and engineers, or adults with finely developed habits of creative thinking and criticism. Schools focused in preparing students for government service or health seek to create productive employees capable of taking full advantage of the career opportunities available in their industry.

The second way in which focus schools resemble one another and differ from neighborhood comprehensive schools is that focus schools are strong organizations with the capacity to initiate action in pursuit of their missions, to sustain themselves over time, to solve their own problems, and to manage their external relationships. Neighborhood comprehensive schools are weak and dependent organizations, whose missions are rendered ambiguous by the compromises worked out in the course of legislative politics and whose capacity to solve problems is constrained by regulations, contracts, and inflexible staffing patterns.

Focus schools need not all be alike. One focus school can prepare students for elite universities while another seeks to help students enter a trade or industry. Career-oriented focus schools can also differ, some preparing students for highly technical or artistic careers and others educating for simpler service occupations. Schools can also tailor their instructional methods to the interests and learning styles of the students that attend them: Some can be designed for the abstract learners who usually profit from classics-oriented instruction, and others for students who learn "hands on" or through problemsolving. Focus schools need not be unique or radically innovative; they need not all use the most up-to-date, "constructivist" pedagogies. Their organizational independence means, however, that students and staff in each focus school consider their school special, a creation that reflects their efforts and meets their needs.

Neighborhood comprehensive schools, in contrast, have diffuse missions defined by the demands of external funders and regulators. They are also profoundly compromised organizations, with little capacity to initiate their own solutions to problems, define their internal character, or manage their relationships with external audiences. Because neighborhood comprehensive schools are essentially products of decisions made elsewhere, staff and students have little reason to consider the schools uniquely their own.

The broad categories of mission and organizational strength include other, more specific features that both distinguish focus schools from neighborhood comprehensive schools and explain the focus schools' capacity to lead and motivate students. Under the category of school mission, the critical differences include the following:

- **Focus schools concentrate on student outcomes before all other matters.** Those outcomes are, further, meaningful in the real world, stated in terms of graduates' ability to succeed in adult studies and occupations, not simply in terms of course completion or test scores. Focus schools expect their best graduates to compete with the best students anywhere. But they also expect their average and below-average students to learn basic skills, mathematics, laboratory science, and literature, and to be capable of reflection and debate. Though neighborhood public schools can also have high aspirations, their day-to-day concerns center on delivering programs and following procedures.

- **Focus schools have strong social contracts that communicate the reciprocal responsibilities of administration, students, and teachers and establish the benefits that each derives from fulfilling the contract faithfully.** The contracts differ depending on the schools' goals, but they all make clear what opportunities the school promises to provide, what work and achievement is required of students, and what the student will be able to accomplish as an ultimate result. The focus school takes responsibility for the actions of staff and students alike, working to ensure that student and faculty peer cultures support the school's mission. Neighborhood comprehensive schools also try to give students valuable opportunities, but they do so diffidently, leaving it up to students to define personal goals and find the connection between school work and their future opportunities. The faculty is obligated to provide instruction and students are obligated to receive it. The neighborhood comprehensive school considers the student and faculty peer cultures to be noninstructional phenomena, rather than intrinsic parts of its educational strategy.

- **Focus schools aggressively mold student attitudes and values.** They regard students as children who should be led and influenced, and faculty as adults who should lead and set examples as well as instruct. Because their social contracts make them collaborative enterprises, focus schools must live by the secular ethics of reciprocity, reliability, fairness, and respect for others. Catholic schools base their ethical teaching on religion, while special-purpose public schools base theirs on the practical requirements of work in a productive organization. Both kinds of focus schools teach these ethics by demonstrating them in everyday life, not just by designating them as the subject matter of didactic courses. In contrast, neighborhood comprehensive schools see themselves primarily as transmitters of information and imparters of skills. They do not think it appropriate to impose on students' values and preferences: Ethics is a subject of study, not a set of principles that can be learned by the experience of being in the school.

- **Focus schools have centripetal curricula that draw all students toward learning certain core skills and perspectives.** The school's dedication to preparing students for a certain kind of adult life means the school must work to ensure that all students master core subject matter; students cannot be left behind because the teacher does not have time to explain a key point, and no student may be relegated permanently to basic-skills workbooks. Students who enter with basic-skill deficits are given special instruction and required to study nights, summers, and weekends in order to catch up. But they are all ultimately exposed to the curriculum that the school defines as essential for all its graduates. In contrast, neighborhood comprehensive schools distinguish among students in terms of ability and preference. They offer profoundly different curricula to different groups. Many students who would be drawn toward the core curriculum in a focus school spend their entire high school careers in comprehensive school remedial programs.

Under the broad category of organizational strength and resiliency, the critical differences include the following:

- **Focus schools operate as problem-solving organizations, taking the initiative to change their programs in response to emerging needs.** If graduates are not measuring up to the school's standards, or if the needs of external clienteles such as employers or college admissions officers change, school leaders know they must change their own methods. In contrast, comprehensive neighborhood schools are powerfully constrained by external mandates and rigid internal divisions of labor. Course offerings are difficult to change because state and local curriculum mandates and teacher contracts limit the extent to which instructional offerings can change. School leaders, lacking the freedom to solve problems, often perceive themselves as not responsible for the results.

- **Focus schools protect and sustain their distinctive character, both by hiring staff members who accept the school's premises and by socializing new staff members.** Focus schools draw from the same pool of teachers who staff the neighborhood comprehensive schools, and they cannot always get the very best. But their clear missions and public images help discourage uncooperative staff members from applying and provide a definite basis for selecting and influencing new teachers and administrators. Neighborhood comprehensive schools have no grounds, other than training and experience, to choose among applicants, and no well-defined basis on which to influence the attitudes or behavior of new staff members.

- **Focus schools consider themselves accountable to the people who depend on their performance**—parents, students, neighborhood and parish groups, and, in the case of schools preparing students to work in a particular industry, employers who hope to find productive employees among the school's graduates. Regular neighborhood public schools answer primarily to bureaucratic superiors: outside rule-making, auditing, and assessment organizations.

These different models of schooling can have sharply different effects on student motivation and learning. Focus schools intend to influence and change students, and they do so. Though differences in student ability and motivation remain, student outcomes are much more uniform and positive in focus schools than in neighborhood comprehensive schools. In special-purpose public schools, as in the Catholic schools studied by Coleman, Hoffer, and Kilgore [1982], the influences of students' race and income on achievement are attenuated. Disadvantaged students particularly benefit from the strong pressure and linkage to adult outcomes that focus schools provide.

Replicating Focus Schools

From our observations of school operations and extensive interviews with students, administrators, and teachers in all the schools, we concluded that the key features of focus schools can be reproduced broadly in public schools. Based on the research, my collaborators and I also think that the vast majority of public school teachers can work effectively in such schools and that students, including those who are disaffected from existing public schools, can profit from them. Our reasons for thinking this include the following:

- **The neighborhood comprehensive school model has lost its support.** Such schools are based on decades of interest group negotiation and mandated responses to particular problems. The schools are so encrusted with rules and procedures that no one in them can work to his or her full potential. Virtually all of the comprehensive school teachers and administrators we interviewed said they could not work effectively in their current situations and expressed preferences for simpler and more collegial environments.

- **Near universal dissatisfaction with neighborhood comprehensive schools** predisposes administrators, teachers, students, and the broader community in favor of dramatic changes.

- **Most public school teachers and administrators say they would prefer to have the freedom and responsibility to solve problems that focus schools have**. Though some public school staff members may be reluctant to take on the additional work and responsibility imposed by a focus school situation, most say they would rather bear the additional burdens than continue to work in schools that are internally divided and ineffective.

Students in neighborhood comprehensive schools are even clearer about their desire for structured, integrated, and demanding environments. The interviews show that

- The vast majority of students now in neighborhood comprehensive public high schools would prefer to live under a strong social contract and to be led and guided by adults whom they trust.

- Students who pose the worst behavior problems in regular neighborhood schools are often the most responsive to the expectations of trustworthy adults. Most, though not all, of these students "turn around" when placed in a focus school environment that both encourages effort and self-discipline and screens out contrary pressures.

- Most inner-city minority students would be willing to take more demanding courses in high school language, history, and mathematics if they thought they could count on help from teachers and if the social climate of the school made it seem like a normal activity.

Focus schools may not work for all students. Some students who refuse to attend any school or to accept any responsibility for study and work are beyond any school's help. But from all evidence these numbers are small, and the number of now-unmotivated students who would respond well to a demanding and productive school environment is much larger.

Some focus schools already exist in public school systems. Most large city and suburban school systems have at least one school that, by virtue of its special mission or magnet status, is free from the prevailing norms of uniformity, has a definite capacity to influence students and faculty, and can solve problems and account for its own performance. Reform efforts like the Annenberg Challenge and the New American Schools Development Corporation are intended to help large districts increase their numbers of focus schools. The charter school movement, which increases school autonomy in return for accountability for results, is also intended to increase the numbers of schools that can pursue clearly defined missions and recruit students and teachers on the basis of their commitment to particular approaches to learning.

Some local school systems are also pursuing site-based management and shared decisionmaking among staff and parents. These efforts create some necessary-but-not-sufficient conditions for focus schooling. Focus schools are site managed, but with a difference. Most site-management schemes transfer the politics of interest-group bargaining from the school district to the school building.[2] A focus school, in contrast, is built around specific educational and ethical principles, not around accommodating the interests of all parties.

Because existing neighborhood comprehensive schools are designed to be fragmented, strong agreements on principle are unlikely to emerge within them. Focus schools are best developed from the ground up, around a small core of committed individuals, not by superimposing procedural templates on existing neighborhood comprehensive schools. The effort to create a focus school should start with a commitment to build a certain kind of school—a school intended to produce artists, scientists, civic activists, environmentalists, candidates for admission to elite liberal arts colleges, or competent entrants to industries with good jobs to offer, such as health, government services, and data processing. Making these commitments is the job of the superintendent and school board, who can move toward a system of focus schools by deciding to create a varied portfolio of schools, each of which has its own purpose and character.[3]

Nonfocus schools can seldom be transformed wholesale into focus schools,[4] but a group of administrators and teachers assembled expressly for the purpose of creating a focus school can often do so within one or two years. Some *a priori* demonstration of good faith from the principal and lead teachers, establishing the intention to create a focus school of known character and to cooperate with one another in doing so, is required.

Students and staff members must also be able to sort themselves among schools. No school can gain or keep a focus if individuals are kept on who have no intention to cooperate in the joint effort that focus schooling requires. In itself, choice does not create focus schools— some school systems have declared open enrollment without making any effort to create a supply of desirable alternative schools. But choice is an indispensable part of a focus-based educational reform.

Though most focus schools should aim to serve a cross section of students, some schools should target students with special talents or students who have failed in other settings. But most focus schools need not and should not succeed simply by handpicking the ablest students. The strength of focus schooling is that it can motivate and mold students. Most focus schools should admit a cross section of students, requiring only that all students agree in advance to respect the school's mission and do the required work.

A period of organizational trial and error is essential. No current focus school sprang into existence fully formed, and even the best ones have developed over time through trial and error. Focus schools must be built one by one, not mass-produced as identical versions of a fixed model.

Implications for Youth Connectedness

As the foregoing implies, preparation for adult life is the basic mission of all focus schools. The adult activity for which students are being prepared provides external validation for the school's programs and its demands on students. This is true whether a school prepares students for higher education, eventual entry into the professions, for work in particular industries, or for competent navigation of a local labor market. In a school focused on preparing students to work in a particular industry or labor market, students can see the jobs for which they are preparing and can understand the real payoff for diligent work. Faculty and staff can use the demands of the future work environment as criteria for setting priorities among curriculum offerings and can understand the levels of skill proficiency that students need to attain. Students can see that knowledge is used differently in work than it is taught in school—that important problems often require simultaneous application of logical, linguistic, and mathematical skills. Finally, the industry or labor market's requirements for interpersonal behavior give the school a definite warrant for upholding and teaching ethical standards such as honesty, reliability, and reciprocity.

Industry- or labor market-based schools are certainly not more focused than college preparatory schools or schools designed to preserve a distinctive culture, such as Judaism or Catholicism. But they can be as motivating for students and as productive educationally. They are also much more likely to mold and motivate students than are regular comprehensive high schools or "shopping mall" vocational schools.

The distinction between a school designed to prepare students for an industry or labor market and a multipurpose vocational school is important. The latter schools can provide excellent instruction, but they often provide coursework related to a wide variety of occupations, as diverse as automotive repair, computer maintenance, landscaping, carpentry, and secretarial work. Students may be preparing for a wide variety of industries; furthermore, most are assigned to the school only part-time while they complete academic courses in their neighborhood comprehensive school. Such schools are too atomized to provide a focus school experience, and they cannot readily use a single industry as a validator of their programs and demands.

In contrast, a school related to a particular industry can give students a definite set of goals, standards, and role models. It can also more readily help students understand how the occupations in an industry complement one another, and how a person working in one component occupation can prepare herself to move into a more lucrative or satisfying one. For disadvantaged urban students, who frequently do not fully understand what it means to work in a complex organization, such schools can provide more than just a start: They can help students learn that people work interdependently, that relatively lowly jobs can be important, and that an aggressive and skillful worker need not stay stuck at the entry level.

Focus schools differ in their instructional tactics and specific goals for students. But they are all alike in two ways. First, they intend to help a student develop as a whole person, intellectually, socially, and morally. Second, they intend to connect a student with the adult world, and to help him or her understand the broader society in order to act competently in his or her own interest. In an uncertain world, some focus schools might train students for jobs or industries that might disappear before students are able to enter them. Focus schools also typically offer a narrower range of electives than do neighborhood comprehensive schools. But focus school students learn the basics deeply, and they expect to continue learning on their own. Because they prepare young people to be effective agents, not dependent victims of circumstance, focus schools still offer benefits that many regular neighborhood public schools cannot match.

References

Bimber, B. (1994). *The decentralization mirage.* Santa Monica, CA: RAND.

Bryk, A. S., Lee, V. E., & Holland, P. (1993). *Catholic schools and the common good.* Cambridge, MA: Harvard University Press.

Coleman, J. S., Hoffer, T., & Kilgore, S. (1982). *High school achievement, public, private, and Catholic schools compared.* New York: Basic Books.

Hill, P. T. (1995). Private vouchers in New York City: The student-sponsor partnership program. In T. M. Moe (Ed.), *Private vouchers* (pp. 120-135). Stanford, CA: Hoover Institution Press.

Hill, P. T., & Bonan, J. (1992). *Decentralization and accountability in public education.* Santa Monica, CA: RAND.

Hill, P. T., Foster, G. E., & Gendler, T. (1990). *High schools with character.* Santa Monica, CA: RAND.

Hill, P. T., Pierce, L., & Guthrie, J. W. (1997). *Reinventing public education: How contracting can improve American education.* Chicago: University of Chicago Press.

Lee, V. E., & Smith, J. B. (1993, July). Effects of school restructuring on the achievement and engagement of middle-grade students. *Sociology of Education,* 164-187.

Lee, V. E., & Smith, J. B. (1994). *High school restructuring and student achievement: A new study finds strong links.* Madison WI: Center on Organization and Restructuring of Schools.

Lee, V. E., & Smith, J. B. (1995, October). Effects of high school restructuring and size on early gains in achievement and engagement. *Sociology of Education,* 241-270.

Lee, V. E, & Smith, J. B. (1996, February). Collective responsibility for learning and its effects on gains in achievement for early secondary school students. *American Journal of Education,* 103-147.

Lee, V. E. (1995). *Another look at high school restructuring: More evidence that it improves student achievement and more insight into why.* Madison WI: Center on Organization and Restructuring of Schools.

Meier, D. (1995, July). Small schools, big results. *American School Board Journal,* 37-40.

Muncey, D. E., & McQuillan, P. J. (1996). *Reform and resistance in schools and classrooms: An ethnographic view of the coalition of essential schools.* New Haven, CT: Yale University Press.

Newmann F. M., & Wehlage, G. G. (1996). *Successful school restructuring.* Madison, WI: Center on Organization and Restructuring of Schools.

Sizer, T. R. (1984). *Horace's compromise: The dilemma of the American high school.* Boston: Houghton Mifflin Co.

Sizer, T. R. (1992). *Horace's school: Redesigning the American high school.* Boston: Houghton Mifflin Co.

Notes

1   For complementary findings see Coleman, Hoffer, and Kilgore [1982]; Bryk, Lee, and Holland [1993]; Hill [1995]; Newmann and Wehlage [1996]; and Lee and Smith, [1993, 1994, 1995, 1996].

2   See, for example, Hill and Bonan [1992] and Bimber [1994].

3   For ideas about how a local public school system can be transformed into a system of strong, focused schools see Hill, Pierce, and Guthrie [1997].

4   For a vivid discussion of the difficulty of transforming existing schools see Muncey and MacQuillan [1996].

9. Extending the Time of Learning

Andrew Hahn

Research has long focused on the failures of urban adolescents. Drop-out rates, crime rates, and unemployment rates are all readily available metrics by which to measure these problems. This necessary knowledge is, by now, well-disseminated in the academic and popular press. Less attention has focused on success. While harder to measure, and certainly less dramatic than failure, the resiliency of inner city adolescents is a relatively new and extremely important focus in the fields of youth and community development research. The more we know about what enables young people to defy difficult odds and develop into healthy and productive young adults, the more we can do to design strategies that enhance and support healthy youth development opportunities in our most undercapitalized urban neighborhood environments.

Why do certain children rise above tremendous odds and graduate from high school, delay parenting, stay out of trouble, and go to college or begin meaningful career-oriented employment while others cannot escape the poverty into which they were born? The literature on resilient adolescents suggests several factors to consider. While many characteristics may be innate, others are learned. These include internal loci of control, high achievement orientations, positive self concepts, and high degrees of social maturity [Werner 1990; Wang & Gordon 1994; Reed-Victor & Strong 1997].

Can youth programs be designed to enhance these learned characteristics? Will such programs work effectively? How can program structures contribute or bring out the resiliency of urban minority disadvantaged youth? This chapter explores some of these questions based on the operation of a pilot project tried in four cities between 1989 and 1993, the Quantum Opportunity Program (QOP).

Individuals come into contact with circumstances and choices that may serve either to foster or to compromise the learned traits such as self-esteem and high achievement. In the scholarly literature, these are referred to as protective factors and risk factors. Much recent literature on resiliency makes clear that schools alone can not effectively ensure optimum access to protective factors and healthy development [Freiberg 1994]. Additionally, the daunting problems that crop up in urban adolescent development rarely can be dealt with as isolated needs with narrow or "quick fix" specific interventions. After examining the disappointing results from program evaluations of many short-term, single-service programs, researchers have noted that effective programs must be comprehensive in scope and intensive in delivery [Barton et al. 1997]. Curiously, this recommendation is based more on the failure of the short-term programs rather than the success of real field-based experiences with comprehensive and long-term programs. QOP with its unique design, as described later, is one of the first studies to evaluate an actual long-term program offering children a variety of services.

QOP is special for an additional reason: the role of a caring, consistent adult helper. One key protective factor that has been identified as essential for healthy development is a strong relationship with a caring adult [Masten 1994]. The presence of a caring adult in a youth program that provides comprehensive services over a long period is a remarkable opportunity for study of the effect of changing the out-of-school and out-of-home environment for inner city youth on resiliency outcomes. As an intensive, comprehensive, non-school-based intervention to promote positive development in poor adolescents, the Quantum Opportunities Program used a long-term relationship with a caring adult worker in a community program in an attempt to improve the outcomes for participating low-income youth from welfare backgrounds. In other words, QOP sought to foster resiliency in randomly assigned high-risk teens who participated in the pilot projects.

History of the Program

In the late 1970s and early 1980s, economist Robert Taggart of the Office of Youth Programs, U.S. Department of Labor, administered a research and development effort to identify effective strategies to ameliorate chronic youth unemployment. He began with the assumption, well-supported in the literature, that the learning environments of community-based youth programs should be as dissimilar as possible to the traditional school environments disadvantaged youth fled in the first place [Whalen & Wynn 1995]. He started U.S. Basics—Comprehensive Competencies Program (CCP), a national network of learning laboratories featuring computer-based instruction in basic skills, life skills, and vocational training. The program featured computer-assisted instruction in neighborhood centers run by community groups, including La Raza, the Urban League, Opportunity Industrial Centers of America (OIC), and others.

Working with Benjamin Lattimore of a community-based organization, an affiliate of OIC that specialized in services for urban African American youth, Taggart turned his attention to a new program design. He wanted to add a caring adult who would provide consistent support within the existing CCP-OIC computer instruction-neighborhood center. Thus the Quantum Opportunity Program was designed to be located in OIC neighborhood centers with strong U.S. Basics' CCP learning labs within them.

Gordon Berlin, then a program director at the Ford Foundation, supported the idea of a comprehensive long-term program with a caring adult and the availability of computer-assisted instruction. Robert Curvin, also at Ford, was concerned about the public perception of urban minority males. He was interested in studying the uptake of a comprehensive intervention program. Would at-risk inner city teens take advantage of it? Or would they fear that they would be perceived as "acting white" and selling out their history and peers? With their interest in various aspects of long-term comprehensive programming, these individuals joined forces to design QOP.

Program Design

The Quantum Opportunity Program was a multiservice, four-year, year-round demonstration project funded by the Ford Foundation in five communities: San Antonio, Philadelphia, Milwaukee, Saginaw, and Oklahoma City. Each program was run by an affiliate of Opportunity Industrial Centers of America. It encouraged community, responsibility, opportunity, and investment. The program is described best by two participants, Jacqueline Jones and Cherise Woffel:

> The program was hard. Education was the main thing. QOP helped us further our education, helped us succeed in high school, and plan for college and beyond. We had to think about career goals, family life, and each other. We had homework, computer-assisted instruction, SATs, math tests, tutoring. . . . The program helped us understand the world. It widened our horizons and exposed us to the world outside our own neighborhood. We had to dress properly, and we had constant nagging, motivation, and support from our two mentors.

A typical day in QOP might mean a safe and supervised afterschool place for doing homework, some time on the computers learning important literacy or life skills, perhaps a field trip to a museum, a speaker on health issues, or time spent on a part-time job or community services project. This typical day might also mean telephone calls or home visits by youth workers to check in on youth assigned to QOP but who, for one reason or another, are not participating at that moment. Guardians too might be involved, for example, in an evening program about the importance of summer jobs or college financial aid procedures.

The program was designed to test the ability of the community-based organizations to foster the achievement of academic and social competencies among high school students from families receiving public assistance. The program design called for a multiyear effort starting in ninth grade and continuing through high school. The planners and funders identified six specific demonstration goals:

- to serve disadvantaged youth, such as those from families receiving public assistance

- to test the acceptance rate when a rich set of services is offered

- to learn not only about the dynamics of recruitment and retention but also about the relative impacts of diverse program components, such as education, life skills, and community service

- to assess the capacity of a community-based organization to manage a complex demonstration over several years

- to test a financial incentive structure that rewards youth and program staff for sticking with the programs

- to use the QOP experience to increase the field's basic understanding of the barriers and the pathways for serving poor, primarily minority youth in multiyear programs

The programs were organized around education activities, such as participation in computer-assisted instruction, peer tutoring, and homework assistance; service activities, such as community service projects, helping at public events, and holding regular jobs; and development activities, such as curricula focused on life and family skills, alcohol and drug abuse, arts, and college or job planning.

A financial incentive also was built into the program. Students received small stipends for participating in approved services, as well as bonus payments for completing segments of program activities. They also received matching funds in an accrual account to be used for an approved activity in the post–high school period, such as college or training. Payments to agencies administering QOP also were based on student participation levels.

Programs delivered services in different settings. All programs provided services in the community agencies during the afterschool hours. In several cases, the public schools provided space and time for services. At some sites, individuals pursed a self-paced set of activities in their homes, along with occasional group activities.

The Philadelphia program corresponded most closely to the QOP blueprint. The program operated primarily during the after school hours, at the Opportunities Industrialization Centers of America. The center was open from 2:00 P.M. to 7:00 P.M. Mondays through Fridays, and on some Saturday mornings and afternoons. At the Center, students did their lessons on computers or talked with the adult counselors.

The QOP experience began with a three-day orientation. Parents were invited to learn about the program on a special parents' night. Both parents and students signed a year-long contract. Adult counselors also committed to spending four years with the students. Most of the counselors did not have their own children, so they were able to devote many afterschool hours and weekends to the QOP students.

The next step was an educational assessment to place youth at the proper academic level. Once the youth knew where to start, they went to the community center after school and practiced vocabulary, mathematics concepts and applications, and language mechanics on the computer. The CCP, developed by Taggart at the U.S. Department of Labor, categorized academic subjects by levels K-12. Each participant worked at his or her own pace. According to one 16-year-old, "If not for the learning center, I would probably just be hanging out after school, cutting classes, knowing I wanted to go to college and what I wanted to be, but not knowing really how to get there."

The philosophy and the persistence of the staff were fundamental to QOP. The staff's unswerving determination to enable and encourage the young people to succeed was a crucial element for program success. Lattimore argued that adults were an integral part of the program, and must be both supportive and tough. He noted, "How do you treat your own kids? You reward them when they behave well, and punish them when they don't. It's a simple idea, really, but it works."

The program administrators and counselors gained the confidence of the QOP students by talking with them daily, spending time with them after school, and counseling them about personal problems. They track the whereabouts and the activities of each young person, often making home visits, and monitor school attendance, particularly on sunny, warm days. Lattimore adds

> These youngsters belong to an extended family whose sole purpose is to nurture their success. What other social program for disadvantaged youth tracks them down when they cut class, follows them if they move to a new neighborhood, stays with them if they go to prison, takes them to cultural events and fine restaurants, tutors them with their schoolwork, worries about their health, fitness and cholesterol levels, urges them to excel?

In addition, the students could reach their counselors at any time. Each counselors wore a beeper and could be reached through an 800 number.

Thus, even in the face of pregnancy, delinquency, dropping out, acting out, or failing in school, participants were encouraged, cajoled, and coaxed back on track. This was an anti-attrition philosophy. Young people were seen as individuals with specific needs and great potential, not as program slots to be filled and replaced. "Once in QOP, always in QOP" was the motto that informed the design and actualization of the program. Nothing the participants could do would be bad enough to be expelled from the program.

The funding for QOP came from an initial $1,050,000 grant made by the Ford Foundation, followed by another grant of $130,000. The national OIC office was allowed to use the interest payments for administration of the national program activities, as well as for other program-related expenses.

In the Philadelphia program, average per-participant direct payments were $3,000 for stipends, $900 for completion bonuses, and $4,100 for the "opportunity account" accrual to be used in the post–high school period. Another $7,000 per person was spent in Philadelphia over the four years (9–12 grade) on staff, agency, and program delivery, for a total of $15,000 per student. Since average QOP hours reached 2,300 hours over the four years, the average per-hour cost was approximately $6.50. About half of this figure represents direct payments to the young participants.

On a programwide basis, with the less intensive sites added in, the total QOP cost per participant was roughly $10,600 over all four years of high school. About half of this figure was spent on program activities; the rest was for stipends, bonuses, opportunity accrual accounts, and payments to QOP coordinators. Less than one-third of all QOPers spent less than 500 hours participating in the program over the four years. The remaining 70% enjoyed anywhere from 500 to 3,000 or more hours in the program over the four years. The average number of hours was 1,286. This cumulative participation level is considerably more than the contact hours of most American youth programs.

More remarkably, students (all on public assistance in eighth grade) randomly assigned to the program took advantage of it over the four-year period. At the start of the fourth year, Saginaw was able to serve 24 of the original 25 youth randomly assigned to it. Philadelphia served 23, Oklahoma City 16, and San Antonio 12 of its original 25 youths.[1] The average accrual account with interest reached approximately $2,300. Even with allowing for inflation in counting hours, the total number of hours adds up to what might be thought of as an extra school year for participating youth.

Thus, in contrast to most youth programs in the add-on or second-chance tradition, QOP was designed to encourage long-term involvement through an array of services. Meaningful relationships with adults would be encouraged without fear of bonds being abruptly severed when the programs ended. Community groups would provide all this in friendly, often familylike environments with deep ties to the neighborhoods. The national office of OIC would provide guidance, technical assistance as needed, and other replication interventions. Modern learning technologies, such as individualized computer-based literacy instruction delivered in high-tech learning labs, would be used.[2] QOP was described as a quantum leap in opportunities because it built on lessons from the past and on the best practices from the present.

Methodology and Limitations

QOP began in the summer of 1989 with the recruitment of disadvantaged students entering the ninth grade. In each of the five sites, 25 students were randomly assigned to an experimental group, and another 25 students were assigned to a control group. All students were chosen from a pool of students who were entering ninth grade and were receiving some form of public assistance. Sites were urged to retain contact with members of both the experimental and the control group so that their progress could be compared through the results of periodic questionnaires. By any reasonable standard, young people in QOP were highly disadvantaged.

The knowledge development goal was to learn about "take-up," that is, a community-based group's ability to serve and sustain young people from impoverished backgrounds in a structured program of services over a relatively long period. Will youngsters living in deteriorating urban neighborhood take advantage of a quantum opportunity? Would the program make a difference in their lives? Would the contention that only comprehensive, year-round, multiyear youth development programs, with a strong dose of adult mentoring, work better than single-service, short-term, fragmented programs prove correct? These are the kinds of questions asked in the QOP experiment; the design implemented to answer them is rather unique in the history of youth program evaluations.

As noted, in each site all students (the 25 in the QOP group and the 25 controls) were randomly selected from lists of exiting eighth grade students from families receiving public assistance. In a departure from other social experiments, QOP directors were not allowed to recruit students who had prescreened themselves into the program. In most studies, program operators have been allowed to over-recruit students, and the researchers have selected students randomly from among the equally motivated students who volunteer for the programs. In the QOP demonstration, however, the researchers randomly selected students from a list of entering ninth grade students, all on welfare (either Aid to Families with Dependent Children, food stamps, local general assistance, or free school lunch), and then handed the OIC project directors this listing of the 25 potential QOP youth. Directors were told to see how many of the 25 youth assigned to the experimental group could be encouraged to join the promised program of services and incentives. The project administrators were not allowed to prescreen the youth, and they were told that any young person from the original list of 25 could and indeed repeatedly should be encouraged to join the program at any time.

The evaluation of the program has been criticized for using samples too small to allow for generalized results. But one critical aspect of QOP was a financial incentive, and it was impossible to know how much money would be spent in these accounts. To prevent these expenses from becoming prohibitive, Ford funded the program with a limit of 25 participants per site. Thus, the program design, not the evaluation procedure, set the sample size.

At the beginning of the program in September 1989, experimental and control group members were asked to fill out a questionnaire that included questions about demographic characteristics, work experience, school experiences, health knowledge, and personal attitudes and opinions. In addition, participants were asked to take tests assessing their academic skill levels (Test of Adult Basic Education—Form 5 Level) and functional skill levels (APL 40 Item Version Survey—CCP Tier Mastery Test).

These tests, along with similar questionnaires, were given to the same experimental and control group members in Fall 1990 and 1991. In Fall 1992, similar questionnaires (with the addition of some questions on future plans) were administered. Academic and functional skill testing were postponed until spring 1993 to capture skill levels at a time when most sample members were preparing to leave high school. In addition, a different type of questionnaire, one focused on future plans, was given to experimental and control group members in Spring 1993.

The purpose of these periodic questionnaires was twofold: to compare experimental and control group members as experimental group members accrued more time in QOP activities and to gauge the amount of positive change that experimental group members may have experienced over time.

In late Fall 1993, a follow-up questionnaire was administered to experimental and control group members. The primary purposes of this questionnaire were to find out what members were doing several months after their scheduled departure from high school and to examine experimental group attitudes toward the QOP. We focus here on the results of this analysis of the Fall 1993 post-high school questionnaire. Before that, however, consider the impact of QOP during the high school years.

Accelerating Results

A review of effects of QOP during the high school years presents several noteworthy conclusions, all relevant to the broad field of adolescent development. (See Table 9-1.) First, the rate of differentiation between the experimental and control groups accelerated after the first two years of high school. Analysis of the two groups at sample entry indicated that the groups were largely free of systematic differences. After one year (the freshman year in high school), we concluded that evidence to support a hypothesis of positive influence on the experimental group was not present. Test scores for many academic and functional skill levels declined for both the experimental and control groups. In several areas, such as vocabulary, math concepts, and language, the experimental group decline was greater.

After two years, however, the positive QOP effect was readily apparent. Experimental group average scores for all 11 academic and functional skills were higher than control group scores, and five of these differences were statistically significant. This finding is important for the field of youth programming: Apparently a program may require more than two years to begin to show statistical impacts. Areas of improvement for the experimental group follow.

- **Skills.** By the time most of the sample were leaving high school in Spring 1993, average experimental group scores for all 11 skills (functional and academic) were higher than control group scores, and all these differences were statistically significant. Average aca-

Table 9-1. The QOP Effect: QOP's Statistically Significant Results Increased over Time

Fall After Scheduled High School Graduation

There were significant differences overall and positive differences in each site:

• more high school graduates

• more college

• more honors and awards

• fewer teens having children

End of Senior Year

Performance in all 11 academic and functional skill areas is stronger among QOP youth and the differences in all skill areas are statistically significant.

End of 10th Grade

Average scores in academic and functional skill areas are greater for QOP participants.

Performance in five of the 11 skill areas is significantly better than controls. Education expectations favor QOP participants over their peers in the control group.

End of 9th Grade

Test scores decline for QOP youth.

No significant differences in education expectations comparing QOP participants to the control group.

demic skill levels (vocabulary, reading comprehension, computation, concepts, mechanics, and expression) had increased more than three grade levels for 27% of the experimental group compared with 14% of the control group. Similarly, average functional skill levels (knowledge of occupations, consumer economics, understanding of government and law, understanding of healthy behavior, and knowledge of community resources) had increased by 20% or more for 38% of the experimental group compared with 16% of the control group.

• **Expectations.** There were accelerating differences between the experimental and control groups regarding their orientation toward and expectations for postsecondary education. After one year, there were no significant differences in educational goals and expectations between the two groups. After two years, however, the educational expectations of the experimental group were much higher than the expectations of the control group, and this difference was statistically significant. Interestingly, the divergence between the two groups resulted from both an increase in the educational expectations of the experimental group and a decrease in the expectations of the control group. By the time most sample members were preparing to leave high school, these differences had expanded even further. QOP members were significantly more oriented toward postsecondary education than were control members on indicators including plans for college, plans for a year from test date, and expected educational achievement.

• **Constancies during high school.** Postulated effects on other characteristics were not detected during the high school years. There were no statistically significant differences between the two groups on the likelihood of having children, or on self-reported school grades (verified on a sample basis by the research team). Similarly, experimental group members were not significantly more likely to improve their contraceptive knowledge and AIDS knowledge than control group members during the high school years.

- **Major differences by site.** There were large differences in the QOP effect between the four sites on which we focused. This is not at all surprising, given the organizational differences among the sites. As reported in Brandeis reports to the Ford Foundation, Philadelphia stood apart from the other sites because of its ability to create a group identity among QOP members, its reliable menu of program offerings, and its success in providing stable, consistent relationships between QOP youth and program staff. As a result, experimental group members in Philadelphia were able to forge supportive relationships with their QOP peers as well as with their site coordinators. Group morale remained strong, and attendance stayed at high levels. In contrast, by the senior year, programs in Saginaw and Oklahoma City reached a point where institutional ties and structured activities between youth and the programs were modest to minimal. Attendance had declined greatly. Yet, even in these sites, personal ties encouraged by the program and made possible by the program design between some QOP members and their program coordinators remained strong, and these ties have often been of significant value to young individuals. By the last year of the pilot, service in these latter two sites often took the form of home visits, weekend events, "just checking-in" phone calls, and individual assignments involving college planning.

In some of the qualitative research associated with the evaluation, the Brandeis authors describe site effects and factors that help to explain the implementation of QOP. In particular, we have focused on the following:

- the extent to which staff turnover can rupture a program's sense of integrity and security and thus lead to emotional disinvestment by youth

- the importance of knitting together solidarity of purpose among those who plan, administer, and evaluate national demonstrations like QOP (in the absence of such cohesiveness, the likelihood increases that local implementation will fall prey to competing values and orientations)

- the need to forge a sense of group ethos early in the multiyear initiative (because the pressures and competing loyalties with which youngsters from low-income families must struggle tend to increase during the teen years, successful bonding between participants and programs is often easier to achieve among early rather than late adolescents)

Net Outcomes after High School

The most profound program effects were discovered only after the close of the four-year program period. Analysis of data from the follow-up telephone and mailed surveys in the late fall following scheduled high school graduation shows a much more significant differentiation between the experimental and control groups than had previous data analyses.[3] Tables 9-1 (on p. 244) and 9-2 show comparisons of educational, demographic, and behavioral variables in four sites for the experimental control group. (Milwaukee, the site dropped after the first year, is not included.)

Education

Members in the experimental group are much more likely to have graduated from high school and to be in a postsecondary school (Table 9-2). They are much less likely to be high school dropouts. Sixty-three percent of the QOP members have graduated from high school, compared with 42% of the control group. Of the experimental group, 42% are in some type of postsecondary school compared with 16% of the control group. And 23% of QOP members are high school dropouts compared with 50% of the control group. All these group differences are statistically significant.

The statistical difference in the dropout percentage contrasts with findings from the spring 1993 survey, a result of question variation between the two surveys. In the spring survey, we asked whether each

Table 9-2. Summary of Net Impacts of QOP Pilot at Four Sites

Characteristic	All Four Sites	Philadelphia
Graduated from high school and in postsecondary school	+26	+48
Graduated from high school	+21	+28
Received honors or awards in past 12 months	+22	+48
Donated time to a nonprofit, charitable, school, or community group in past 6 months	+30	+56
Served as a volunteer counselor, mentor, or tutor in past 12 months	+20	+36
Responded "strongly agree" to the statement, "I am hopeful about the future"	+21	+37
Lives with parents		-24
Has children	-14	
High school dropout	-27	-36
Unemployed, not in school, and not a high school graduate	-32	

individual had ever dropped out of school. Thus, an individual did not have to be a dropout at the time of the survey to answer the question affirmatively. In fact, many "dropouts" were back in school at the time of the survey. In the fall survey, we counted as a dropout anyone who was not a high school graduate and who was not presently in school. This method more accurately pinpoints those who permanently dropped out of high school.

Most encouraging is the evidence that QOP had some positive effect on educational goals and dropout rates in all four sites. As expected, the differences are most dramatic in Philadelphia, the site that best met QOP program design expectations. Seventy-six percent of Philadelphia QOP members are high school graduates, compared with

48% of the control group. The dropout rate among control members is more than five times greater than among QOP members (44% compared with 8%). The percentage of the experimental group who are in postsecondary school is three times higher than the percentage for the control group (72% compared with 24%). All these differences are statistically significant. The college attendance rate in Philadelphia is nothing short of remarkable.

In Oklahoma City, the differences between the experimental and control groups in the dropout rate and attendance in postsecondary schools are both statistically significant. The difference in high school graduation rate is not statistically significant, but QOP members are nearly twice as likely to be high school graduates (50% compared with 26%). In San Antonio, members of the experimental group are more likely than control group those in the control group to be high school graduates and to be enrolled in postsecondary schools. While these differences are not large enough to be statistically significant, they are substantial.[4]

The results in Saginaw are similar to those in San Antonio. Though substantial, differences between the experimental and control groups are not large enough to be statistically significant. Nevertheless, the high school dropout rate of the experimental group is only slightly more than half that of the control group (21% compared with 39%).

For all four sites combined, there are statistically significant differences between the experimental and control groups for attendance at both four-year and two-year colleges. The attendance rate at four-year colleges for the experimental group is more than three times higher than for the control group (18% compared with 5%), and their attendance rate at two-year colleges is more than twice as high (19% compared with 9%).

Children

There is evidence that QOP members are less likely to have children than control group members in the postprogram period. Twenty-four percent of the experimental group have children, compared with 38% of the control group. This is a statistically significant difference and an important finding: While estimates vary, some experts have noted that low-income families begun by teenage mothers cost the nation $34 billion a year in health and welfare benefits. Nearly half of all single mothers in AFDC (the national welfare program in place during QOP) had their first child as a teenager.

The likelihood of having children varies substantially by site for the experimental and control groups. Unlike most other variables, the QOP effect in Philadelphia appears to be less than in the other three sites. There, the QOP group likelihood of having children is 32% compared with 36% for the control group. The largest difference between the experimental and control groups appears in San Antonio (7% compared with 30%). The differences in Oklahoma City and Saginaw are smaller than in San Antonio but substantially larger than in Philadelphia. None of the single site differences in the likelihood of having children are statistically significant.

Honors and Awards

Both experimental and control groups were asked whether they had received any honors or awards during the previous 12 months. The proportion of QOP members receiving honors or awards was nearly three times higher than the proportion of control group members (34% compared with 12%). This is a statistically significant difference.

QOP members had a greater likelihood of receiving an award or honor in all four sites. The greatest differences were in Philadelphia, where the rate for QOP members was five times higher than for control group members (60% compared with 12%), and in San Antonio, where no member of the control group had received an award while 21% of the members of the experimental group members had.

Community Service

Given the service component in the QOP plan, it is perhaps not surprising to find extreme differences between the experimental and control groups in the proportion of individuals who have performed some sort of community service. During the six months after QOP participation, 21% of the experimental group had taken part in a community project; 28% had been a volunteer tutor, counselor, or mentor; and 41% had given time to a nonprofit, charitable, school, or community group. The corresponding percentages for the control group were 12%, 8%, and 11%.

As with other variables, site differences are noteworthy. As expected, the greatest difference in the likelihood of being a volunteer counselor or tutor between the experimental and control groups occurred in Philadelphia: 52% of QOP members, compared with 16% of control group members. There was also a large difference in Saginaw (35% of the experimental group compared with 6% of the control group), but there was no difference between the two groups in Oklahoma City. In addition to these largest differences between the groups in Philadelphia and Saginaw, members of the experimental groups there were far more likely to be volunteer counselors and tutors than members of the experimental groups in other cities.

Regarding those who donated time to a nonprofit, charitable, school, or community group in the previous six months, differences between the experimental and control groups are substantial in all four sites. Again, the biggest difference (76% of the experimental group compared with 20% of the control group) is in Philadelphia. This is the only site difference that is statistically significant.

Attitudes and Opinions

The fall 1993 survey asked a number of questions to gauge respondents' state of mind, sense of the future, and self-assessed need for various types of help. Respondents were asked to note their level of agreement or disagreement with six statements:

- My family life is happy.

- I am hopeful about the future.

- I am depressed about life.

- I am bothered about things.

- I am lonely.

- My family life has been a success.

In addition, those surveyed were asked about the extent to which they knew what steps to take in the future and about their need for help in improving reading and math skills, in training for a good job, in finding a job, and in getting alcohol or drug treatment. The hypothesis was that QOP members would be more upbeat about their lives, would have a clearer sense about the future, and would express less need for special academic and training help than the control group members.[5]

On most of these dimensions, members of the experimental group were at least slightly more positive than members of the control group. There were statistically significant differences between the two groups regarding their agreement or disagreement with two statements: "I am hopeful about the future" and "My life has been a success." Despite these differences, a large proportion of both the experimental and the control group gave a remarkably positive assessment of their lives. Ninety-eight percent of QOP members and 86% of control group members "strongly agreed" or "agreed" with the statement that they were hopeful about the future, and 74% of QOP members and 51% of control group members strongly agreed or agreed with the statement that their life has been a success.

The positive self-assessment by members of both groups is also noteworthy where experimental-control group differences are not statistically significant. Ninety-three percent of the experimental group and 82% of the control group "strongly agreed" or "agreed" with the statement that their family life is happy. Only 9% of QOP members and 17% of control group members "strongly agreed" or "agreed" with the assertion that they were lonely. More than half of both groups disagreed with the statement that they were bothered about things.

Differences between the two groups regarding their knowledge of steps to take in the future were not statistically significant. A lower percentage of QOP members (5%) than control group members (13%) did not know what steps to take, but a slightly higher percentage of the control group professed to know their future steps exactly.[6]

There were also no significant differences between assessments of the experimental and the control group of their need for reading and math help, help in training for a good job, and help in finding a good job. Members of the control group were significantly more likely to express a need for help with an alcohol or drug problem (no QOP members expressed such a need), though the actual number admitting this need was small.

As with other variables, there are some notable differences by site in attitudes and opinions. The clearest QOP effect is in Philadelphia, where the percentage of QOP members who strongly agree that they are hopeful about the future is more than twice the percentage of control group members. There also appears to be a strong QOP effect in Saginaw, but little effect in Oklahoma City.

In contrast, differences between the experimental and the control group in the percentage who say that they need help with reading and math skills are small in all four sites. More noteworthy, the expressed need for such help is lower in Philadelphia and San Antonio than in the other two sites.

Subgroup Comparisons

We divided both the experimental and control groups into four subgroups: those in some kind of postsecondary school, those still in high school, those not in school (they could be graduates or dropouts) and working (full or part-time), and those not in any school and not working. The last group is of particular interest, as it signals "inactivity" among a group of young "at-risk" people. Those in postsecondary school make up a much larger proportion of the experimental group than of the control group (55% compared with 24%). A somewhat higher percentage of the control group is not in school but working (26% compared with 15%). Turning next to the most at-risk group, a substantially larger percentage of the control group is neither in school nor working (50% compared with 30%) than of the QOP group. The difference between these two distributions is statistically significant.

Nearly half of the experimental group and one-third of the control group in postsecondary education are attending four-year colleges. Three-quarters of both groups are full-time students, and nearly all receive some form of financial aid. Only small percentages (9% of the experimental group and 17% of the control group) work full-time while going to school. Among those who graduated from high school but are not now in school, nearly all plan to return to school at some point. Relatively small percentages of both groups are working full-time (6% of the experimental group and 30% of the control group). Even when part-time work and apprenticeship and on-the-job training categories are included, approximately half this subgroup is not working. Of the small number of youth still in high school, nearly all are in the 12th grade. All expect to complete high school. Three of the 17 people in this subgroup are working while going to school. Fifty-six members of the experimental and control groups are not high school graduates and are not working. Nine of these individuals are full-time homemakers. Only 12 of the 56 individuals are working full-time or part-time; this figure reflects the difficulty of getting jobs for those without a high school degree.

Crime and QOP

The Brandeis evaluation of QOP for all four sites together did not report especially strong or meaningful differences in criminal involvement in the first postprogram follow-up survey. We did find that in Philadelphia the percentage reporting arrests was 20%, compared with 33% among controls. We also found that the average number of arrests differed between the two groups: 0.32 for QOP youth in Philadelphia and 0.50 in the controls. Robert Taggart, now an independent consultant writing for OIC, administered a second survey to QOP and control group youth; his survey was timed to represent the two years after high school at three sites: Philadelphia, Saginaw, and Oklahoma

City [Taggart 1996]. With this additional year of follow-up activity, he documented that the "average number of arrests ever" was 0.28 among QOP youth and 0.56 among controls in this second postprogram survey, for a 28 percentage point difference. This finding has led other researchers to place QOP among a handful of programs that apparently help combat lawlessness among teens [Bushway & Reuter 1996].

Table 9-2 enumerates results of the QOP pilot during 1989–1993. The first column cites the average results of all four sites combined. The second column displays the exemplary results in one of the four sites, Philadelphia. Numbers represent the percentage point difference in both columns between the experimental group and the control group.

Implications

The story of QOP is an encouraging one. We learned first and foremost that something works for these children. This finding stands in sharp contrast to the many negative effects reported in the media, in political circles, and in an earlier generation of youth development evaluation.[7] Other lessons follow.

- **Opportunity matters.** Many children took advantage of the combination of hard and soft resources, such as help from adults and college preparation and guidance. While talk shows and theories about the culture of poverty speculate that children who live in such bad neighborhoods will not participate in "connecting" activities—or even are prevented from doing so by their peers—this study finds no statistical proof of this proposition.

- **A community-based group.** OIC generally fulfilled its promise. Although QOP is now being replicated in school-based settings in a new initiative funded by the U.S. Department of Labor and the Ford Foundation, the positive role of the community-based organization (CBO) was demonstrated in the pilot project. Conversely, the demonstration showed great unevenness across the various sites. CBOs do bring the advantage of being able to recruit and serve some of the most vulnerable groups in society, but they often face problems retaining staff and program quality factors are a persistent problem.

- **Continuity matters.** Even when regular services were interrupted, relationships with caring adults mattered, as in the Oklahoma site. MDRC's evaluation of Career Beginnings and Public/Private Ventures' study of the Big Brothers/Big Sisters mentoring program supports this finding from QOP [Cave & Quint 1990; see also Public/Private Ventures [1995]).

- **Money matters.** Although money does matter, how much is unclear. Young people in QOP called the financial incentives "chump change" but were upset if checks were late. The money allowed many to do things in the postsecondary period that would otherwise have been unattainable. Our research was not able to separate neatly the effects of money from mentoring and other services. Another recently completed study—the Baltimore CollegeBound evaluation of 16 Baltimore high schools—found that students must receive a mixture of services, including "last dollar" scholarships, counseling and information about postsecondary financial aid, rather than one or the other, to achieve net effects on attendance rates at four-year college. Providing financial resources with counseling is a pairing that made a significant difference in young peoples' college attendance [Hahn & Bailis 1995].

- **Investments matter.** Outcomes of investments gain strength over time. When evaluating this or similar programs, it is important to allow sufficient time for programs to mature. The short-run results from QOP were negative: Perhaps this is one reason why an earlier generation of programs was often thought to yield disappointing results. The tracking and follow-up periods may have been too short, or the program designs themselves may not have been sufficiently intense, without sustained follow-up. QOP's results accelerated over time as a result of both deterioration of the prospects of the control groups and the beneficial effect of QOP on participants.

- **Age matters.** Similarly, age matters in the design of youth programs. We speculate QOP would have produced even more dramatic outcomes had it started with early adolescents between the ages of 10 and 15. A recent report by Hahn [1995] shows how public policy and, to a large extent, programs made possible by policy are silent on the importance of age in the design and delivery of youth strategies. QOP worked at the intersection of middle and high school, easing the transition and providing support throughout the high school years, but who knows what would have happened if it began in the late elementary school years?

- **Families matter.** Families count, of course, in both positive and negative ways. Deep parental and guardian supports were never assumed in QOP; the CBO staff often acted as surrogates. Our ethnography revealed many sad instances where parents let the children down, failed to show up for program activities, or even used the young peoples' financial incentives inappropriately. But there were many positive family influences as well. In an important design decision, however, QOP never assumed deep parental or guardian involvement and was able to demonstrate significant positive outcomes for participants without substantive parental support. This important finding makes clear that the assumption that without parental support adolescent interventions are necessarily doomed to failure is a false one. Programs can randomly select at-risk kids and help them regardless of parental involvement.

- **Programs matter.** Programs can support resiliency, yet the concept of programs is in retreat. Conservatives often argue that formal program structures create dependency and rob people of initiative. Liberals may argue that programs like QOP are too small to bring to scale and that systemic change of mainstream youth-serving organizations such as public schools should be the focus of intervention. Obviously QOP is not a good example of systemic change or work with mainstream institutions. It was a small program, and its future success likely depends on the program staying small. But, regarding the conservative critique, nothing in QOP suggests that multiyear investments rob young people of personal responsibility or initiative.

Summary and Conclusions

To review, in QOP, there were comprehensive achievements and positive differences at each site:

- QOP members are more likely to be high school graduates.

- QOP members are more likely to be attending postsecondary schools.

- QOP members are less likely to be high school dropouts.

- QOP members are more likely to have received an honor or award in the past year.

- QOP members are less likely to have children.

There were also significant differences for all the sites combined:

- QOP members are more likely to be involved in community service.

- QOP members are more likely to be hopeful about the future.

- QOP members are more likely to consider their life a success.

Together with the significantly higher academic and functional skill levels that we found in our analysis of the late senior year 1993 data, we have a picture of a QOP population that has been considerably aided by its participation in QOP.[8]

Perhaps the most encouraging finding of this analysis is that QOP members are better off in all four sites. As mentioned, it is more difficult to find statistically significant differences between the experimental and control groups in individual sites because of the small sample sizes. Nevertheless, there are clearly positive QOP effects in all the sites. The first five comparisons listed above (high school graduation rates, postsecondary school attendance rates, dropout rates, receipt of an honor or award, and the likelihood of having children) all hold true in each site, even though not all the differences are statistically significant.

The implications from these site differences in all four sites are far-reaching. It is, of course, most beneficial to have a site like Philadelphia, where project administrators have successfully created a group identity and designed tangible program services to support QOP members throughout their high school years. The positive effects of such a program are readily apparent.

Apparently, however, there is a substantial positive effect even when programs could not achieve a consistent group identity or deliver a steady stream of formal program services like those in Philadelphia. Why? This has often been achieved by the caring and concern shown by coordinators who visit and call students, frequently on a weekly basis. Even when group activities in these sites dwindled, a "case management" and youth development approach was used by staff throughout the entire high school period, thus affording QOP a mentoring component thought by many to be a crucial protective factor in the development of resiliency [Masten 1994; Werner 1990]. The most optimistic finding of this study is that teenagers are able to benefit significantly even when formal group services provided to them are modest. If young people are connected with caring adults for sustained periods, year-round, positive results do emerge. The program motto, "once in QOP, always in QOP," was taken to heart by enough counselors to have made a real difference.

Though this report shows that even a little adult attention for sustained periods can produce impressive effects on participating youth from poor backgrounds, it should not obscure the importance of leadership, skill, talent, motivation, and organization in project sites. The differences, for example, between San Antonio and Philadelphia cannot be attributed to the neighborhood setting, the characteristics of participants, or the program model.[9] What distinguishes these sites is the degree of buy-in from the host organizations and the commitment of staff at all levels. A central lesson from the past decade of evaluations is that, in multisite demonstrations, the differences among sites is often greater (and more interesting) than the differences between the aggregated results for the treatment group and the average results for the control group. QOP supports this observation well.

Perhaps most important in the current political and cultural climate is the discovery that in a well-run project, such as Philadelphia, the take-up rate and pattern of program persistence from the ninth grade through the senior year defies the usual generalizations about poor youth, three-quarters from minority backgrounds. Simply put, when a quantum opportunity was offered, young people from public assistance backgrounds—African American males, females, whites, Asians, others— took it! They joined the programs and stayed with it for long periods.

Philadelphia had a near-perfect record of involving young people for a sustained period (one youth in the treatment group was jailed; Philadelphia served all other youth assigned to it over the four years), all the more remarkable considering the artificial method devised by the researchers that required the program to "sell" its approach to a list of unscreened potential recruits. The social science literature on the "underclass," not to mention lurid headlines in daily newspapers, predicts that some inner city youth are so estranged as to defy or to reject invitations to participate in programs like QOP. The policy and program management literature can also be found to predict that staff would not and could not work with the same group of young people year-round for four years. These predictions were not supported in the unfolding of the QOP project in Philadelphia and, to a lesser extent, in the other sites.

There are many reasons for the general success of QOP's pilot program. The demonstration was designed intelligently. It was led by caring staff. Conventional theories that predict failure have not been formulated on the basis of street-level experiences with true, enriched, high-quality program models of engagement and youth development. QOP did not operate close to the ideal in several sites, but when it did in others, the results were impressive. Even when formal program activity was minimal, we found evidence that informal but relentless adult attention was beneficial to participants.

Still another explanation is surely the early intervention one. Programs that engage adolescents early in their training and education experience more success than programs that attempt a quick fix in the later adolescent years. This is especially true during the "bridge" years such as the middle school to high school transition.

Finally, QOP was not immune from the sad headlines and quiet disasters that strike routinely in the nation's inner cities. Consider some reasons that the Brandeis team did not receive follow-up surveys from the small program in Saginaw, Michigan:

- One student was shot by the police and died in the incident.

- For three students, counselors wrote: "Made on-site visits to last known addresses...many calls...families no longer there...contacted high school counselors...no forwarding addresses given for school records. Disappeared."

- Staff wrote: "Reputed drug dealer...new residence is known as crack house. Interviewer refused to enter residence."

- "Made on-site visit only to find house condemned...no forwarding address."

In other sites there were accidents, beatings, drugs. A number of children were lost; they just disappeared despite extraordinary efforts to monitor and track them anywhere in the country. Some of these young people may reappear in another city, in another program, in a shelter, or in a college graduation line. We will never know: poor families have a high degree of geographical mobility. If the replication of QOP works, the dream might be to have a network of well-run QOP projects with interlocking supports across America's cities and neighborhoods.

The literature suggests that intensive comprehensive interventions involving a competent adult mentor can make a lasting change in the lives of young people. QOP found this to be true for a group of randomly selected at-risk young people. And yet most adolescents are not offered such program opportunities. In our unpublished tabulations using the National Education Longitudinal Study (NELS), we found that among African American eighth graders, only one-fifth are involved in programs organized by community groups like OIC. Religious programs reach perhaps 44% of African American eighth graders, as do sports programs. The frequency of contacts with organized activities drops from there. Many more young people can benefit from well thought-out programs. The QOP experiment found that when offered the chance to become involved in a long-term program, kids took it. The potential for programming is enormous, and the need is great. The principles of a successful program models have been identified. The time is right to begin using these principles for children who need them.

References

American Youth Policy Forum. (1997). *Some things do make a difference for youth.* Washington, DC: Author.

Barton, W. H., Watkins, M., & Jarjoura, R. (1997). Youths and communities: toward comprehensive strategies for youth development. *Social Work*, 42, 5.

Bushway, S., & Reuter, P. (1996). Labor markets and crime risk factors. In Lawrence Sherman et al. (Eds.), *Preventing crime: What works, what doesn't and what is promising?* College Park, MD: University of Maryland

Cave, G., & Quint, J. (1990). *Career beginnings impact revaluation: Findings from a program for disadvantaged high school students.* New York. Manpower Demonstration Research Corporation

Freiberg, Jerome H. (1994). Understanding resilience: implications for inner city schools and their near and far communities. In Margaret C. Wang and Edmund W. Gordon (Eds.), *Educational resilience in inner city America: challenges and prospects.* Hillsdale, NJ: Erlbaum.

Hahn, A. (1995). *Making age count in the development of national youth policy.* Waltham, MA: Brandeis University, Center for Human Resources.

Hahn, A., & Bailis, L. (1995). Executive summary. *A new field emerges: The Baltimore CollegeBound Program and other college access programs.* Waltham, MA: Brandeis University, Center for Human Resources.

Masten, A. S. (1994). Resilience in individual development: Successful adaptation despite risk and adversity. In M. C. Wang and E. W. Gordon (Eds.), *Educational resilience in inner city America: Challenges and prospects* (pp. 3-26). Hillsdale, NJ: Lawrence Erlbaum Associates.

Public/Private Ventures. (1995). *Making a difference: An impact study of Big Brothers/Big Sisters.* Philadelphia: Author.

Public/Private Ventures and Brandeis University, Center for Human Resources. (1992). *Dilemmas in youth employment programming: Findings from the Youth Research and Technical Assistance Project.* Vol. 1-2. Report for the U.S. Department of Labor. Washington, DC: U.S. Government Printing Office.

Reed-Victor, E., & Stronge, J. H. (1997). Building resiliency: Constructive directions for homeless education. *Journal of Children and Poverty, 3,* 1.

Taggart, R. (1993). *Quantum Opportunities Program: Promise for the future.* Philadelphia: Opportunities Industrial Centers of America.

Taggart, R. (1996). *Quantum Opportunities Program: An introduction.* Philadelphia: Opportunities Industrial Centers of America.

Wang, M. C., & Gordon, E. W. (Eds.). (1994). *Educational resilience in inner city America: Challenges and prospects.* Hillsdale, NJ: Lawrence Erlbaum Associates.

Werner, E. (1990). Protective factors and individual resilience. In S. Meisels and J. Shonkoff (Eds.), *Handbook of early childhood intervention* (pp. 97-116). New York: Cambridge University Press.

Whalen, S. P., & Wynn, J. R. (1995). Enhancing primary services for youth through an infrastructure of social services. *Journal of Adolescent Research, 10,* 1.

Notes

1   Milwaukee was dropped from the analysis for reasons described in the research reports submitted to the Ford Foundation. Milwaukee did not implement the program after the first year. Dropping the site from the analysis has led to a number of comments from reviewers of the Brandeis evaluation. Some reviewers agreed with dropping Milwaukee since the study was a pilot project rather than a planned replication; other commentators disagreed. Another comment about methodology came from reviewers who observed that although rigorous random assignment procedures were used, the Brandeis team was required to use a random replacement policy to launch the project. The study randomly replaced youngsters who had died or had moved from the neighborhoods under study whether in the treatment or control groups. These were the only reasons to replace randomly the names originally assigned to the categories, not motivation or personal characteristics.

2   Taggart has written an interesting and lively evaluation report on QOP using his own follow-up survey data. Although there are slight discrepancies between his "internal" study for OIC and the official Brandeis study for the Ford Foundation, the key findings do correspond. Both studies use the same information from the program on costs and hours of participation in various program activities. Taggart's study [1993] is available from OIC. See also, *Introducing the Quantum Opportunities Program* [Taggart 1996], which includes a second year of post-high school follow-up information. The latter extends one year beyond the Brandeis follow-up used in this publication.

3   The QOP sites conducted the follow-up surveys following a training protocol designed by the Brandeis researchers. Researchers verified 10-15 % of survey responses to all sites for both treatment and control groups. There was not one discrepancy in responses.

4   It is extremely difficult to have statistically significant differences when sample sizes are as small as they are in San Antonio.

5   We recognized that an alternative hypothesis regarding the expression of need for academic and training help also made sense;

namely that QOP members who were more familiar with the "culture" of help through their QOP activities might be more willing to express their need for further help.

6   In unpublished tabulations of the National Education Longitudinal Survey (NELS), we found that only half of all African American eighth graders discuss the planning of their high school programs with counselors and teachers. Even less—a third—discuss jobs or careers with teachers or counselors. Since students and their families can easily make the wrong choices about high school courses and curricula, these findings are alarming. They support the need for programs like QOP that bring resources into the transition from middle school to high school.

7   So pervasive is the belief that youth programs for poor adolescents rarely achieve results that a new publication from the American Youth Policy Forum is entitled *Some Things DO Make a Difference for Youth* [1997]. It reports positive findings in three dozen programs with evaluations.

8   These findings stand in sharp contrast to the many negative or modest results found in other youth employment and training programs. See, for example, reviews in a report for the U.S. Department of Labor [Public/Private Ventures and Brandeis University 1992].

9   One possible "structural" explanation for Philadelphia's success may have to do with the close proximity of the OIC-QOP site to the participating school and the fact that OIC-QOP negotiated a presence in the high school for some QOP activities.

10. Youth Development Programs

Jodie Roth, Lawrence F. Murray, Jeanne Brooks-Gunn, & William H. Foster

The Carnegie Council On Adolescent Development [1996] offers this elegant, yet simple characterization of the rewards of successful adolescence, capturing the hopes of all parents for their children and setting the tone for our nation's efforts at designing public policies supportive of our young citizens' progression toward becoming satisfied, productive and healthy young adults:

> Adolescence is one of the most fascinating and complex transitions in the life span: a time of accelerated growth and change second only to infancy; a time of expanding horizons, self-discovery, and emerging independence; a time of metamorphosis from childhood to adulthood.... The events of this crucially formative phase can shape an individual's life course and thus the future of the whole society. [Carnegie Council 1996, p. 7]

Growing concern for the health of America's youth, such as the national initiative *Healthy People 2000* [DHHS 1991], is driven, in part, by the increasing evidence that many of our young people are experiencing just the opposite outcome—that the quality of their lives is rapidly declining. Adolescents are dying from violence, drug and alcohol use and abuse, motor vehicle accidents, and unsafe sex [Lerner 1995]. Seventy-five percent of adolescent deaths are caused by injuries, homicide, and suicide, and the consequences of substance use. Injuries and disabilities related to motor and recreational vehicles, repercussions of unprotected sexual activity, mental disorders, and chronic illness account for significant sources of adolescent morbidity [Millstein et al. 1993]. For others, engagement in risk behaviors—drug, alcohol and tobacco use, juvenile delinquency, and chronic school truancy and underachievement—limit their life chances. Dryfoos [1990] estimates that approximately half of our nations' adolescents engage in two or more of these risk behaviors and 10% engage in four.

Positive youth development, a promising framework for addressing these problems, focuses on how adolescents develop in healthy ways. Service efforts within this framework, known as youth development programs, have their intellectual, empirical, and applied origins in a long-standing tradition of health advocacy and disease prevention efforts. Study of the various abstract models and service delivery systems for confronting health-compromising behaviors in high-risk communities reveals common characteristics among successful strategies. Conceptual and practical attempts to integrate and coordinate these various components lead to the emergence of a comprehensive approach to healthy development that goes beyond traditional prevention or intervention models.

With the emergence of the positive youth development framework, a renewed hope in the possibility of assisting even troubled adolescents toward healthy adulthood has captured public attention. Although youth development programs are touted as a means of optimizing the development of all adolescents, they can also provide the framework for helping to prevent at-risk populations from falling headlong into health compromising behaviors. And, some hope that it can be an effective treatment strategy in the rehabilitation of adolescents in trouble, including substance abusers, violent gang members, and the like.

In this chapter, we address the effectiveness of the positive youth development framework for promoting healthy behavior among at-risk and troubled youth. In the first section, we delineate the characteristics of positive youth development programs. Next, we review the evaluation literature on youth development programs indicative of their efficacy for promoting healthy behavior for at-risk youth with a particular focus on urban youth. In the third section we discuss the potential value of consciously applying the youth development strategy to institutions and systems serving adolescents out of the mainstream, youth already in trouble. In the last section, we draw conclusions and suggest potential additional directions for youth development programs.

Principles of Positive Youth Development Programs

Positive youth development encompasses all our hopes and aspirations for a nation of healthy, happy and productive individuals. Clearly, achieving this goal requires more than preventing problem behaviors. Problem free is not fully prepared [Pittman 1991]. In *Turning Points*, the Carnegie Council on Adolescent Development [1989] delineated five goals of successful adolescent development. Youth should be intellectually reflective, en route to a lifetime of meaningful work, good citizens, caring and ethical individuals, and healthy [Carnegie Council 1989]. Youth development practitioners typically translate these goals into a framework of competencies—desirable attitudes, behaviors, and skills—necessary for positive development [Urban Institute 1994; Pittman 1992; Camino 1992].

There is growing consensus among youth development leaders, based on more than 200 research studies and numerous taskforces, synthesis reports, and roundtables, of what types of experiences help a young person acquire the competencies necessary for a healthy and productive adulthood (see Dryfoos [1990]; Pittman and Fleming [1991]; Pittman, O'Brien, and Kimball [1993]; Urban Institute [1994]; and Zeldin, Kimball, and Price [1995]). Simply stated, young people need access to safe places, challenging experiences, and caring people on a daily basis [Zeldin et al. 1995]. A more elaborate answer specifies the opportunities and supports adolescents need. Table 10-1 illustrates the competencies, opportunities, and strategic supports related to each of the five goals for healthy development. These opportunities and supports, also referred to as protective or risk factors depending on their presence or absence, exist in the different contexts influencing adolescents' lives—family, peers, school, workplace, neighborhood, commu-

Table 10-1. Relation Between Developmental Goals, Competencies, and Strategic Supports

Developmental Goals	Desired Competencies	Needed Opportunities	Needed Supports
Ability to be intellectually reflective	Broad base of knowledge. Good oral, written, and problem-solving skills. Ability to demonstrate creative expression. Ability to learn.	Formal and informal instruction and training. Skills practice. Acquisition of cognitive skills (reading, writing, and mathematics). Reflection, exploration, and discussion of ideas and choices. Expression through different, creative media and in different settings.	Assistance in gaining access to current and future resources through involvement and connections to people and information. High expectations for achievement, as well as the encouragement and rewards necessary to meet these expectations.
Preparation for a lifetime of meaningful work	Understanding and awareness of life options. Knowledge of steps needed to make choice. Preparation for work and family life. Understanding value and purpose of family, work, and leisure. Academic achievement.	Formal and informal instruction and training. Skill practice. Acquisition of cognitive skills. Reflection, exploration, and discussion of ideas and choices. Making positive contributions to others.	Guidance in options assessment, planning, and goal setting. Assistance in gaining access to current and future resources through involvement and connections to people and information. High expectations for achievement, as well as the encouragement and rewards necessary to meet these expectations. Clear messages about standards of behavior, discipline, and values.

Table 10-1. (continued)

Developmental Goals	Desired Competencies	Needed Opportunities	Needed Supports
Becoming a good citizen	Historical knowledge. Understanding own group's history and values. Appreciation of difference. Development of interpersonal skills. Desire to be ethical and involved in efforts that contribute to the broader good.	Fully taking on responsibilities of group membership. Making positive contributions to others.	Caring relationships with peers and adults. Help in understanding the importance of working well with others. Ability to discuss and modify boundaries as appropriate.
Developing caring and ethics	Intrapersonal skills, such as self-discipline, judgment, coping, ability to understanding emotions, and personal and ethnic identity. Interpersonal skills, such as working with others, understanding difference, sustaining friendships, communication, cooperation, and negotiation.	Fully taking on responsibilities of group membership. Making positive contributions to others. Reflection, exploration, and discussion of ideas.	Clear messages about standards of behavior, discipline, and values. Nurturance, friendship, and affirmation. Caring relationships with peers and adults.
Attaining and maintaining good health	Good current health status. Knowledge of effects of unhealthy behaviors on mind and body. Health-enhancing skills to ensure future health.	Formal and informal instruction and training. Skill practice.	Clear messages about standards of behavior, discipline, and values. Guidance in options assessment, planning, and goal setting.

nity, and country (see Bronfenbrenner [1979, 1986]). When circumstances prevent both economically affluent and disadvantaged families, schools, and communities from providing their youth with these needed opportunities and supports, youth development programs offer one avenue for fulfilling these needs.

A parsimonious definition of youth development programs has been elusive, however. Most simply, youth development programs can be understood as age-appropriate programs designed to prepare adolescents for productive adulthood by providing opportunities and supports to help them gain the competencies and knowledge needed to meet the increasing challenges they will face as they mature. Although variation exists in how programs actually do this, an emerging consensus identifies what types of program characteristics might fill the void left by inattentive families, schools, and communities [Carnegie Council 1996, 1994; Lerner 1995; McLaughlin et al. 1994; Dryfoos 1990; Pittman 1991].

Youth development programs share a common conception of young people as resources to be developed, not as problems to be managed. Characteristics of this philosophy are seen in the individual attention, cultural appropriateness, and choice and responsibility given to adolescents. Youth development programs are often described as familylike environments, where adolescents can feel safe, and caring adults support and empower them to develop their competencies. Like ideal families and neighborhoods, these programs create a strong sense of membership with explicit rules, responsibilities, and flexibility [Roth et al. 1998]. Such programs demonstrate a commitment to supporting the development of ethnic identity as well as personal identity. They view youths' ethnic and cultural backgrounds as part of their individuality and uniqueness [Camino 1992].

Youth development programs often include life skill development, community service, and formal and informal activities that allow youth to nurture their interests and talents, practice new skills, and gain a sense of personal or group recognition. Regardless of the specific activity, the emphasis lies in providing opportunities for active participation and real challenges. Adolescents are typically involved in all stages of activity, from idea generation to implementation. The activities often result in a recognizable product, such as a performance, team record or newspaper. The activities can have both direct (i.e., homework sessions and tutoring) and indirect (i.e., encourage youth to stay in school and try harder and opportunities to practice academic skills) links to education [Roth et al. 1998].

This philosophy of youth development programs reflects the potential for such programs when the existing systems of community, neighborhood, school, and family fail to encourage the development of competencies needed for positive development. Youth development practitioners emphasize changes not only in adolescents, but also in the institutions and adults affecting adolescents' lives. For example, Bazemore and Terry [1997] suggest that communities need to cultivate new opportunities for youth to make productive contributions.

Program efforts focused solely on the prevention of a single problem behavior, such as violence or substance abuse, do not equip adolescents with the tools for a responsible and productive adulthood. Youth development programs are gaining prominence as a way to best help our youth because they are grounded in the complexities of adolescents' experiences and assumptions about the positive capacities of youth. However, few programs incorporate all of the elements described above. It is more realistic to view the above discussion of the philosophy of youth development programs as a framework for maximizing positive youth development through a comprehensive mix of service and strategies.

Evaluations[1]

In 1992, the Carnegie Council on Adolescent Development commissioned a taskforce to review the state of evaluations of youth-serving organizations for preparation of *A Matter of Time*. The taskforce concluded that many of the nation's oldest and largest youth organizations' failure to allocate financial and staff resources for outcome evaluations led to unsubstantiated claims about effectiveness. They also noted that many proposals to funders from youth-serving organizations have weak evaluation designs.[2] Furthermore, program staff sometimes saw evaluations as threatening, and were therefore likely to resist participation. The Council considered it crucial to bridge this gap between evaluators and practitioners. In addition, they noted that no consensus on appropriate outcomes for youth-serving programs existed. Categorical funding streams often call for measurement of outcomes related to problem behaviors, but taskforce members believed that positive outcomes needed to be evaluated as well [Carnegie Council on Adolescent Development 1992].

To update and expand on the Carnegie report, we conducted a multistep review of the literature to locate empirical evidence of the efficacy of the youth development framework for programs serving at-risk youth. We conducted an extensive search of social science databases for evaluations of prevention and intervention programs for adolescents, excluding curricula-based programs. In addition, we supplemented the sparse number of evaluation studies located through the database searches by soliciting evaluation reports from program staff as part of a questionnaire mailed to 230 youth-serving agencies.

Since the 1992 Carnegie Council report, our review suggests few, if any, improvements in the quality or quantity of the evaluations of youth development programs.[3] We reviewed more than 60 evaluation studies of youth-serving programs, including journal articles, reports to funders, and unpublished documents. These studies varied in the quality of their design, the appropriateness of the data collection measures, and the validity of their conclusions based on the data presented. Too often, pieces of information necessary for our task of understanding the effectiveness of programs in generating positive outcomes for youth were missing.[4] Furthermore, the programs evaluated varied in their articulated adherence to any youth development approach, such as the framework described above. Most of the programs stressed the prevention of specific risk behaviors, such as substance abuse or dropping out of high school, rather than focusing on enhancing positive behaviors. Additionally, few programs espoused an integrated view of adolescents, or offered an array of services and supports.

A limited number of rigorous evaluations of positive behavior-focused competency-enhancing programs do exist. These programs aggressively embrace the youth development philosophy. (See Roth et al. [1998] for a more comprehensive review of youth programs.) This small body of evaluation literature suggests that programs, if implemented well, can promote the acquisition of youth development competencies by adolescents, including at-risk youth.

Our search of the evaluation literature identified six such programs that embrace the youth development framework. All of the programs follow an integrated approach by offering a wide range of services and opportunities, including social, academic, recreational, cultural, and skill- and competence-building supports (see Table 10-2 for program descriptions). All six target poor urban youth, and all but one serve young adolescents ages 10 to 16.[5]

The following three evaluations employed random assignment (see Table 10-2 for details of evaluation methods):

- Big Brothers/Big Sisters (sites used in evaluation include Columbus, OH; Houston, TX; Minneapolis, MN; Rochester, NY; Philadelphia, PA; Phoenix, AZ; San Antonio, TX; and Wichita, KS)

- Quantum Opportunities Program (Philadelphia, PA; Oklahoma City, OK; San Antonio, TX; Saginaw, MI; and Milwaukee, WI)

- Woodrock, Inc. (Philadelphia, PA)

Three other evaluations of interest used a comparison group design in generating their findings.

- ADEPT (New Orleans, LA)

- LA's BEST (Los Angeles, CA)

- South Baltimore Youth Center (Baltimore, MD)[6]

Table 10-2. Summary of Program Evaluations

About the Program	About the Evaluation	Main Findings
Big Brothers/Big Sisters of America (BB/BS) is the oldest, best-known, and most sophisticated mentoring program in the country. Local affiliates create and support one-to-one relationships between adult volunteers and youth living in single-parent households. The program does not specifically target any problem behaviors, but offers a supportive environment and the caring of an adult friend intended to help the youth develop. The local affiliates and matches are governed by carefully established procedures and criteria. National operating standards provide uniformity in recruitment, screening, matching, volunteer training, and match supervision, while allowing for minor variations to accommodate local demands. On average, the youth and adult meet for three to four hours three times per month for at least a year.	Authors: Tierney et al. [1995] Source: Public/Private Ventures report Design: Random assignment; eight sites; 18-month follow-up. Sample: 487 program and 472 control youth with follow-up date; youth ranged in age from 10 to 16 at baseline (93% between 10 and 14); 23% were minority girls, 15% white girls, 34% minority boys, and 28% white boys.	After 18 months of participation, program youth were 46% less likely to start using illegal drugs and 27% less likely to initiate alcohol use during the study than were the controls. The results were equally impressive for both boys and girls. The effect was even stronger for the minority participants, who were 70% less likely to initiate drug use. Program youth were 32% less likely to report hitting someone during the previous 12 months. There were no differences between the two groups in the number of times they stole or damaged property, were sent to the principal's office, did "risky" things, fought, cheated on a test, or used tobacco. Program youth earned moderately higher grades, skipped half as many days of school, skipped fewer classes, and felt more competent about doing their school work than did control youth. The impacts were larger for girls, particularly minority girls. Program participants reported better relationships with peers and parents than did the controls at the end of the study. The effect was strongest for white boys. There were no statistically significant gains in self-concept, or in the number of social and cultural activities participated in.

About the Program	About the Evaluation	Main Findings

Quantum Opportunities Program was a community-based, year-round, multiyear, multiservice youth development program for students from families receiving public assistance. Twenty-five students began the program in the ninth grade, and continued with the program until the end of the twelfth grade. The explicit goals of the program were to foster academic and social competencies. Each year, the students participated in 250 hours of education-related activities (tutoring, computer-assisted instruction, homework assistance, etc.), 250 hours of development activities (acquiring life/family skills, planning for college and jobs), and 250 hours of service activities (community service projects, helping with public events, holding regular jobs). Students received hourly stipends and bonuses for completing each segment of the program.

Authors: Hahn et al. [1994]

Source: Report sent with survey

Design: Random assignment at 4 sites before recruitment; 5-year longitudinal study, beginning in 9th grade to one-year post-high school.

Sample: 100 experimental and 100 control participants at pretest. Eighty-eight experimental and 82 control participants at follow-up. All were highly disadvantaged.

The rate of differentiation between two groups accelerated after the first two years in the program. By the end of high school, program participants showed significant increases in academic skills and educational expectations, but no differences in dropout or childbearing rates, grades, or knowledge about contraceptives and AIDS. There were differences in the extent of success by site. One year after the end of the program, there were significant differences in dropout and childbearing rates: Program participants were significantly more likely to have graduated from high school or received their GED (63% vs. 42%), be in a postsecondary school (42% vs. 16%), and have fewer children (24% vs. 38%). In addition, 22% more participants received honors or awards during the past 12 months and 30% more participants were involved in community service during the six months since finishing the program. Also, they were less likely to have been in trouble with the police within the previous 12 months.

The goal of the 25-year-old Woodrock, Inc., is to promote interracial, interethnic, and intercultural harmony among youth. The recent addition of a Youth Development Program encourages youth to resist the negative culture of drugs and violence, develop resiliency skills, and build positive support systems that transcend ethnic and racial boundaries. The program operates in two elementary and two middle schools in two inner-city

Authors: LoSciuto [1996]

Source: Materials sent with survey

Design: Randomized assignment of two cohorts; pre- and posttest measures.

Sample: 244 treatment and 471 control youth from inner cities; youth ranged in age from 6 to 14 years old (mean age=10); 47% female, 45% Latino, and 12% African American

There were significant differences (p<.05) between the groups in reported school attendance, race relations, and drug and alcohol use in the past month favoring the program participants after controlling for pretest difference. There was a trend (p<.10) for program participants to report higher self-esteem, less drug and alcohol use for the last year, and greater control of aggression.

Table 10-2 (continued)

About the Program	About the Evaluation	Main Findings
communities. School-based activities include weekly human relations classes designed to provide youth with resiliency skills, peer tutors, homework assistance, individual guidance sessions, and monthly teacher-advocate meetings. Out-of-school activities include special events, weekend retreats, afterschool clubs, crisis intervention, and a summer program. As part of the family support component, youth advocates conduct home visits and serve as intermediaries between school personnel and parents.		
The ADEPT Project was a comprehensive afterschool program focusing on building positive self-esteem and providing homework assistance and activities for social and emotional growth. Children participated in two-hour sessions offering self-esteem building exercises, free play, creative dramatics, and assistance on homework assignments throughout the school year.	Authors: Ross et al. [1992] Source: Journal article Design: Comparison group; pre- and posttest measures. Sample: 540 program and 296 comparison participants; 60% low-income latchkey children in grades K-6	The results indicate that the program did not have any measurable positive effects on personality variables, such as self-esteem, risk-taking, depression, or in class behavior. There was also no positive effect on standardized test scores. However, there was a statistically significant improvement in average standardized test scores for students who received the self-esteem building curriculum.
LA's BEST is a comprehensive afterschool program intended to combat obstacles to educational achievement by offering an alternative support system. The program provides kindergarten through sixth grade students with opportunities for educational and developmental enrichment through academic tutoring, instruction, and content activities; computer	Authors: Brookes et al. [1995] Source: Report sent with survey Design: 10 programs, comparison group, two-year longitudinal study Sample: 80 fifth through seventh graders who participated for two or more years and 66 comparison stu-	Despite lower pretest grades for program youth, they received significantly higher grades than the comparison students two years later in math, science, social studies, reading, and composition. Furthermore, they showed greated improvement in their reported effort in science and social studies. The stu-

About the Program

activities; cultural enrichment; recreation; and nutrition. This free program is offered Monday through Friday after school until 6 p.m. at 19 of the most disadvantaged and poorest performing schools in the city.

South Baltimore Youth Center was a demonstration program modeled on the elements of successful programs identified by the Eisenhower Foundation. The Center was designed to be a grassroots community-based safe haven for youth from high-risk community or home environments and to offer positive social activities, including mentors, tutoring, and job training. The staff created a familylike atmosphere where adults provided emotional support and guidance in a caring, informal manner. Case management, agency collaboration, and empowering decisionmaking by the youth were also key components. The explicit goal of the Center was to reduce the risk for neighborhood youth by building on their resiliency. The program operated during nonschool hours—six hours after school and during the day on weekends and summers.

About the Evaluation

dents from the same schools with 0-3 months of participation; youth were mostly minority students and 65% were non-native English speakers.

Authors: Baker et al. [1995]
Source: Journal article
Design: Multiple comparison groups, three-year longitudinal study and process evaluation.
Sample: 68 program participants and 132 comparison youth at pretest, but only 38 program and 35 comparison at posttest. All youth were from inner cities, but their ages are not specified.

Main Findings

dents who participated for two or more years held significantly more positive attitudes about themselves and school, felt safer during the afterschool hours, knew more people in college, had higher educational expectations, and liked school more than comparison students.

The outcome evaluation showed a positive effect for the program from the pretest to the posttest three years later. The amount of self-reported alcohol consumption increased significantly less for the program youth than for the comparison youth between the pretest and posttest. The self-reported amount of drug use decreased significantly for the program youth during the study. The largest decrease was among the program youth who had a positive peer group. The amount of self-reported minor and serious delinquent behavior decreased significantly for the program youth, particularly for those youth in negative peer environments during the pretest. There were no differences in the prosocial behavior of either group.

All of the evaluations measured pre- to posttest change in both behavioral outcomes (such as school performance and substance use) and psychological outcomes (such as beliefs and attitudes about themselves and the future).

All of the programs report positive changes in the attitudes and/or behaviors for program participants (see Table 10-2 for specific outcomes). For example, the 88 participants in the Quantum Opportunities Program (QOP) fared statistically significantly better than the 82 controls the year after the four-year program: 21% more QOP participants graduated from high school or received their GED (63% vs. 42%); 26% more QOP participants were attending some type of postsecondary school (42% vs. 16%); 14% fewer QOP participants had children (24% vs. 38%); 22% more QOP participants received honors or awards during the past 12 months; and 30% more QOP participants were involved in community service during the six months after finishing QOP (41% vs. 11%). In addition, there were significant differences between the two groups in their attitudes and expectations for the future. QOP participants were more likely to be hopeful about the future (98% vs. 74%) and to believe that their life has been a success (74% vs. 51%) [Hahn et al. 1994]. The magnitude of the findings varied by site.

The impact evaluation of Big Brothers/Big Sisters of America (BB/BS) [Tierney et al. 1995] also shows positive changes in program youth's risk behaviors. Since BB/BS takes an integrated positive-focused approach to adolescents, there is no direct focus on reducing problems. Nevertheless, the evaluation demonstrated the program's impact on several risk behaviors. After 18 months of participation, the 486 participants were 46% less likely to start using illegal drugs than the 472 control group youth. Youth of color were 70% less likely to initiate drug use. In addition, participants were 27% less likely to initiate alcohol use, and Little Sisters of color were less than half as likely to start drinking. Participants were also 32% less likely to report hitting someone during the previous 12 months. Participation in BB/BS also positively impacted youths' school behavior. Participants received slightly higher grades, skipped half as many days of school, cut fewer classes, and felt more competent about doing their schoolwork than did youth in the control group. Participants also reported better relationships with their parents and improved relationships with their peers [Tierney et al. 1995].

Similarly, LoSciuto [1996] found statistically significant, but modest, differences between the 244 participants in the Youth Development Program of Woodrock, Inc. and the 471 adolescents in the control group after controlling for pre-test differences. More specifically, program participants reported better school attendance (experimental group mean=4.31, control group mean=4.12); more positive attitudes towards race relations (experimental group mean=4.04, control group mean=3.90); and lower reported use of alcohol, tobacco, and drugs during the previous month (experimental group mean=1.10, control group mean=1.15).

As detailed in Table 10-2, all of the programs report positive changes in the attitudes and/or behaviors for program participants. No program evaluation, however, reported positive outcomes for **all** the attitudes and behaviors measured. The pattern of findings suggests caution when proclaiming the benefits or failure of youth development programs. The evaluated programs do have some positive impacts on outcomes of interest, such as school performance, drug use, and attitudes. However, not all of the evaluations measured or found effects on the same behaviors.

The limitations of the research do not preclude us from drawing some preliminary conclusions about youth development programs. First, findings from the multisite, random assignment evaluation of the QOP provide evidence of the strength of the youth development framework. The sites varied in their adherence to the QOP model in their implementation of the program. Not surprisingly, the Philadelphia site, where the program was more fully and consistently implemented, showed greater positive impacts on the participating students. For example, more than 70% of participants in Philadelphia graduated from high school and were in postsecondary schools one year after the program. The rate in the other three sites was under 30%. Even when the program implementation was not ideal, however, the program still positively impacted participating adolescents [Hahn et al. 1994]. Thus, more limited programs may still be of some benefit, but the closer to the overall youth development framework, the better the outcomes for adolescents.

Second, the evaluations described in Table 10-2 provide insight into the relative importance of different characteristics of the youth development framework. Yet, it should be noted that none of the evaluations tested the relative efficacy of individual characteristics directly (i.e., no systematic variation of components in randomized design). Implementation differences between the QOP sites and findings from the process evaluation of the South Baltimore Youth Center suggest elements that may be critical to successful programs. The characteristics of staff, such as their level of commitment and caring, their personal contact with the students, and their skill at relating to the adolescents seemed to be associated with program success [Baker et al. 1995; Hahn et al. 1994]. Unfortunately, specific information about the quality of adult-youth relationships was not measured.

Further support for the importance of the staff comes from an ethnographic study of more than 60 inner-city youth-serving organizations [McLaughlin et al. 1994].[7] They found that, although organizations took many forms, all shared adults who created and nourished "places of hope" through their skills of community building, listening to youth, and bringing adults and youth together for concrete, productive purposes. Every one of the leaders operated, to varying degrees, outside the conventional institutional framework; they were individuals who made the system work despite itself.

The importance of a relationship with an unrelated caring adult for at-risk young adolescents has been well documented [Werner 1990; Furstenberg 1993; Rutter 1987; Scales 1991; Carnegie Corporation 1989, 1994]. Although not the only way, many programs match youth with mentors to provide the opportunity for a one-on-one relationship with an adult who can augment family networks. Mentors furnish adolescents with an avenue for establishing their identity as separate from their family while maintaining the guidance and protection of a caring adult. Mentors also serve as an important source of support, offering both instrumental supports such as job contacts and information, and personal support and guidance. Despite their popularity, research on the effectiveness of programmatically supported mentoring relationships is just becoming available. We found only one rigorous evaluation of mentoring-only programs: Big Brothers/Big Sisters.

This evaluation provides evidence for the value of caring relationships between adults and youths created and supported by programs. Tierney, Grossman, and Resch [1995] write that the benefits from mentoring programs do not occur automatically. Rather, they argue that the integrated body of standards and supports provided by the BB/BS organization are critical to making the matches work, which in turn generate the positive outcomes. The results of Public/Private Venture's ongoing research initiative of mentoring programs provides further information on how successful matches are formed (see Sipe [1996]). Mentors who do not attempt to change their mentee, but instead focus on building a trusting relationship by letting the youth drive the pace and activities, proved to be longer lasting and more successful. At an organizational level, careful screening, orientation and training, and support and supervision of the volunteers by program staff are the most influential program structures.

Second, program duration appears to be an important design aspect of successful programs. Hahn and colleagues [1994] suggest that QOP is effective because it reaches adolescents early and provides continuity by engaging participants throughout high school. In other words, it offers sustained services. Big Brothers and Big Sisters typically met with their Little Sister or Little Brother approximately three times a month for four hours over the course of a year, totaling 144 hours of direct contact [Tierney et al. 1995]. Although not tested directly,

Tierney and his colleagues believe this high level of contact contributed to the program's success.

Similarly, findings from the evaluations of QOP, BB/BS, LA's BEST, and ADEPT suggest the potential for cumulative effects with prolonged participation in a youth development program. There were no differences between the QOP and control adolescents after the first year of the program. However, differences between the groups accelerated after the first two years, and continued into the postsecondary period [Hahn et al. 1994]. Similarly, youth attended LA's BEST for two or more years, BB/BS for more than a year, and ADEPT for one year. Unfortunately, the length of participation is not reported for the participants in the other programs evaluated.

Even with these well-designed studies, this review highlights the paucity of high-quality outcome evaluations of programs fitting the youth development framework. Given this state of considerable promise and unsubstantiated effectiveness, we conducted interviews with 13 key informants in the field of youth development to expand our understanding of the promises and pitfalls of the youth development framework. We asked our informants what they would do to promote youth development programs or to better understand their value. They offered the following suggestions:

- Build public will and awareness with a focus on the most influential groups, including the business community, clubs, and fraternal organizations.

- Spread the youth development message to other environments that interact with youth.

- Create a separate funding stream for young people in every community in America.

- Create strategic alliances.

- Create more kinds of programs.

- Provide more support for community based organizations (CBOs).

- Create networks of organizations to share ideas and implementation strategies.

- Focus on infrastructure and organizational issues, as well as quality control.

- Find out who is doing good work and expand it; saturate communities with programs.

- Support improvements in the quality and quantity of evaluations and documentation.

These perspectives give direction to new efforts to investigate the merits of youth development programs and additional hope for the emergence of a body of comprehensive practice and research on the approach.

As noted earlier, there has been little improvement in the state of program evaluation since the 1992 Carnegie Report. Noteworthy exceptions are the evaluations of Big Brothers/Big Sisters and Quantum Opportunities Program. This limitation is partly due to the relative newness of the field of youth development; we can expect continuing improvement in the literature as the field matures. Nevertheless, despite the early stage of the evaluation literature, the available evidence points to the potential of the youth development framework for promoting healthy behaviors among at-risk youth.

Adolescents Out of the Mainstream

The emerging evidence of the efficacy of the youth development framework for poor urban youth raises the question of its usefulness for more disconnected youth—such as those in the nation's juvenile justice and mental health systems. Indeed, some efforts at preventing adolescents from entering these systems use aspects of the youth development framework (e.g., community policing and substance abuse and violence prevention curricula). Its value may be broader.

The founders of the juvenile court intended to create a flexible and individualized system that could provide the best in justice and rehabilitation [Krisberg & Austin 1993; Bernard 1992; Needleman 1983]. The primary purpose was rehabilitation rather than punishment [McNeece 1983]. Original intent aside, practice has demonstrated that our current juvenile justice system is not primarily concerned with the rehabilitation of adolescent offenders. As part of this larger system, the juvenile court has a range of options in processing an alleged delinquent or status offender, ranging from dismissal of the charges to placement under probation supervision to confinement in a secure institution [McNeece 1983]. Ideally, an adjudicated delinquent is matched with an intervention option that the court deems appropriate based on an adolescent's needs. However, interventions are generally selected on jurisdictional, funding, or space availability considerations, rather than on adolescent needs analysis. Problems particular to the adolescent or the family, ecological issues, and clinical concerns are rarely factored into decisions [Chamberlain et al. 1996; Colton 1990].

Considerable energy has been devoted to exploring effective alternatives to institutionalization for juvenile offenders. A result of this exploration has been the development of service programs that could serve as the basis for the introduction of a youth development program framework. Three of the most popular community-based services for adolescent offenders are intensive probation supervision, restitution, and wilderness programs [Roberts 1987; cited in Borduin 1994]. Intensive probation involves frequent contact (several times per week) between the adolescent and the probation officer [Borduin 1994]. Restitution requires the offender to pay a sum of money or to perform a useful service for the victim as a way of imposing a sanction and as an attempt to hold adolescents accountable for their antisocial behavior [Borduin 1994]. Wilderness approaches vary in some respects, but are generally based around the physical and psychological challenges posed by a wilderness setting. The objective of the arranged challenges is to promote personal development and group cooperation [Greenwood & Turner 1987].

Studies of both institutionalized treatments and alternative treatment programs, however, fail to show their effectiveness [Borduin 1994].

The failure of existing options indirectly suggests the potential value of incorporating a youth development approach in designing interventions for troubled and disconnected youth. We can point to two primary limitations of juvenile justice practices that hint at this potential. First, these interventions fail to account for the fact that delinquent behavior is linked with family variables, peer relations, school performance, neighborhood contexts, economic realities, and racial and ethnic forces. Second, they are rarely delivered in the adolescent's natural environment where the antisocial behaviors have meaning. On these fundamental points, then, juvenile justice diverges sharply from the principles of youth development.

Mental health systems that deal with troubled youth also deserve the attention of youth development programs. While juvenile justice and mental health constitute distinct jurisdictions, considerable overlap and integration is evident. Researchers in mental health have criticized mental health therapies that are designated restrictively for the individual with the disorder, thereby neglecting the larger contextual needs that impact on the individual, such as the family systems, offspring, and the functioning of adults in need of mental health therapy [Cicchetti & Toth 1998; Petersen et al. 1993]. The recognition that adolescents typically demonstrate a high degree of comordibity also presents difficulties for traditional mental health treatment [Birmaher et al. 1996]. For example, depressed adolescents have been found to have higher rates of illicit drug use and alcohol use or abuse [Hammen & Compas 1994]. A critical recognition by mental health research about the rehabilitation of problem behaviors reflects a youth development perspective: "Much of what we thought we knew or understood about the syndrome of depression in children and the course of the disorder, may be based not just on the depression but on the nature and extent of concurrent disorders" [Hammen & Compas 1994]. Coupling this recognition with the fact that mental health problems simultaneously have direct consequences for other areas of an adolescent's life (e.g., academic performance) and are impacted upon by a young person's interrelated life realms (e.g., peer relations), lends further credence to the multimodal treatment approach advocated by youth development programming.

The youth development perspective offers a balanced lens that neither blinds us to the harm caused by adolescent offenders, in the case of juvenile justice, nor limits our ability to identify needs for services, such as mental health therapy [Bazemore & Terry 1997]. In this sense, youth development does not advocate the simplistic replacement of incarceration or treatment. Instead, it promotes the integration of services around a solid belief that the particular needs of an adolescent (and of the state, in the occasion of a delinquent or status offense) do not preclude the adolescent's needs for growth, support, and development. Our investigation reveals little in the way of self-conscious youth development programming in systems dealing with troubled youth such as the juvenile justice and mental health rehabilitative systems. Rehabilitation from unhealthy behaviors and situations is uncharted territory, as is the efficacy of youth development programs.

Conclusions

Our review of the small number of evaluation of youth development programs provides preliminary support for the efficacy of the youth development framework in enhancing the positive development of poor urban youth. Although numerous examples of youth development programs exist for at-risk youth, much remains to be done to determine whether or not such programs make a difference in the lives of all young people and subgroups (such as those defined by poverty status or disconnected behavior). We also need to know if such programs improve the life chances of disconnected youth who are already involved with the juvenile justice and mental health systems. As our investigation into the systems serving disconnected youth demonstrated, little is being done by way of positive youth development to assess the merits of this approach with such individuals.

We liken the present state of knowledge as to the value of youth development programs to the early childhood intervention program movement, circa 1970. At that time, a series of innovative programs had been developed and implemented and the first results of well-designed evaluations were just beginning to appear. Little had been done in the way of specifying the impact of particular program components or child outcomes. That is, there was little systematic comparison of the variation in programs, such as type, intensity, onset and length of programming [Brooks-Gunn et al., in press; Berlin et al. 1998]. Child outcomes, for the most part, focused on intelligence test scores, even though scholars were advocating a more integrated view of early development [Zigler & Trickett 1978; Bronfenbrenner 1979; Meisels & Shonkoff 1990]. Since that time, early childhood intervention programs have gone through a number of stages to the point that current programs might be best termed "fourth-generation" programs.

The field of youth development is poised to begin their "second-generation" of programmatic efforts. Nationally, there is a strong interest in expanding adolescents' access to youth development programs. The current mismatch between the enthusiasm and experiential testimony for these programmatic efforts, on the one hand, and definitive empirical evidence, on the other hand, however, calls into question the efficacy of such efforts. Despite considerable support for a sound theoretical model, without more than the beginnings of convincing empirical evidence is still sparse, so that making generalizations across communities, regions, scales, and thus across cultures, becomes treacherous.

In addition, concerted attention by policymakers and youth development practitioners to rehabilitative systems such as the juvenile justice and mental health is warranted. This agenda describes a new level of service for youth where research and practice, evaluation, and advocacy must converge to implement policy and programming that reconnect youth to critical support systems.

References

Baker, K., Pollack, M., & Kohn, I. (1995). Violence prevention through informal socialization: An evaluation of the South Baltimore Youth Center. *Studies on Crime and Crime Prevention, 4*, 61-85.

Bazemore, G, & Terry, W. C. (1997, Sept/Oct). Developing delinquent youths: A reintegrative model for rehabilitation and a new role for the juvenile justice system. *Child Welfare, 76*, 665-719.

Berlin, L. J., O'Neal, C. R., & Brooks-Gunn, J. (1998). What makes early intervention programs work? The program, its participants, and their interaction. *Zero to Three, 18*, 4-15.

Bernard, T. J. (1992). *The cycle of juvenile justice.* New York: Oxford.

Birmaher, B., Ryan, N. D., Williamson, D. E., Brent, D. A., & Kaufman, J. (1996). Childhood and adolescent depression: A review of the past 10 years. *Journal of the American Academy of Child and Adolescent Psychiatry, 35*, 1575-1583.

Borduin, C. M. (1994). Innovative models of treatment and service delivery in the juvenile justice system. *Journal of Clinical Child Psychiatry, 23* (Suppl), 19-25.

Bronfenbrenner, U. (1979). *The ecology of human development: Experiments by nature and design.* Cambridge, MA: Harvard University Press.

Bronfenbrenner, U. (1986). Alienation and the four worlds of childhood. *Phi Delta Kappan, 67*, 430-436.

Brooks-Gunn, J., Berlin, L. J., Fuligni, A. (in press). Early childhood intervention programs: What about the family? In J. Shonkoff & S. Meisels (Eds.), *Handbook on Early Childhood Intervention* (2nd ed.). New York: Cambridge University Press.

Camino, L. A. (1992). *What difference do racial, ethnic, and cultural differences make in youth development programs?* Washington, DC: Carnegie Council on Adolescent Development.

Carnegie Council on Adolescent Development. (1989). *Turning points: Preparing American youth for the 21st century.* Washington, DC: Author.

Carnegie Council on Adolescent Development. (1992). *Consultation on evaluation of youth development programs: Report on the meeting.* Washington, DC: Author.

Carnegie Council on Adolescent Development. (1994). *A matter of time: Risk and opportunity in the out-of-school hours.* Washington, DC: Author.

Carnegie Council on Adolescent Development. (1996). *Great transitions: Preparing adolescents for a new century.* Washington, DC: Author.

Chamberlain, P., Ray, J, Moore, K. J. (1996). Characteristics of residential care for adolescent offenders: A comparison of assumptions and practices in two models. *Journal of Child and Family Studies, 5*, 285-297.

Cicchetti, D., & Toth, S. L. (1998). The development of depression in children and adolescents. *American Psychologist, 53*, 221-241.

Colton, M. (1990). Specialist foster family and residential child care practices. *Community Alternatives, 2*, 1-20.

Dryfoos, J. G. (1990). *Adolescents at risk: Prevalence and prevention.* New York: Oxford University Press.

Furstenberg, F. (1993). How families manage risk and opportunity in dangerous neighborhoods. In W. J. Wilson (Ed.), *Sociology and the public agenda* (pp. 231-238). New York: Sage.

Greenwood, P. W., & Turner, S. (1987). *The Vision Quest Program: An evaluation.* Santa Monica, CA: Rand.

Hahn, A., Leavitt, T., & Aaron, P. (1994). *Evaluation of the Quantum Opportunities Program. Did the program work? A report on the post secondary outcomes and cost-effectiveness of the QOP Program (1989-1993).* Waltham, MA: Brandeis University, Heller Graduate School, Center for Human Resources.

Hammen, C., & Compas, B. E. (1994). Unmasking unmasked depression in children and adolescents: The problem of comorbidity. *Clinical Psychology Review, 14*, 585-603.

Krisberg, B., & Austin. J. F. (1993). *Reinventing juvenile justice.* Newbury Park, CA: Sage Publications.

Lerner, R. M. (1995). *America's youth in crisis: Challenges and options for programs and policies.* Thousand Oaks, CA: Sage Publications.

LoSciuto, L. (1996). *Outcome evaluation results for the woodrock youth development program: 1994-95 and 1995-96.* Presented to Woodrock, Inc. Board of Directors, November 14.

McLaughlin, M.W., Irby, M.A., & Langman, J. (1994). *Urban sanctuaries: Futures of inner-city youth.* San Francisco: Jossey-Bass Publishers.

McNeece, C. A. (1983). Juvenile justice policy. In A. R. Roberts (Ed.), *Social work in juvenile and criminal justice settings* (pp. 34-56). Springfield, IL: C. C. Thomas.

Meisells, R, & Shonkoff, J. (Eds.) (1990). *Handbook on early childhood intervention* (2nd ed.). New York: Cambridge University Press.

Millstein, S. G., Petersen, A. C., & Nightingale, E. O. (Eds.). (1993). *Promoting the health of adolescents: New directions for the twenty-first century.* New York: Oxford University Press.

Needleman, C. (1983). Conflicting philosophies of juvenile justice. In A. R. Roberts (Ed.), *Social work in juvenile and criminal justice settings* (pp. 215-223). Springfield, IL: C. C. Thomas.

Petersen, A. G., Compus, B., Brooks-Gunn, G., Stemmler, M., Ely, S., & Grant, K. (1993). Depression in adolescence. *American Psychologist, 48*(2), 155-168.

Pittman, K. (1991). *Promoting youth development: Strengthening the role of youth-serving and community organizations.* Paper commissioned for the USDA Extension Service, National Initiative Task Force on Youth at Risk, Washington, DC.

Pittman, K. (1992). *Defining the fourth R: Promoting youth development through building relationships.* Paper commissioned for Big Brothers/Big Sisters of America.

Pittman, K., & Fleming W. E. (1991). *A new vision: Promoting youth development.* Testimony of Karen J. Pittman before the House Select Committee on Children, Youth, and Families, Washington, DC.

Pittman, K., O'Brien, R., & Kimball, M. (1993). *Youth development and resiliency research: Making connections to substance abuse prevention.* Washington, DC: Center for Youth Development and Policy Research.

Roth, J., Brooks-Gunn, J., Murray, L., & Foster, W. (1998). Health promotion and youth development: Synthesis of current program evaluations. *Journal of Research on Adolescence, 8,* 423-459.

Rutter, M. (1987). Psychosocial resilience and protective mechanisms. *American Journal of Orthopsychiatry, 57,* 316-331.

Scales, P. (1991). *Portrait of young adolescents in the 1990's: Implications for promoting healthy growth and development.* Chapel Hill, NC: Center for the Study of Early Adolescence at the University of North Carolina.

Sipe, C. L. (1996). *Mentoring: A synthesis of P/PV's research*. Philadelphia: Public/Private Ventures.

Tierney, J. P., Grossman, J. B., & Resch, N. L. (1995). *Making a difference: An impact study of Big Brothers/Big Sisters*. Philadelphia: Public/Private Ventures.

Urban Institute (1994). *Nurturing young black males: Programs that work*. Washington, DC: Author.

U.S. Department of Health and Human Services [DHHS]. (1991). *Healthy people 2000*. Washington, DC: United States Government Printing Office.

Werner, E. (1990). Protective factors and individual resilience. In R. Meisells & J. Shonkoff (Eds.), *Handbook of early childhood intervention* (pp. 97-116). Cambridge, England: Cambridge University Press.

Zeldin, S., Kimball, M., Price, L. (1995). What are the day-to-day experiences that promote youth development? Washington, DC: Center for Youth Development and Policy Research.

Zigler, E., & Trickett, P. K. (1978). IQ, social competence, and evaluation of early childhood intervention programs. *American Psychologist, 33*, 789-799.

Notes

1   This section is drawn from Roth et al. [1998].

2   For example, many evaluation designs suffer from small sample sizes, limited administrative record keeping (i.e., no Management Information System [MIS]), and rapid staff turnover. In addition, vague program goals make identifying expected outcomes for youth difficult.

3   Conversations with experts in the field confirm the general lack of quality evaluations of youth development programs and organizations.

4   For example, not all reports included basic demographic information about the youth. This was true of both published and unpublished evaluations. Similarly, many failed to describe the methods used to collect and analyze the data, or how they reached their conclusions. This was particularly the case for many of the unpublished evaluations.

5   Participants in the Quantum Opportunities Program begin in the ninth grade and continue throughout high school. Three more of the programs serve both younger and older adolescents. Specific ages of adolescent participants were not reported in the study of the South Baltimore Youth Center.

6   Findings from this study need to be judged cautiously because of the high rate of attrition between the pre- and posttest.

7   They judged organizations "successful" in large part because the community youth held them in high regard and credited the organizations with enabling them "to find a different path."

Epilogue

Hugh Price

As their children's first teachers and principal caregivers, parents bear the primary responsibility for the socialization of their children. But the plain fact of the matter is that those who work cannot afford to be home in the afternoons and over the summer when their youngsters are out of school. Youth development programs help to fill that gap.

Karen Pittman of the International Youth Foundation tells me that youngsters must acquire certain competencies to become successful citizens and adults. These competencies include health and physical competency, personal-social, cognitive-creative, vocational, and citizenship competence. Successful youth development programs meet these myriad needs. According to Pittman, family, peers, school, community groups, religious organizations, and places of employment are all important players in the developmental process.

The Carnegie Task Force found that young adolescents do not want to be left to their own devices. It reports that in national surveys and focus groups, America's youth express a serious longing for more regular contact with adults who care about them and who respect them, as well as a longing for greater access to constructive and attractive alternatives to the loneliness many now experience [Carnegie Corporation 1992].

I will never forget watching the videotapes of those focus groups. There is more than longing. There is real anger at adults for bringing young people into the world and then abandoning them.

The crux of everything in youth development is relationships. Because successful youth programs function like families, drawing youth into activities that enable them to move beyond the dead-end or deadly experience, staff in these programs function as family members, caring adults, helpful older brothers and sisters, concerned aunts and uncles, and grandparents. They assume, in effect, these roles.

The *New York Times* reported on March 9, 1995, on the Quantum Opportunities Program, which illustrates what youth development is all about in operation [New York Times 1995]. Key features of the QOP program include a sustained relationship between the youth worker and young people, coupled with modest financial stipends and college saving plans for kids.

The youth workers in the QOP program win the confidence of the young people, interact with them daily, hang out with them after school, and counsel them about personal concerns. Workers also check whether students are attending school and on sunny, warm days whether they not only go to school in the morning but stay in school throughout the day. They make sure that the young people do their homework, that they study vocabulary on computers, attend cultural events, and visit colleges.

I was a youth worker while I attended law school. I will never forget an interaction with the youngsters who had invested in our relationship. We met generally at about 3 P.M. three times a week. I was once about 20 minutes late, and they said to me: "Mr. Price, don't ever be late again. If you expect us to invest in this relationship, we need to know that it is the single most important thing in your life at 3 o'clock, because it is the most important thing in our lives at 3 o'clock. And the moment you're late, you have blown the relationship and blown the trust." That is what bonding and relationships are about.

Research shows that youth development programs produce the kinds of outcomes that society values and curtails those behaviors that we abhor. According to Richard Mendel, the author of a terrific essay, "Prevention or Pork: A Hard-Headed Look at Youth-Oriented Anti-Crime Programs" [1995], a number of strategies have begun to demonstrate impressive results in reducing criminal behavior, as well as delinquent and predelinquent behavior among young people. In his essay, he cites several notable examples.

In Fort Myers, Florida, a program called "Success through Academic and Recreation Support" (STARS), works with young people who are ages 11–14. That program has reduced juvenile crime rates by almost one-third; among 11- and 12-year-old offenders citywide, the rate of repeat criminal activity dropped by 64% [Mendel 1995, p. 18].

Mendel also cites an effort in Lansing, Michigan, where crime went down by 60% in two troubled Lansing neighborhoods after police, local schools, and social service agencies opened up a neighborhood network center and launched an extensive youth development program.

On February 23, 1996, the National Urban League staged an urban policy forum on the subject of youth development, which was broadcast on C-SPAN [National Urban League 1996]. We were joined in that forum by David Wolchak, chief of police in Concord, New Hampshire, and also the president of the International Association of Chiefs of Police. We were also joined by Eric Holder, at that time the U.S. Attorney for the District of Columbia.

Both of these individuals are tough as nails on the issue of crime and criminal justice. But both had a fundamental message: society needs to wake up and realize that there is no way to prosecute or jail or imprison your way out of the teenage crime problem. It simply will never happen. Investments must be made in prevention-oriented programs.

As you learned from Chapter 8, crime reduction is not the only welcome dividend from youth programs. QOP found that the youngsters involved in the experimental group, compared with the control group, improved their basic skills, graduated from high school, and went on to college at a higher rate than those in the control groups, and they also had fewer babies.

What, then, is the basic message of all this experience and research? The QOP experience and research undergird intuition, but we do need research. The basic messages are these:

- First, youth development is essential to the healthy academic and social development of young people.
- Second, youth development programs provide working parents of all complexions and income groups with an assurance that their

youngsters are safe from harm and in the hands of caring adults who will engage them in constructive activities while the parents are earning a living.

Youth development programs significantly reduce youth crime by keeping teenagers off the streets during the peak hours of violent juvenile crime, by helping them to forge close relationships with adult mentors who care about their fate, and by involving them in constructive activities that engage their minds and consume their energy. These programs produce other beneficial results, including boosting academic achievement and reducing teen pregnancy. As a result, cities become healthier environments for young people, and cities become safer and more attractive places for citizens, commuters, shoppers, tourists, and convention-goers. The most basic message is that youth development is a cost-effective and a humane public investment that pays handsome dividends for everyone.

The Urban League's youth development strategy includes several elements. First, we are working with the creative team from an advertising firm that is undertaking a Public Service Announcement (PSA) campaign for us under the auspices of the Ad Council. The theme is, "Do you know where your children are?" The hours of 3 P.M. to 6 P.M. are a time of enormous peril for young people if we do not fill that hole in their lives—but it is a time of great promise if we do. And we are pounding that message home for five years, subject to the availability of funding.

What is interesting is that the knowledge that 3 P.M. to 6 P.M. is such an important time is fairly new knowledge. Now that we have this knowledge, we can close the loop in the argument; namely, the evidence substantiates intuition. And we are going to drive that message home and say, "Hey, world, do you realize this?"

Second, we have funding from three foundations to launch youth development mobilization campaigns in several Urban League-affiliate communities, and we are trying to raise more. The campaigns are well underway in Miami, Hartford, Detroit, and Springfield, Massachusetts.

The St. Louis program has been launched. One of the goals was to get the African American middle class to step up to the plate. A dinner raised $19,000 on the spot, with an average gift of $500. The St. Louis project is one of our lead horses in this effort. This project has also identified a list of about 45 African American organizations—fraternities, sororities, civic groups, and the like—that they intend to make presentations to over the next six months.

Finally, the Urban League affiliate communities across the country will be working with tenant associations and block clubs and so forth to celebrate young people who are doing the right thing. And we will be doing this in virtually all 114 Urban League sites. And folks will be staging parades and block parties and assemblies.

Our affiliates are deeply involved in the school-to-work activity and deeply involved with young adults in actual job placement. And one of our strengths is that Urban League affiliates essentially operate at the intersection between all sectors of their communities. They have the relationships with the business community, media, inner-city organizations, and parents. And one of our particular strengths is "making deals" with employers or with sectors to link the supply and demand side of the question of how to get a job. We are involved in skill training and attitudinal preparation, and we also have contractual relationships with specific companies to take people who emerge from our programs. And we want to accelerate that. We deal most with young adults and displaced workers, but we are working increasingly with youngsters.

My picture of what might be called a youth development infrastructure in a community consists of lots of places where good things happen for kids. Good things happen in schools like the Beacon schools in New York City. Good things happen in Boys Clubs and Girls Clubs and settlement houses. Good things happen in Urban League affiliates. Good things happen in wonderful programs operating out of storefronts.

Not every youngster wants to go to the same program every day, and so an infrastructure is one with lots of options and enough space to take everybody. But it is also one which recognizes that the bricks and mortar are not the important issue. The relationships are the issue. When I was a youth worker, we operated out of a raggedy old school, and the home base was the least important thing.

I had to go out and connect with the young people where they were and invest months of time in building the relationship to reel them into the building, or into my home, or into the science museum. The key is the human connective tissue between the youngster and the youth worker, and then the entire community is the venue for doing this work.

The all-too-familiar response to this evidence and this experience is, "Sounds good, I may be a little skeptical, but, yeah, you've marshaled some evidence. But where's the money going to come from? How will we finance all of this good stuff?"

We have to look inside the pockets of other public programs. We cannot get to the level of scale needed for our young people solely through private giving.

I was the human resources administrator for the City of New Haven in the late 1970s. Those were halcyon days of community development block grants. We took a chunk of money from the social services portion of the block grants and also from Title XX, and we funded afterschool programs all over the city: in churches, in Boys Clubs, in Urban League affiliates, and in schools. And the other program we funded in the 1970s was senior citizen centers so the folks would have a place to go. And those were also wonderful programs.

I went back to New Haven in 1990 to give a speech, and by that time the city was really terrified of its children. They were running wild. There were shootouts on the courthouse steps on the New Haven Green. I asked: "You're terrified of your children. Are the afterschool programs still here?"

"Oh, no, the tax base has eroded; we do not have the funds for them. We had to shut them down."

"Fine. Are the senior citizen programs still here?"

"Oh, yeah, they're still here."

"Now, I know you're going to misconstrue what I'm about to say, but what kind of sense does it make for you to defund the programs that promote safety and development in your community and fund the programs for seniors who are probably too terrified of the kids to go out of their houses to the centers? What kind of fundamental sense does that make?"

The principal source of potential support in a parsimonious world is from alternative ways of using criminal justice funds. Now, again, I am not an anarchist. I believe in strong police protection. I live in a small city, but a real city, and all three of my adult daughters live in real cities. I want them protected. But the question is, "Are we spending taxpayers' dollars in the smartest way to reduce crime?"

We all remember the debate a few years ago of the anticrime bill and the idea of putting 100,000 more policemen on the streets of America's cities. The question that was never posed—because we really did not quite have the data, but I want to pose it today—is, "Is adding 100,000 more police officers the most cost-effective way to use taxpayers' money to curb youth crime?" Let us consider the impact of using exactly the same amount of money in a radically different way.

Assume that a police officer's salary and benefits come to about $50,000 a year. How else might you use that money? A part-time youth worker working in a typical afterschool program situated in an Urban League facility or a Girls Club or a Boys Club earns these days about $15 an hour. If that youth worker worked from 3 P.M. until 6 P.M. (the peak times of day for violent teen crime and sexual activity) from Monday through Friday, the weekly salary would come to $225. If that youth worker worked, say, 44 weeks of the year, or basically from Labor Day through July 4, he would earn about $9,900 a year. In other words, we could fund five youth workers working Monday through Friday from 3 P.M. until 6 P.M. for every single police officer we fund who works a five-day shift, eight hours a day, only three of which are during the peak time of day for violent juvenile crime.

When I did this work, I worked with about seven young people; given inflation, the typical youth worker works with about eight these days. That means that the money society would spend on 100,000 extra police officers could instead pay the salaries of 500,000 youth workers working from 3 P.M. until P.M., Monday through Friday, Labor Day through July 4, with perhaps 4 million young people.

The interesting question that has to be put by taxpayers to policymakers is, does anybody really believe that 100,000 police officers working an eight-hour shift, only three of which are during the peak time of day for violent juvenile crime, will detect more crime than what 4 million kids will not commit if they are with youth workers five days a week during the peak hours of the day for violent juvenile crime, not to mention the potential impact of that on reducing teen pregnancy?

I do not mean to single out the police or to suggest that adequate police protection is not indispensable. A fundamental point is that some of the money that society would spend on expanding the criminal justice system—namely, on more police, prosecutors, judges, prisons, prison guards, and probation officers—would be more productively spent on dramatically increasing the availability of prevention-oriented programming during the peak time of day for violent juvenile crime.

New prisons, as has been proposed by governors, will cost taxpayers dearly in debt service and guards' salaries for 50 years to come. Afterschool youth development programs operate out of schools, YMCAs, Girls Clubs, Urban League affiliates, and churches—facilities that taxpayers have already paid for once.

We all buy cars for $25,000, when basically we can get the same car for $20,000, except we get only two speakers instead of four. And that car comes with regular hubcaps instead of alloy hubcaps, but lug nuts are standard equipment so the wheels will not fall off. So we can get the same basic car for $20,000 and put $5,000 into the kids.

In the 1950s, when I was a teenager in Washington, D.C., everyone in our town, be they parents, educators, taxpayers, or politicians, considered afterschool and summer programs an indispensable feature of a balanced, well-functioning community. In other words, these programs for young people were the essence of what we now rather esoterically call a civil society.

Once upon a time, communities had a ready response to that haunting question, "Do you know where your children are?" Today, as never before, the compassionate and cost-effective answer is afterschool programs instead of all-day prisons.

When Mayor Giuliani, in one of the budget-cutting spasms in New York City, threatened to shut down the afterschool programs, the parents in Staten Island went ballistic. I wish that I had every name and telephone number so that the parents in Bay Ridge, Queens, and the parents in Harlem can all get ballistic together, and maybe some politicians will pay attention to them.

There is no organized constituency around this issue just yet, but it is waiting to happen. If you can organize people, they do understand the problem—and they make certain that politicians get the point as well. Ernie Cortez and his organizers at the Texas Interfaith Education Fund mobilized parents in San Antonio to get the schools open from 3 P.M. until 6 P.M.; I sat in one of their so-called actions. I saw 1,500 parents in an auditorium to testify to the mayor and the head of the chamber of commerce that they wanted the schools open. Because the mayor knew there were going to be 1,500 parents there, they had actually already cut the deal. This was an affirmation of everybody's efficacy—it was a magnificent thing to behold. Keep in mind that this is a high school auditorium chock-full of people—it could hold only a thousand; another 500 were in the gymnasium with television monitors. They also had the cheerleaders and the band out there.

One of the parents diagnosed the afterschool issue. Ernie had brought down experts to educate folks about the issue. Another parent said, "This is what we are after; we want these schools open and a good program there."

And then the mayor said, "I hear you, so I pledge to do this." The cheerleaders cheered and waved their pompons. The band banged on their kettle drums. And everybody applauded their visionary mayor who looked out into a sea of 1,500 constituents. Everybody won that night.

Ernie substantiated the case. But he also needed 1,500 parents to drive the issue into the end zone. And that is the subtext of our mobilization effort: Create a constituency on call for kids that will ante up out of their own pockets but will also be on call to say to elected officials: I pay taxes and I want my money spent this way rather than that way.

Our thrust is to work with the parents directly to help them understand what they need from the schools and to organize themselves into a constituency of consumers. Parents themselves may not be able to reallocate criminal justice funds, but they can make a dramatic change in the quality of education that is provided. But we also need to get taxpayers who may not be the parents of the kids involved to understand that they have a stake in making sure that youngsters who are not their own have a place to be, because a constituency of taxpayers must be behind this issue.

Everyone should be concerned with the quality of education that young people receive from 8:00 A.M. until 3:00 P.M. We will not see a reallocation of public resources toward prevention until there is a constituency that is educated about needs and current expenditures and then stands up to elected officials.

References

Carnegie Corporation of New York. (December 1992). *A matter of time: Risk and opportunity in the nonschool hours*. Report for the Task Force on Youth Development and Community Programs. New York: Author.

Mendel, R. A. (1995). *Prevention or pork? A hard-headed look at youth-oriented anti-crime programs*. Report prepared for American Youth Policy Form. Washington, DC: American Youth Policy Form.

National Urban League. (February 23, 1996). *Youth development: The overlooked piece of the anti-crime puzzle.* Presentation made at the National Press Club, broadcast on C-SPAN.

New York Times. (March 9, 1995). Guiding hand to college for ghetto youth, A10.

About the Authors

Douglas J. Besharov is a resident scholar at the American Enterprise Institute and a professor at the University of Maryland School of Public Affairs, where he teaches courses on family policy and welfare reform. From 1991 to 1992, he was the administrator for the AEI/White House Working Seminar on Integrated Services for Children and Families. Mr. Besharov began his career as an assistant corporation counsel of the City of New York and later was the executive director of the New York State Assembly's Select Committee on Child Abuse. He was the first director of the U.S. National Center on Child Abuse and Neglect. Mr. Besharov contributes articles on social welfare policy to the *New York Times*, *Washington Post*, and the *Wall Street Journal*, and other publications. His books include *Enhancing Early Childhood Programs: Burdens and Opportunities*; *When Drug Addicts Have Children: Reorienting Child Welfare's Response*; and *Recognizing Child Abuse: A Guide for the Concerned*.

Jeanne Brooks-Gunn is the Virginia and Leonard Marx Professor of Child Development and Education at Teachers College, Columbia University. She is the first director of the Center for Children and Families at Teachers College. In addition, she has directed the Adolescent Study Program at Teachers College and the College of Physicians and Surgeons at Columbia. She is also a visiting scholar at the Princeton Child Research Center at Princeton University. Dr. Brooks-Gunn was a Senior Research Scientist at Educational Testing Service and a visiting scholar at the Russell Sage Foundation. In 1996, she was awarded the John B. Hill Award from the Society for Research on Adolescence. She has written more than 250 articles and 15 books, including *Conse-*

quences of Growing Up Poor, Escape From Poverty: What Makes a Difference for Children? and *The Encyclopedia of Adolescence.*

Brett V. Brown is a senior research associate at Child Trends, a nonpartisan, nonprofit research center that studies children and families. He directs many of Child Trends' projects on social indicators of child and family well-being, and conducts research on fatherhood and the transition to adulthood. Dr. Brown is a consultant to the Federal Interagency Forum on Child and Family Statistics, a member of the Healthy People 2010 Adolescent Health Working Group, and provides technical assistance to both the national and state Kids Count organizations. He codirects, with Dr. Kristin Moore, Child Trends' work on the Assessing the New Federalism project, which monitors welfare reform and the well-being of children and families.

Carol Emig is the director of Public Information and Policy at Child Trends, a nonpartisan, nonprofit research center that studies children and families. She was previously Senior Associate at the Center for the Study of Social Policy and the Deputy Director of the bipartisan National Commission on Children, a Congressional-Presidential body chaired by U.S. Senator John D. Rockefeller IV. She also was director of a Chicago-based children's advocacy organization, and a Research Assistant to former First Lady Rosalynn Carter.

William H. Foster is the senior vice president and chief operating officer at the National Center on Addiction and Substance Abuse (CASA) at Columbia University. He was staff director for the bipartisan Congressional Commission on the Social Security "Notch" Issue. Dr. Foster was chief of staff and then deputy commissioner of the New Jersey Department of Labor. He served as the senior policy advisor to Senator Bill Bradley on the 1988 welfare reform bill. He has written more than 60 scholarly publications, and is the recipient of numerous awards, including the Congressional Science Fellowship from the American Association for the Advancement of Science, and the Ester Katz Rosen Fellow from the Society for Research in Child Development.

Karen N. Gardiner is a senior associate at The Lewin Group, where she focuses on employment and training issues. She was a research associate at the American Enterprise Institute, where she studied youth development, teenage pregnancy, and welfare. Along with Douglas Besharov, she edited a monographs series on sexuality and American social policy, and a special triple volume of *Children and Youth Services Review*, which focused on the evaluation of teenage pregnancy prevention programs. Ms. Gardiner has coauthored and contributed to articles that appeared in *The Public Interest* and *The Washington Post*. Prior to her work at AEI, she was an LBJ Intern in the office of Rep. Barbara Boxer, and a research assistant for Women in Charge, a Chicago-based organization dedicated to promoting women into leadership roles in social service organizations.

Andrew Hahn is professor and associate dean at the Heller Graduate School, Brandeis University. Dr. Hahn's work focuses primarily on workforce policies for young people, as well as evaluation of community, youth, and economic development interventions. He assisted the U.S. Department of Labor on the development of the School-to-Work Opportunities Act and has led for many years a variety of projects in the Heller School's Center for Human Resources. Dr. Hahn works extensively with groups around the country on evaluation methodologies for assessing community needs and the impacts of community interventions. He was a designer and codirector of Career Beginnings, a national mentoring program for disadvantaged youth. He is guest columnist in *Youth Today*. Dr. Hahn is the author of *What Works in Youth Employment* (with Robert Lerman) and *Dropouts in America: Enough is Known for Action* (with Jacqueline Danzberger).

Paul T. Hill is research professor in the University of Washington's Graduate School of Public Affairs. He directs the Center on Re-Inventing Public Education, which develops, tests, and helps communities adopt alternative governance systems for public K-12 education. He is also a nonresident senior fellow of the Brookings Institution. Dr. Hill's current work has focused on reform of public elementary and secondary education. His most recent book is *Fixing Urban Schools*, a guide for community leaders who need to transform big-city school systems. He is also author of *Reinventing Public Education: How Contracting Can Transform America's Schools* (with Lawrence Pierce and James Guthrie). That book concludes that public schools should be operated by independent organizations under contract with public school boards, rather than by government bureaucracies.

Shawn V. LaFrance is vice president for planning and development at the Foundation for Healthy Communities in Concord, New Hampshire, a nonprofit organization dedicated to improving health and health care in northern New England. He was a program officer for Children and Youth at The Commonwealth Fund, and has held a number of positions in management and research with the New York City Department of Health. He was also a policy advocate with the Citizen's Committee for Children of New York, and served as a volunteer board member with several national and local children and youth organizations.

Robert I. Lerman is director of the Human Resources Policy Center at The Urban Institute and professor of Economics at American University. He has worked on reforming the nation's income maintenance and training programs as a staff economist for both the Congressional Joint Economic Committee and the Office of the Assistant Secretary of Policy, Evaluation, and Research at the U.S. Department of Labor. His article with Hillard Pouncy, "The Compelling Case for Youth Apprenticeship," in *The Public Interest*, influenced the policy debate that ultimately led to the School-to-Work Opportunities Act of 1994. In December 1997, Dr. Lerman published the award-winning article, "Reassessing Trends in U.S. Earnings Inequality," in the *Monthly Labor Review*. He is coeditor of *Young Unwed Fathers: Changing Roles and Emerging Policies* (with Theodora Ooms).

Linda Datcher Loury is an associate professor of economics at Tufts University. Her main areas of research are group differences in earnings, intergenerational mobility, and the relationship between education and earnings. Ms. Datcher Loury was a postdoctoral fellow at the John F. Kennedy School of Government at Harvard University. She also served as an assistant research scientist at the University of Michigan Survey Research Center. Her recent articles have been published in the *Journal of Labor Economics*, the *Review of Economics and Statistics*, and the *Journal of Human Resources*.

Kathryn Taaffe McLearn is assistant vice president for The Commonwealth Fund, where she is responsible for the Foundation's children and youth grantmaking. She recently co-authored the Fund's *Survey of Parents with Young Children*. She is a visiting research scientist at the Bush Center for Child Development and Social Policy at Yale University. Dr. Taaffe McLearn served as the director of studies for the Task Force on Meeting the Needs of Young Children at the Carnegie Corporation of New York, and was principal author of the task force's report, *Starting Points: Meeting the Needs of Our Youngest Children*. She was a senior program officer at the Smith Richardson Foundation, where she directed the work of the Children and Families at Risk program.

Lawrence F. Murray is the Senior Program Associate in the Program Demonstration Division at the National Center on Addiction and Substance Abuse (CASA) at Columbia University. He was the urban hub director at the Washington Business Group On Health's National Network for Child and Family Mental Health. Mr. Murray was the assistant commissioner for community-based services at the New York Department of Juvenile Justice. In Nassau County, he was the director of postinstitutional/runaway homeless youth services and the assistant director at Big Brothers/Big Sisters. Mr. Murray was selected as a member of the inaugural class of the Annie E. Casey Foundation Children and Family Fellowship Program.

Hillard Pouncy is a fellow at the Center for Community Partnerships, University of Pennsylvania. He is a political scientist and independent consultant to several projects on youth opportunity, employment training, and education reform, He has published recently on child support enforcement policy including: "Paternalism, Child Support Enforcement, and Fragile Families," with Ronald B. Mincy in *The New Paternalism: Supervisory Approaches to Poverty*, edited by Lawrence Mead, and "There Must be Fifty Ways to Start a Family: Social Policy and Fragile Families of Low-Income, Noncustodial Fathers," in *The Fatherhood Movement*, edited by Wade Horn, David Blankenhorn, Mitch Pearlstein, and Don Eberley (1998). Dr. Pouncy was associate professor of African and African-American Studies at Brandeis University and associate professor of Political Science at Swarthmore College.

Hugh Price is president and chief executive officer of the National Urban League. Previously, he was vice president at the Rockefeller Foundation, where he was responsible for managing domestic initiatives in education for at-risk youth. Mr. Price was a senior associate and subsequently a partner in Cogen, Holt & Associates, an urban affairs consulting firm. He was senior vice president of WNET/Thirteen, New York City's public television station, and was a member of the Editorial Board of the *New York Times*. Mr. Price served as the first executive director of the Black Coalition of New Haven, an organization dedicated to restoring neighborhood vitality and intergroup cooperation, and was a neighborhood attorney for the New Haven Legal Assistance Association. His articles have appeared in numerous publications, including the *Wall Street Journal*, the *Los Angeles Times*, and the *San Francisco Chronicle*. He also writes a weekly column, entitled "To Be Equal," for African-American newspapers across the country.

Jodie Roth is a research scientist at the Center for Children and Families at Teachers College, Columbia University. She received her Ph.D. from the Combined Program in Education and Psychology at the University of Michigan. She is interested in how schools and other institutions affect adolescents' development. Her research has examined the connection between adolescent childbearing and schooling. Currently, Dr. Roth is investigating how out-of-school programs can promote healthy adolescent development.

Patricia Stern is a doctoral student in Sociology and Urban Studies at the University of Pennsylvania. She is completing her dissertation, an ethnographic community study of a white working-class and poor neighborhood in Philadelphia and as the recipient of an HUD Doctoral Dissertation Grant for this field research, 1997-98. While doing her fieldwork, Ms. Stern was a community organizer with a Community Development Corporation in the neighborhood. Her Masters' research focused on teen sexuality and inner-city white youth. Prior to her graduate work at the University of Pennsylvania, Ms. Stern ran a community service program and taught a seminar on urban social issues at the University of Chicago Laboratory School. While in Chicago, she researched housing policy for the Uptown Task Force on Displacement and Housing Development.

William Julius Wilson is Lewis P. and Linda L. Geyser University Professor at Harvard University. He has been elected to the National Academy of Sciences, the American Academy of Arts and Sciences, the National Academy of Education, and the American Philosophical Society. He is also past president of the American Sociological Association, and is a MacArthur Prize Fellow. In June 1996, he was selected by *Time* magazine as one of America's 25 Most Influential People. Finally, he was awarded the 1998 National Medal of Science.

He is author of numerous publications, including *The Truly Disadvantaged*, which was selected by the editors of the *New York Times Book Review* as one of the 16 best books of 1987. His latest book, *When Work Disappears: The World of the New Urban Poor*, received the Sidney Hillman Foundation Award. Dr. Wilson is a member of numerous national boards and commissions, including the President's Commission on White House Fellowships, the National Urban League, and the Russell Sage Foundation.